TESTAME

PI

Unremarkable

A Good Place to Start

by Blake Heathcote
Book Jacket Design by Designwerke Inc.

Published in Canada by Testaments Press
ISBN 978-0-9948722-4-1

TESTAMENTS
PRESS

Other Books by Blake Heathcote

TESTAMENTS OF HONOUR
A SOLDIER'S VIEW
WE WILL MEET AGAIN

Blake Heathcote was born and raised in Toronto, the son and grandson
of Canadian veterans. Blake's father, Lieutenant E.B. Heathcote,
served in WW 2, and his grandfather, Major E.T. Heathcote MM, ED,
served in both wars.

In 1999, Blake founded the Testaments of Honour project, a non-profit initiative
whose objective was, and is, to chronicle on digital video first-hand accounts of
Canadian veterans. The goal is to provide future generations with a richer,
deeper understanding of Canadian history through use of first-person testaments —
but also, and of equal importance, to share and celebrate the stories
of Canadian veterans as they, themselves, told them.

In addition to his books, Blake has written
15 plays and 2 television documentaries.

For Garfield Mitchell

A conservator of Canadian history,
and a generous and insightful friend.

Unremarkable

A Good Place to Start

by Blake Heathcote

Testaments Press

Photographic Acknowledgements

All photographs are from the *Testaments of Honour Historical Archive*, with the following exceptions:

Library and Archives Canada: 6, 78; *City of Toronto Archives*: 11, 14; *United States Air Force Academy Library*: 141, 197, 218, 226, 228, 245, 251, 252, 254, 255, 268, 288, 293, 301, 302, 303, 304, 306, 308, 311, 312, 336, 338; Vic Gammon, 232; *Ley Kenyon*: 250, 257, 300; *Bundesarchiv*: 332, 336; *United Artists*: 370.

Photographs and drawings from the above mentioned sources were copies that were a part of John Weir's personal collection. Every effort has been made to contact all copyright holders. The publishers will be glad to make appropriate corrections in future editions for any errors or omissions that are brought to their attention.

Contents

Prologue 1

1. Beginnings 4

2. Living Off the Land 14

3. Uncle Adrian 32

4. Growing Up 41

5. Per Ardua Ad Astra 58

6. The Turning of the Tide 77

7. War 90

8. Circuits and Bumps 114

9. Battle Orders 130

10. The End of the Beginning 151

11. Stranger in a Strange Land 181

12. Evading 194

13. An Education 204

14. The War Behind the Wire 228

15. The Great Escape 248

16. Second Sight 275

17. The Beginning of the End 288

18. The Long Walk 297

19. At Large 317

20. Family Reunion 347

21. Home 354

22. Postscript 365

Additional Photographs 367

Acknowledgements 373

Bibliography 375

Prologue

By November 1941, England was losing the war. During the Battle of Britain – July to October 1940 – the RAF had managed to stave off a German invasion. Fighter squadrons had been badly battered, and they struggled with shortages of men and equipment well into 1942.

Flights of Hurricanes and Spitfires would cross the Channel into German-occupied France, and assess the Luftwaffe's strength, hunt for vulnerable ground targets, and try to get the enemy up into a fight. Every attack had to count, especially as they only had enough fuel for about 15 minutes in action.

John Weir was a Canadian who'd been flying with 401 Squadron for more than a year. His squadron had been decimated during the Battle of Britain, and much of 1941 was spent rebuilding. By November, losses had mounted again. Seventeen pilots were missing or had been killed since the middle of October, which meant that virtually everyone flying was a replacement. Weir was Flight Leader and had logged almost 1,000 hours of flight time. Because of the shortage of veteran pilots, he had been assigned an inexperienced 'Wing Man,' Gardner, who had seen little combat. That put John on edge. It was the Wing Man's responsibility to watch his Flight Leader's back as well as his own. But pilots who hadn't flown together couldn't anticipate, let alone rely on, how one another

A Hurricane II from 401 Squadron.

would react in combat. That would take weeks of flying against the enemy, and there wasn't time.

Once they were airborne, Weir kept glancing back to see if Gardner was following his lead. A minute after they breached the French coast, a group of German Messerschmitts appeared out of nowhere with the sun behind them, and swept down in an ambush. John glanced back yet again to see if Gardner was in position. That was a mistake. The aircraft were charging towards one another at 370 mph, and in that split second, he lost sight of the Germans. He flipped his Spitfire over hard down and to the left, trying to shake off any pursuers. At that same moment, Gardner screamed over the radio, and was dead before his Spitfire spun out of control.

An ME-109 attacked John from behind, and its cannons blew the left wing off his Spitfire. Machine gun fire raked his instrument panel and pierced the fuel tank, spraying gas back into the cockpit, which erupted in fire and engulfed him. He yanked open the canopy and bailed out at 26,000 feet.

As he drifted down, he did his best to gather his thoughts, and tried to figure out where he was. He landed hard, buried his parachute, then got moving as soon as he could. The Germans would be on the hunt for him. He was bruised and battered, but started walking. A farmer appeared on the road, and John decided to take a chance. In French, he explained who he was and that he wanted to get back to England. The man listened sympathetically, then touched John's face and shook his head. He told John that he had been burned and needed help. He should wait for the Germans, who could give him the medical attention he needed. He said he had to get moving or he would be arrested and shot. Then he walked away as fast as he could move.

The Germans arrived minutes later, and bundled John into a truck. They drove him to a nearby Luftwaffe base for interrogation, and the soldiers ignored him – just as he'd hoped. He listened to what they said to each other. He was fluent in German, and did his best to remember anything he thought might be useful. His thought about his father, Gordon, and his Uncle Adrian, who for years had helped him prepare for such an unlikely situation.

With them in mind, he began mapping out what his next moves should be.

Chapter 1

Beginnings

Gordon Weir, John's father, was born in 1888 and came from a long line of tough, independent Presbyterian Scots. His father owned a successful farm in West Flamborough, Ontario, just outside of Hamilton. Gordon was the youngest – and smallest – of seven children, which possibly helped forge his desire to build a life and career beyond the limits of mixed crop farming. His father died in an accident when Gordon was only two years old, and by the late 1890s, the farm had been sold and most of the family had relocated. By the age of twelve, he knew he had to begin planning for his future.

He loved life in the country, but Gordon had come to understand that only a career in finance, medicine, or law would generate sufficient income to provide him with the comfort and security he envisioned for himself. A solid education would be the necessary first step. In 1906, he entered the University of Toronto to obtain a degree in commerce. Four years later, he rounded out his education with an MBA at Harvard, then returned to Toronto to find work in the financial sector. But Canada was still recovering from a mild recession, and jobs were hard to come by. Gordon settled for a position as financial editor of the Toronto Star, where he stayed for several months.

In 1912, an opening arose at the A.E. Ames Company for work as a bond salesman, and Gordon jumped at the chance. This was the opportunity he had been waiting for.

His responsibilities with Ames, one of the most prominent investment firms in Canada, involved bond sales in corporate and international markets. This provided Gordon with frontline insights and experience into the workings of the Canadian financial industry. While at Ames, he established friendships with Donald McLeod and Ewart Young, two young men who shared his vision for a modern investment company. Theirs would be small, lean, and ambitious. Such a business model would be well suited to take advantage of Canada's evolving industrial and commercial potential.

Gordon, like many young Canadians, received military training with the reserves as part of his education at university, and he earned a commission as a lieutenant with the Argyll and Sutherland Highlanders of Canada. When war was declared between Britain and Germany in August 1914, the reserves were mobilized, and Gordon was called up. By March 1915, he was on his way to France with the Argylls and the Canadian Expeditionary Force (CEF).

He had an extremely distinguished war record. He was, in point of fact, a war hero. By the spring of 1916, he had been promoted to the rank of captain of the 4th Canadian Machine Gun Company. He served with the regiment through the devastation of the Somme, and in September 1916 was promoted to major and assigned command of the 5th Canadian Machine

Canadian machine gunners dig in, in shell holes on Vimy Ridge.

Gun Company. In January 1917, four Canadian divisions moved north from the Somme to begin preparations for the Canadian assault on the formidable German fortifications at Vimy Ridge. Gordon was there from the outset, supervising the construction of machine gun positions amongst the vast network of trenches, as 100,000 Canadian troops mustered for the attack.

On Easter Monday, April 9th, Canadian forces began their assault in driving sleet and snow, and in the wake of a rolling barrage. By 6:00 am they had captured the first line of enemy trenches. The crest of Vimy Ridge was captured by mid-afternoon, and three days later the Ridge had been won. Gordon was in the thick of the battle throughout. He was Mentioned in Dispatches (MID) on June 1st, 1917, and awarded the Military Cross (MC) on July 18th. The official citation for his decoration reads,

Gordon Weir in the trenches at Vimy on April 7, 1917,
two days before the historic assault.

For conspicuous gallantry and devotion to duty. Under heavy fire he supervised the action of eight machine guns, and with great courage led his men forward to best positions in the new line. Throughout he set a splendid example to his men.

His bravery came at a price. Gordon was badly wounded (his third time) by enemy machine gun fire during the battle for Vimy. Earlier in the war, his lungs had been permanently scarred from German gas attacks, giving him lifelong respiratory problems. But he survived, which unto itself was something of a notable accomplishment for *any* officer serving on the front lines during the Great War.

In January 1919, Gordon was promoted to Lieutenant Colonel, and the King awarded him the Distinguished Service

Order (DSO). He was the sole surviving officer from his unit, and ended his posting in London leading his regiment on horseback in a ceremonial Victory March Past before King George V at Buckingham Palace.

More significantly, he had returned to Canada a married man.

History has little to say about the young women of the Great War. Many served overseas as ambulance drivers and clerical staff, and some singular souls served with special distinction as battlefield nurses. In early 1915, two such women met and befriended one another onboard a troopship during

Freda Taylor in 1915.

the five-day Atlantic crossing with the CEF to England. Mary Frederica Taylor, known as Freda, came from Strathroy, Ontario, and Edwina Ratcliffe Lordly, known as Ted, was from Nova Scotia. Both enlisted in the Canadian Army Medical Corps (CAMC) for service on the front line, and their friendship stood fast throughout the rest of their lives. They were both '*New Women*': smart, attractive, and independent.

It is possible that Gordon crossed paths with Freda and Ted on the ship, as they were travelling overseas at about the same time. Nevertheless, five months later, while recovering from wounds in the military hospital in Le Tréport, Normandy, Gordon encountered the fiercely intelligent and strikingly beautiful Freda. Their courtship was brief, and the two were married in London on August 15th, 1915, shortly before he returned to the Front. By the time they returned to Canada in May 1919, Freda was pregnant with their first child and only son, John. A year later, a second child, Nancy, completed the

Freda and Gordon in London, 1915.

family.

Back in Toronto, Gordon focussed on his career. Within months of his return from the war, he once again discussed the idea of forming a new firm with his friends, Donald McLeod and Ewart Young. On February 1st, 1921, all three resigned from A.E. Ames. Between them, they had raised an initial investment of $40,000, with which they formed McLeod Young Weir Limited. Through the 1920s, their partnership demonstrated great insight and prudence, as well as pioneering many innovations in the profession. Over time, their modest firm grew into a $300 million financial giant with offices in Britain, Europe, US, and the Far East.

As the most entrepreneurial and ambitious of the partners, Gordon drove the company forward. From the outset, the partners decreed that the firm would be constructed on new footings. The first significant innovation was that staff would be given the chance to participate in the business as shareholders, making the employees one of the firm's greatest assets. They would truly be invested in their work.

The second innovation was that there would be no patronage or favouritism bestowed on family. While working on his MBA at Harvard, Gordon had studied the British banking system and learned of disasters caused by the ne'er-do-well sons of wealthy fathers. Many young men took advantage of comfortable jobs and high salaries they'd been handed and indulged themselves and their friends to the detriment of the companies that employed them. Corporate America had suffered through similarly inbred patronage for generations. Gordon insisted that McLeod Young

Weir would never become vulnerable in this way. Nepotism was forbidden.

Original thinking such as this helped transform the profession and laid the foundations for one of Canada's great companies. Gordon also made a point of not allowing past success to breed complacency. He drove himself, and those who worked for him, to approach problems and prospects in the same way: rethink them from the ground up. Make no assumptions. Gordon was fiercely proud of his Scottish heritage. He believed the reason the Scots had created so much of the modern world was because they were survivors who had learned to endure in the face of extremely harsh weather and the brutality of English oppression. His service in the Great War affirmed for him that survival was no quirk of fate, nor a dividend of religion or politics. It was the product of a man's willingness to think for himself. Independent thought and determination were what shaped one's future. To succeed, he believed you had to

Forest Hill Village in 1924, looking west from Bathurst.

11

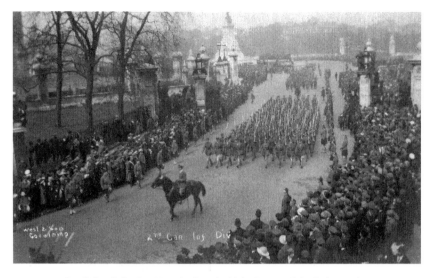

Lt. Colonel Gordon Weir (on horseback) leads men of the 2nd Battalion Canadian Machine Gun Corps past the Victoria Memorial, Buckingham Palace, on a 7 mile Victory March through London, Spring 1919.

establish where you were headed, evaluate the challenges that that entailed, then ensure that you did the work and did it well.

The Weirs had a large gracious home in Forest Hill Village. In the 1920s, this was a pleasant, almost rural, community in the northern part of a very reserved and proper Toronto, which had just begun to expand beyond its 19th century parameters.

Freda and Gordon appeared to be an ideal couple. Both were driven, ambitious, and extremely intelligent. Both loved animals, the outdoors, and excelled at sports. They shared a passionate enthusiasm for skiing in particular, which led them to jointly organizing and funding the first national ski team in the 1920s.

But theirs was not a happy union. Perhaps they were too much alike. Conflict and resentment quickly became the dominant themes in the marriage. Freda sought a divorce shortly after the birth of Nancy in the 1920s, but Gordon, then ascendant in the business world, vetoed discussion of any such thing, concerned about the impact it would have on his professional reputation.

Freda removed herself to Europe, unencumbered by Gordon. In addition to skiing, she was a world-class figure skater, and so enjoyed spending her winters in Switzerland. She oversaw Nancy's education in England, which made it possible for her to spend time with her close friend Ted Lordly, who had married an RAF officer and was now living in London. (Ted was also a world-class athlete, and competed in the 1936 Winter Olympics in Berlin.) And so Gordon and Freda began living lives that were largely separate.

Ironically, it was Gordon's success in business that made Freda's new life possible.

Chapter 2
Living Off the Land

A photograph taken in 1925 a few blocks south of the Weir
home in Forest Hill features Gordon, prominent among a
dozen other businessmen. They are standing in front of a steam
shovel in an undeveloped lot, celebrating the groundbreaking
for the new Granite Club on St. Clair Avenue West. A couple of
hundred yards to the east was the Badminton & Racquet Club,
which had been founded the previous year in a former streetcar

Gordon Weir, centre right in dark bowler, at the ground-breaking
for the Granite Club in Toronto, 1925.

barn. Gordon was integral in establishing and expanding both of these clubs, as is clear by his place of prominence in the Granite Club photo. And yet there is almost no mention of him in histories of the clubs. This was no oversight. Whenever possible, Gordon avoided drawing attention to himself or his work. He knew the value of maintaining a discreet profile when it served his purpose.

Like Forest Hill, these new clubs had been intentionally located north of downtown Toronto. In Gordon's thinking, they would be sporting clubs for workingmen and professionals, not social clubs for the rich. You would be able to play tennis, badminton, go for a swim, curl, bowl, and have a place to bring your family and meet with friends for lunch or dinner in a sanctuary removed from the stuffiness of the city.

During summers, many of those with money escaped the heat of the city for comfortable homes on Lake Muskoka and Georgian Bay. Toronto financial markets slipped into a seasonal hibernation, which left the advisors with little to do. As a result, many stockbrokers took the summer off, too. Not Gordon. Every year he travelled overseas to service his roster of European clients and explore new business opportunities.

He also loved to spend a few weeks in Algonquin Park. He never purchased a summer home or property, because in his mind that meant too much expense and concern about upkeep. He preferred renting modest cabins in remote areas that could take advantage of the best fishing and hunting.

Gordon also decided how John spent his vacation, something he took very seriously. Those twelve weeks away from school were not to be wasted. John spent several summers at Camp Kagawong in Ontario's Kawartha Lakes region, learning the basics of canoeing, shooting a bow and arrow, carving, fishing, and various other outdoor skills (and earned several merit badges that he kept all his life). One summer he spent a month in Trois-Pistoles, billeted with a Québécois family, to improve his French, which his father knew would be an asset. (This imbued his French with a distinctive Québécois accent, which he never managed to shed completely.)

As John's primary parent in Toronto (Freda remained in Europe), Gordon raised him with the same discipline with which he managed his own life and business. When he asked for a report, whether from John or a board of directors, he wanted it presented *'straightforward and without dressing.'* He taught John by example. He wanted him to learn to be self-reliant, prudent, and unostentatious in all things. A balanced life was essential: that meant an abundance of athletics and team sports, good grades, and above all, discipline. You had to work with what you had, and make the most of it. And you did not open your mouth until you were sure of your facts.

Gordon had a sharp temper, which kept John in check, making him think twice before he said or did anything foolish or questionable. Gordon taught him how to hunt, the proper use of firearms, and the inestimable value of a jackknife. In his opinion, nothing could beat that as an all-purpose tool. John was expected to carry his with him at all times.

Gordon stressed that John was responsible for himself at all times, too. No one else would be. Should he fail to prepare properly for some situation or event, it would be no-one's fault but his own. That's what being a survivor meant.

For years, Gordon had been hunting and fishing in Algonquin Park with an Ojibway guide who had the unusual name of *Fiji*. Fiji had been raised in Algonquin and lived there year round. His knowledge of the Park was boundless, and he and Gordon took countless trips throughout the 1920s. Gordon had come to trust and value him as a guide and a friend.

When John was old enough, he was invited to join them, which to him meant he'd earned acceptance from his father: he was no longer a child but was now a young man. But Fiji's acceptance was something else again.

For John, everything about him was an adventure. To begin with, he was an Indian, which was pretty special. He was a taciturn, compact man, lean and solid, who John thought looked as though he had been built for walking instead of riding. He didn't smoke or drink and said little when a look or gesture would suffice. He came and went as it suited him, and appeared to live an entirely solitary life. John knew almost nothing about him, as he only spoke of the day at hand and the place he found himself in. And yet this quiet man had a profound impact on John.

On these trips, Gordon and John typically spent their days fishing, returning late in the day with Fiji cooking supper and few words exchanged. John had been raised to remain silent unless spoken to around adults. But sometimes he'd ask Fiji a question if the moment seemed right. Fiji's quiet manner, so unlike his father's, sparked John's insatiable imagination and

Fiji in Algonquin Park, 1931.

curiosity. He wanted to understand how someone could live their whole life in the woods.

John woke early one morning, dressed quickly, and decided that this was a day for exploring. He was about to turn ten years old and wanted to see what made Algonquin so special. The sun was coming up when he set off, and it was cool, so he walked briskly to warm up, and he kept moving until he had lost sight of the Weir cabin.

When he stopped to look around, he had gone far enough that he might have managed to get himself lost. That made him a little uneasy. He touched the jackknife in his pocket to make sure it was still there, which was reassuring. He remembered he'd stuffed a small bag of raisins in his pocket. He stopped to eat some while he figured out what to do next.

'Hello, John.'

A quiet voice from behind scared him half to death, but he did his best not to show it. He turned around to see Fiji, who had appeared as if from thin air. Fiji smiled, and with a nod walked ahead into the woods. After he'd gone a dozen yards, he stopped and turned around, waiting for John to catch up. John went after him, making a fair amount of noise as he crunched through the leaves and twigs carpeting the ground.

That made him wonder how Fiji had managed to sneak up on him so silently. When he asked, Fiji smiled but said nothing. He indicated that John should stay put. Then he walked away in a wide arc, circling around through the trees and out of sight,

John in Algonquin Park, 1932.

and returned to where John waited.

To John, it looked like Fiji's feet weren't touching the ground, but were sort of gliding along, almost skating. John started to say something, but Fiji held up his hand to stay quiet. He pointed to his feet. Moving slowly, he walked on the outer edges of each foot in a slow, rolling heel-to-toe stride, somewhat pigeon-toed, using the front of each foot to gently feel the ground ahead for anything that might snap or crackle. There was almost no sound. Fiji smiled at John and said, '*Now you.*'

John didn't have moccasins like Fiji, which he really wanted now, but he did his best to copy Fiji's stride. After a few tries, he began to get the feel of it. Fiji smiled and headed into the forest. John followed.

They walked for some time without talking, John following and very attentive to Fiji's every move. Finally, Fiji stopped and stood very still. John did too. He could hear rushing water close by as Fiji moved to the foot of a small rise, then lay down on the moist ground, and crawled up to its crest. He signalled John to do the same. John crawled up after him and peered over the top where he saw a fast flowing stream. A moment later, an oily slip of a thing slithered out of the water and climbed the clay bank on the opposite side of the stream. It paused, listening and watching.

John got very excited and tried to think what those animals were called.

'Otter,' Fiji said quietly. John nodded.

The otter dove down the bank on its belly and slipped into

A River Otter.

the stream, then popped up again with a squeak of delight. This apparently was an *'All Clear'* signal, as five more otters appeared and took turns sliding down the clay, squealing and chirping, perking up their ears to make sure the coast was clear.

John didn't move. He was completely wrapped up in a circus that seemed to have popped up just for them. The otters played for another few minutes, then disappeared back into the woods. When they'd gone, Fiji started moving along the bank of the stream. John hurried after him, trying to walk the 'Indian' way he'd just learned. He rounded a corner and almost tripped over Fiji, who was lying on the ground. John dropped down, too, and waited for instructions. Fiji lay still.

They stayed there without a sound for as long as John thought was possible. He wanted to ask questions, but before he could, a fox appeared from the opposite shore of the stream carrying a morsel of moss in its mouth. It walked into the water, tucked its head down and dipped it underwater, then bobbed up again as it waded deeper until only its snout and the sprig of moss remained visible. The fox let go of the moss, swam back to shore, and disappeared back into the underbrush. John looked at Fiji, who explained that she was getting rid of fleas, and would do the same thing every couple of days. Fleas hate water, and would abandon the fox to escape onto the bit of moss.

From that point on, John couldn't get enough of this silent, gentle man's walks in the woods and the world they revealled. John peppered Fiji with questions, which he sometimes answered, but to which he often just gently shook his head.

Gordon watched the unconventional friendship evolve between his talkative son, who had questions pouring out of him like a spring flood, and the quiet Ojibway guide who seemed content to accept the world as he found it.

Recognizing this keenness in his son, Gordon proposed a plan whereby in a few week's time, John and two of his friends would go on an expedition into Algonquin with Fiji for a week and learn how to live off the land. John was enthusiastic; it would be an incredible adventure.

Once they were back in the city, he invited his friends Bill and Artie to come with him. They were excited to get out of the city in the summer, let alone to be going into the wilderness with a real live Indian.

'No one should die of hunger in the Canadian woods between April and October,' was how Fiji introduced the week-long expedition to John and his friends on the morning they set out. The four of them spent the morning walking deep into the forest until

they had no sense of where they were. The subject of food came up around what the boys thought might be lunchtime. As instructed, each had brought nothing with him except a jackknife; certainly nothing to eat. They assumed they were heading towards some Indian retreat deep in the woods where they'd probably have to cook their own hot dogs and eat beans off a tin plate. But when food was mentioned, Fiji said '*not yet*,' and kept walking.

By mid-afternoon, the boys were getting anxious. Fiji listened to them talk until they ran out of words, and then said if they were so hungry, they should start looking. This was met with baffled silence. He said they would go together to see what they could find. Off he set with the three boys trailing behind, and Artie and Bill grumbling to John. Fiji paid no mind to this. He pointed out edible plants and mushrooms and said that under every rock and fallen log there was food. To show what he meant, he flipped over a rotting log and pulled out a worm. He gave it a quick wipe with his fingers, then dropped it into his mouth and swallowed it whole. He looked at the boys, who were horrified. Nobody made a sound.

Fiji indicated that it was John's turn. He knew he was on the spot. He'd invited the other guys and got them excited about the adventure. What's more, he knew his father would want a full report of all they had done. So he gamely plucked a worm from the earth and swallowed, but it came back up faster than it had gone down. Fiji said that he wasn't hungry enough and that they would try again tomorrow. John promised himself that he would never leave the house again without his pockets full of chocolate bars.

The boys foraged for anything slow enough to lay hands on but came up empty. Now hungry *and* tired, the adventure had lost its charm. By late afternoon, the boys were ready to wrap things up and head home. It had been great and all, but they thought they had better get back before it got too dark.

John spoke up for the others, asking if they shouldn't be looking for their campsite soon? Or maybe heading back to the cabin? Fiji shook his head and said that it was too late to turn back. They would make camp here, and as it would be dark in a few hours, they should make some beds. And if they wanted supper, they had better keep looking.

That put a damper on an already damp day. Bill had a pup tent that he'd wanted to bring, but John had said no, it was against the rules. Rules, Artie asked? Whose rules? What kind of rules? John pointed to Fiji but said nothing.

They were hungry and tired, and it had begun to dawn on them that there were going to be a whole lot of unwelcome surprises on this trip; nothing would be what they had expected.

Fiji got them moving. He said once they'd made their beds he'd help them look for food. Artie said they hadn't brought sheets or pillows or anything, so how was he supposed to make a bed? They didn't even *have* beds. No, Fiji explained. You have to *make* a bed, from pine boughs. He told them to collect a half dozen each, and he would find spruce branches for cover.

Wow, John thought, things were getting even worse. But before the other guys could start griping, he went looking for branches. They spread out and grabbed whatever they thought might work. One by one, they drifted back to the clearing that Fiji had chosen and piled the stuff in front of him for approval. He picked up four or five boughs and demonstrated how you arranged them to make a forest mattress. He showed them how to lay beds twenty or thirty feet from each another, explaining that if one of them ran into any trouble, the others would be at a distance and would have a better chance.

A better chance of *what*, Bill asked John. Was Fiji serious? And if he was, what did that mean? John didn't know. No one was happy. But it was far past that being a consideration. The boys were all well brought up and never used bad language, but they knew a couple of words. During the school year, they had made a pact that if something really needed a swear word, they'd each have their own to use. The words all got discreet airings as the end of the day came on.

The boys grumbled but built their beds, spacing them generously from one another. They took the spruce branches and created simple lean-tos over their beds to provide some cover from rotten weather. Fiji's first lesson kept bouncing around in John's head: *'You'll never go hungry in the woods,'* and the unspoken, *'But you have to catch what you eat.'* Not that night.

It was pitch dark by the time they had finished, and the boys were tired enough that sleep came easily, even with empty stomachs. And then it began to rain.

In the morning, they were cold, wet, and hungry. The spruce branches provided some cover, but they had made their beds on a flat patch of ground, and rainwater had pooled around them. Fiji had been up for some time when they woke and had a fire going. He told them that next time to make sure they set their beds were on a slope.

Then he showed he had a heart. He had gathered fresh worms for breakfast, but this time they would be fried. The boys were hungry enough to give them another shot. Fiji had found a thin shard of rock with a hollow in it, and propped it over the fire to heat. He scooped out some muck from a leather pouch on his belt and dropped it on the rock. Bear grease, he said. Always carry some with you. The boys nodded, knowing that life as they'd known it was meaningless here. Bear grease. Okay, then.

The grease heated up and began to bubble. Fiji added a mouthful of spit into it, making it bubble that much more. The boys just stared. He had some worms at the ready. He split them down their middles, flattened them, then laid them on the sizzling stone surface, frying them up like strips of bacon. The bear fat gave the worms flavour, and all three boys discovered that when you're hungry enough, your stomach gets less particular. John thought they tasted great.

With breakfast over, Fiji established what would become their daily routine. They disassembled their beds and scattered the branches, and then the fire was extinguished, and all traces of it were buried. They made sure they had left no rubbish anywhere, and whatever footprint their campsite had made in the forest had been minimized or completely eradicated. They set off again, deeper into the forest.

Fiji said they were heading towards a lake where they would make camp for the night. It was about eight miles northeast, which meant they would have to navigate without a compass. Bill said they should look for moss on trees because it grew on the north side. Fiji led them to a tall birch that had moss growing all around its base. Clearly, the moss trick wasn't going to work. Fiji showed the boys how to use the sun and shadow to get their bearings, and said if they got it right and kept moving in the right direction, there was no way they could miss the lake. He told them to make note of landmarks or other points of reference, which could come in useful if they had to retrace their steps. This confused them; why didn't he simply take them there? No, they were to lead the way, and he would follow. Today was about them learning to find the way on their own.

The three boys set off without Fiji and walked for what seemed like hours, each one of them spotting outcroppings and twisted or fallen trunks of trees that could be useful landmarks. No sign of the lake, though. Eventually, they came to a clearing they all agreed would be easy to remember. It seemed familiar, and would be useful as a point of reference. Then Artie said, 'There's Fiji.' They wondered how he'd done that – beaten them to a place that they didn't even know how they'd found.

John reminded them that Fiji was very good at tracking because he was an Indian. Really quiet, too. He must have been following them the whole time. Bill noticed some familiar branches and spruce boughs, and then it gradually dawned on them that this was the clearing where they had spent the previous night and had walked away from a couple of hours earlier.

Fiji welcomed them back and offered some advice. The

A clearing in Algonquin Park.

hardest thing to do when you're walking in the forest is to keep to a straight path, he said. The trees will confuse you. As you go forward, sooner or later everyone drifts one way or the other, and you end up looping around back on yourself. This is what you have to do: when you're finding your way through the bush, first decide what direction you want to head in. Use the sun and shadows to orient yourself. Take a fix on something specific about a hundred yards away. Keep your eye on that and walk directly towards it. Don't rethink it when you're moving: just go. When you reach your mark, choose another and walk toward that. Now you're not walking in circles anymore. Keep confirming that you're headed in the right direction and keep moving forward. What's important is to head to a specific target.

Using this approach, the boys eventually found the lake,

where they carved out a new campsite. The mosquitoes and black flies were ferocious by the water, so Fiji had them build a fire and lay cedar boughs on it, which began to smoke. When they sat downwind of the fire, the wind blew the smoke over them and kept the insects away.

They built their beds for the night. Now they were famished. Fiji sent them looking in the sandy shallows of the lake, where they collected clams and crayfish by the handful and brought them back to camp. Fiji boiled the clams until they opened, and the crayfish turned bright pink. He tossed bear grease into the water he'd used, which in turn made a very tasty broth. John thought it was amazing when you learned how things were actually done. Sometimes it was unbelievably straightforward. What's more, deconstructing such small mysteries made life more interesting, not less. That in itself was something of a revelation to him.

In the days that followed, the boys' meals included crayfish, clams, snails, grubs, and even the occasional fish, once they'd learned how to catch them without tackle. Leaves, mushrooms, and berries were often added to the mix. They learned to appreciate the tops of green bull rushes, which tasted like asparagus when cooked. Fiji dried the roots in the sun, pounded them into a paste, then left that to dry until it could be worked into a sort of flour. From this, he made bannock that he stuffed with worms, snails, and whatever else came to hand. He fried the whole works up, and they loved it.

As the days passed, Fiji continued introducing new skills, such as the challenge of making a snare to catch wild game.

This took some doing. But by the sixth day each boy had managed it and caught a rabbit, which they cooked on willow spits over an open fire. To their amazement, the boys found even cleaning and skinning the animals gave them great pride in what they had accomplished using nothing but their knives and their ingenuity. They had learned to do things they wouldn't have believed possible a week before. On their last night in the woods, the boys ate their dinner contentedly around the fire, agreeing that rabbit tasted a lot like chicken. Fiji said he thought it tasted more like cat, which made them think.

The next day was their last. Fiji had them take turns navigating back to the Weir cabin in what they had collectively decided was the direction they'd come from. After many hours, it was clear they wouldn't make it back before dark. Fiji led them through basics such as navigating by the North Star, and reminded them of other tricks they had learned. After a few stumbling starts, they found their way. When the cabin came in sight, the boys were astonished that they'd managed to find it. They were very proud of themselves and full of stories as they nattered away at Gordon. They talked about Fiji. Not just what he had shown them, but *how* he had shown them. When Gordon asked if they'd thanked Fiji, they suddenly realized he'd already disappeared back into the forest before they could say their goodbyes.

It was late, and sleep came easily. What they found odd, though, was that after sleeping on the ground for a week, none of them could get comfortable sleeping in soft beds. It was simply better on the floor.

When they were back home in Toronto, Gordon listened to John chatter about the trip, the stories spilling out as he remembered all they'd done, and asking when they could go again. Gordon said it wouldn't be for some time, as later that week they were sailing to England. They would meet up with Freda and Nancy in London, and then spend the rest of August travelling in Holland and Germany. He would also finally get to meet his Auntie Ted and Uncle Adrian, about whom he'd heard a great deal. They would be coming along, too.

Chapter 3
Uncle Adrian

Uncle Adrian was someone whose name John had heard in passing for many years. But he hadn't a clue who he was, and had certainly never met him or his curiously-named wife, Auntie Ted.

Sir John Adrian Chamier, known to his family and friends as Adrian, had been born in 1883 in Fyzabad, Uttar Pradesh, India. He was the son of a British general serving in India, was educated in England, and earned his officer's commission from the Royal Military College, Sandhurst. He was posted to the British Indian Army's Punjabi regiment in Jharkhand, India, where he remained until the outbreak of WWI in 1914, when he returned to England and transferred to the Royal Flying Corps (*RFC*), the *'air arm'* of the British Army, as a pilot.

The use of aircraft during the war meant aviation was no longer a novelty: it had become a prominent feature of modern warfare. Accordingly, the RFC merged with the Royal Naval Air Service in 1918 to form the modern Royal Air Force (*RAF*). Adrian had served with great distinction throughout the war, and in 1919 he was promoted to the rank of Lieutenant Colonel. In 1921, he was appointed Deputy Director of the RAF's new Intelligence Section.

'Ted' Lordly with Adrian Chamier at the time of their marriage, London, 1918.

Adrian met Edwina Ratcliffe Lordly – 'Ted' – in London in 1917, and so began a courtship that led to their marriage in February 1918. Ted's maid of honour was Freda Ferguson, the nursing sister she had met onboard ship in 1915. Freda subsequently introduced Ted and Adrian to her husband, Lieutenant Colonel Gordon Weir, when he was home on leave from the front.

Gordon and Adrian were kindred spirits politically and militarily, and became close friends almost at once. Although they worked in different professions and lived on opposite sides of the Atlantic, both men were very attentive to post-war politics in Europe. In particular, they shared apprehensions about the political, social, and economic upheavals taking place in Germany.

During the 1920s, millions of Germans seethed with resentment. This was largely in reaction to the terms and repercussions of the Treaty of Versailles of 1919, one of the peace treaties negotiated between Germany and the Allied Powers. Among its many provisions, the Treaty required Germany to *'... accept the responsibility [with her allies] for causing all the loss and damage* [during the war...]'. It further required that the country disarm, surrender key territories, and pay staggering war reparations of $31.4 billion dollars (roughly equivalent to $500 billion in 2015). Most nations affected by the Treaty were neither pleased nor pacified by its daunting terms. Those terms motivated Germany to forge more favourable treaties with other sympathetic European nations (such as Russia).

For all the strictures it imposed, the Treaty did not hobble the German economy permanently. On the contrary, in many ways, the Treaty empowered it, fueling patriotic indignation, which Germany's National Socialist Party was able to manipulate to their advantage. After struggling through a crippling depression, Germany's economy found new strength in ways that gravely concerned both Adrian and Gordon. For several years, Gordon had been expanding McLeod Young Weir's client base in Europe, particularly in Germany and Holland. Each year during his trips overseas, he was a first-hand witness to the massive changes that Germany was undergoing.

Tremendous financial opportunities arose as Germany rebuilt its fractured economy into a nascent industrial force. However, much of that new strength came with a price: Adolph Hitler's political ambition.

As Hitler rose to power, Gordon believed there were serious flaws in what international investment in Germany's industrialization was actually underwriting. He shifted his focus to ways and means of protecting the assets of his clients. Even as early as 1931, he saw ominous clouds gathering over certain sectors of Europe's financial communities. Adrian shared those concerns.

In his work for RAF Intelligence, one of Adrian's responsibilities was monitoring Germany's adherence to, and violations of, the strict limits imposed by the Treaty, specifically with regard to the constraints regarding rebuilding military resources. By the late 1920s, he could see that certain political forces were using Germany's military heritage as a foundation on which to construct new aggressive political objectives. Adolph Hitler touted the rebirth of national pride, guided by the authoritarian ideology of his Socialist party, as a means of restoring economic and social stability.

That alone was cause for concern. However, what most troubled Adrian was that which was being hidden. The Versailles Treaty explicitly stated that Germany was forbidden to have any air force whatsoever, but by 1930 Adrian had discovered that German pilots were being trained in discreet locations, typically making use of Russian instructors. He felt certain that Germany's production of aircraft would not be far behind. In an attempt to prevent disaster, he relentlessly lobbied the British government to acknowledge his reports and all but demanded that they closely monitor how their old enemy was beginning to stir. But no one wanted to listen to such war mongering. No one wanted to believe that another war might be possible.

England's losses in WWI had been catastrophic, and the post-war population enthusiastically advocated and embraced pacifism. Other European countries were equally anti-war and seemed willing to undertake whatever conciliatory steps necessary to avoid the catastrophe of another global conflict. But few countries were in concert with one another about what actions to take, and so fragile balance of the Versailles Treaty was constantly at threat.

Gordon and Adrian believed that Germany should be considered the primary threat because of its volatile economy, and its historical predilection for military aggression. Again, no one wanted to listen.

They also argued that the most dangerous force in Europe was Fascism, which employed antagonistic propaganda and manipulative dogma to win mass support and submission. Fascists played a kind of confidence game, in which its advocates guaranteed security and well-being in exchange for the extensive surrendering of essential liberties and rights. The tipping point would be when countries began challenging international borders newly redefined at Versailles. Adrian believed this was coming soon; Gordon agreed. Together they resolved to lobby their respective governments to be pro-active in maintaining the peace, and to put meaningful safeguards in place before serious problems erupted.

Both men had an enormous impact on young John. Both were committed to the same ideals, and yet they were an unlikely pair. Gordon was an outdoorsman and an athlete, but paradoxically (in John's words) he barely knew how to screw in a light bulb, or which end of a hammer to use. He established for John solid examples of self-discipline, social conduct and manners – largely by example, not lecturing – and ensured that he acquired essential survival skills. But at heart, he was a hard-nosed businessman and ex-soldier, and his relationship with his son was more formal than easy-going. Adrian was a contrast.

When Gordon and John arrived in London in August 1929, they went first to the Chamier's flat in Chelsea, where Freda and Nancy were waiting. John was shy meeting Uncle Adrian and Auntie Ted for the first time, in addition to his being expected to remain silent, as was the rule in the Weir household. At the Weirs, there was a strict code of behaviour for the children. They were expected only to use the back door and stairs, never the front: those were for parents and guests only. In the dining room, children were also expected to stand until their parents came in, to sit only after their parents had done so, and to keep their hands folded in their laps. There was no talking allowed unless they had been spoken to. It was not unusual for dinner to pass with the parents only talking to each other, and the children not saying a word.

The Chamiers were a distinct contrast to this. John found Auntie Ted to be warm, which his mother wasn't naturally inclined to be. Adrian could be formidable, but John liked him

Adrian Chamier.

immediately. He was friendly and talkative with John, asked him questions, and really listened to his answers. He was most struck by how Adrian never treated him like a child. Adrian was so very different from his father. He was inventive and mechanically inclined and loved nothing more than to tinker, invent, repair, and just generally *make* things. John's limitless curiosity about all manner of people, man-made objects, and the natural world drew him to Adrian, who in turn recognized the boy's keen intelligence and enthusiasm. (Over many summers, they worked together on several imaginative projects, including building an ingenious solar heating system for the Chamier's house in Portugal.) John regarded Adrian with enormous admiration and respect.

After the two families had finished pleasantries that first day, Gordon excused himself to make some phone calls, while Freda, Ted, and Nancy disappeared to go shopping. Adrian took John on a tour of the expansive flat, chatting to him about school and other such small talk. He then surprised John by off-handedly asking if he could remember how many windows there had been in the room where they'd had tea that afternoon. John asked if he meant the sitting room, which he did. He could picture them clearly; there had been four. Then Adrian asked about the number of doors, the colour of the walls, what was on the windowsills. John found this to be a very unusual conversation, and it was even a little nervous-making. But he liked being able to rise to the task.

Two days later, John again found himself with Adrian, who asked more challenging questions. This time, the questions were about life out on the street: what people were wearing, who was sitting, and who was standing. John asked if this was a kind of game. Adrian said that it was indeed, one that he had learned in India when he was a young man. He called it the 'Observation and Memory Game,' and said it was a variation on 'Kim's Game,' which he had picked up from Rudyard Kipling. You didn't play to win or lose. It was simply a memory exercise and a different way of looking at the world. Adrian added that he thought John had a knack for it.

John was often present during long conversations between his father and Adrian. There was nowhere else to go, for starters.

Like most boys, he had no interest in politics. But years later in high school, as the threat of war grew in intensity, he was surprised how familiar he was with the names and details of the forces that were then re-shaping the world. Newspapers and radio broadcasts resonated with ideas and points of reference that he had repeatedly heard in conversations between the two men who were having such a formidable impact on his view of the world.

The Weirs and the Chamiers sailed to the continent the following day.

Chapter 4

Growing Up

On John's first trip to Germany with his family in the summer of 1929, the Weimar Republic was still enjoying the financial and social resurgence of its Golden Era (1924-1929). Financial challenges had been subdued, and economic growth was flourishing, accompanied by a tremendous cultural renaissance. But Gordon felt the German people had unrealistic expectations for continued unlimited economic gains, and believed that the state of the nation was precarious at best.

Much of his reservation had to do with the Germans' ambivalence towards its parliamentary system, whose moderate political parties were unable to control a rise in extremist challenges from both right and left-wing extremists. The global depression following the 1929 crash of the U.S. stock market would further weaken the government, providing opportunities for marginalized organizations to aggressively pursue their political agendas through nationalistic manifestos and agitation in the name of patriotism. Nowhere was this truer than with the ambitious and ruthless National Socialist Party (Nationalsozialismus), which came to be known by its acronym, Nazis.

The Weirs were staying at the Hotel Metropole in Wiesbaden,

30 miles southwest of Frankfurt (am Main). Staring out a hotel window, John was surprised to see a squad of young men dressed in brown shirts and black belts come marching from a side street and parade through the crowds in the busy square below. This delighted him. Here, in this foreign country, was a street full of young men who looked just like troops of boy scouts back home. He called to his father and told him there was a parade of scouts marching through town, looking every bit the same as his friends in Toronto. Gordon said they were nothing like boy scouts, and that in time John would come to understand what he meant.

As he continued to watch them, John was struck by the arrogance with which they marched through the peaceful streets. They acted more like soldiers than scouts. This was neither good nor bad; it was just very different from what he was used to. He watched these German boys, and tried to imagine what they were feeling and thinking.

Between 1929 and 1933, Hitler and the Nazis worked to establish themselves as a credible political power, worthy of serious consideration in coming elections. Through crafty manoeuvering, Hitler seized power in 1933 and achieved full control over the legislature and the executive branches of the government. With the Nazis in power, foreign nationals were increasingly treated with hostility and suspicion, as propaganda encouraged fear and distrust and instilled a culture of paranoia and suspicion.

Each year, Gordon would visit his German clients in the summer, with John accompanying him. By 1933, Hitler had taken full advantage of his new role as chancellor, and the Nazis had insinuated themselves into all facets of German life. John sensed a palpable difference in the charged atmosphere of the cities they visited.

On their trip that year, there was much less informality about foreigners travelling into and around the country. Even at age fourteen, John felt greater tension and inhibition among the adults. Everything and everyone seemed to have been seized with a more intense and fervent spirit. Gordon decided that it was no longer safe for his son to wander outside, even though Cologne – where they had gone after Wiesbaden – was an old, conservative city. John was instructed to stay in the hotel unless accompanied by an adult. Freda, Uncle Adrian, and Auntie Ted were with them, and so there were more than enough people around should he want to do some sightseeing.

One morning John decided he was going to venture out on his own. He thought it would be safe to have a quick look at the city square, which he could see from his window and was only a few minutes walk from the hotel. He went out, keeping the hotel in sight. He hadn't forgotten his father's warning but was willing to chance getting caught.

The towering Cologne cathedral was a focal point of the city. It was a few blocks away. John could see its spire from the square, known as the Alter Markt, and used it as a landmark. He found a spot by a fountain where he could sit and watch people passing by. Everything looked so clean and orderly, and he felt completely safe.

Then, like something out of a movie, a swarm of uniformed

men trooped into the square, and forced the crowd back with barked orders and open hostility. John stood there galvanized, watching the soldiers bully people into obedience, astonished by how loud and angry they appeared to be. One of the officers, a Hauptmann (captain), saw John watching them, presumably not responding in an appropriately respectful manner, and stormed over to him. With his face inches from John's, he began to scream at him. It terrified John, who spoke no German, and

Adolph Hitler in Nuremberg, 1928. Hermann Göring is in front on the left.

hadn't a clue what he had done wrong. But it seemed clear that he was about to be arrested and carted off.

At that moment, Auntie Ted came walking through the Alter Markt and caught sight of this standoff. It took her a moment to realize that it was John who was caught up in it; but when she did, she acted swiftly. She moved in, stepping between the Hauptmann and the boy, and took him on. She knew that when you found yourself face to face with German authority, they paid more attention if you didn't talk, but shouted, especially at close quarters, and square in the face.

At age forty-three, Auntie Ted was trim and fit, with an athletic figure, and a voice that announced that she was a force to be reckoned with. She spoke German fluently and was in possession of an extremely rich and colourful vocabulary. She shouted at the officer that John was a child, had no passport, and was not a member of any party, all in a lively mixture of English and German that stunned John with its colour and coarseness. He had never heard such profanity, let alone from an aunt. She rounded off her tongue-lashing with a concussive *scheißkopf*. He looked startled, tipped his hat, then walked away with a perfunctory salute. John returned to the hotel with a new appreciation of Auntie Ted.

The Weirs and the Chamiers moved on to Frankfurt, where John was now confined to the family's hotel room. From the window, he watched a bustle of activity in Römerberg Square, one of the most beautiful public spaces in the old city. It had been the site of markets and fairs for centuries and was lined on one side with a magnificent façade of half-timbered 16th century houses.

On that day, hundreds of people had gathered to demonstrate against the increasingly violent tactics of the Gestapo and the SS. These were the early years of Hitler's Chancellorship when the ability for civilians to express discontent, while not welcomed, had not yet become grounds for being shot, sent to a camp, or summarily guillotined (a chillingly common method of dispatch for political dissenters during the height of Nazi authority).

An SS officer, resplendent in his black Hugo Boss uniform, faced off against the mob. He was in command of three armoured trucks, each equipped with water cannons capable of firing jets of water powerful enough knock people flat hundreds of feet away.

Sizing up the situation, the officer saw the odds were against him. He didn't hesitate. He picked up his flare gun and fired two flares directly into the body of the crowd. This created some mild panic and split the mob into three smaller groups. The officer followed this with blasts from the water cannons, injuring dozens and making the crowd disperse. John never forgot how cold-blooded. Nazis could be once they had decided to take action.

He asked his father and Adrian questions about what was happening, and why the cities they visited no longer felt safe. Gordon and Adrian never hesitated to talk about such matters with John. Adrian encouraged him to pay close attention to what he saw, and to ask questions about anything that he found unclear. Gordon stressed the importance of thinking, and not being a passive bystander.

At the end of each day, back at the hotel, Gordon and Adrian would sit and talk. John liked being a part of those adult conversations, even though much of it went over his head, and he usually stayed quiet. He knew that if he were to say anything in response to a question, his father would expect thoughtful answers. John had learned that unless he was clear about what he was talking about, it was better to remain silent. He developed a deep appreciation for listening to the two men talk and learned a great deal from watching their faces reveal feelings they hadn't expressed.

One of the greatest pleasures of travel in Europe for John was walking through the old cities, which were so different from any place in Canada. His father and Adrian asked questions such as, what made a city square in Cologne distinct from one in Amsterdam? Or London? Or Paris? How did people use the public spaces? What did people do when they interacted with one another? There were conversations about customs and manners of dress, and the peculiarities of different languages and cultures. When Gordon was busy, Adrian would come with him as they wandered around the cities. He revived the Observation and Memory game as part of their walks, and at the end of the day would ask John questions about things they had seen, and what stood out in his memory.

While in Frankfurt that summer, Adrian added a new twist to their exploring. Adrian had a specific starting place in mind: the 400-year-old Fountain of Justice in Römerberg Square.

Fountain of Justice, Römerberg Square, Frankfurt.

Once there, he pointed to a small medieval church, Old St. Nicholas, and asked John if he had a good sense of where they were. John said he did. Adrian said that they were going to try something a little more complicated than the Observation game. This would be more of a challenge. He wanted John to follow him like he was a detective. John wanted to know what the rules were, and Adrian said there was only one: not to be seen. He could move as fast or slow as he wanted when he was following Adrian, but he had to keep out of sight. If Adrian spotted John, then the exercise was over, and they would start again.

John was enthusiastic: this was something very new and quite

Römerberg Square, Frankfurt.

different. Adrian set off but didn't hurry or try to be evasive. In fact, to John it looked as though Adrian had forgotten they were playing a game, and that he had become distracted with sightseeing. When Adrian was about 20 metres ahead of him, with dozens of people between them, John set off in pursuit. While the Square was busy, it certainly wasn't crowded. But it couldn't have been more than a minute or two before John lost sight of him. It was like he had evaporated. Adrian had been dressed in a light coloured summer suit, unlike the more sombre colours worn by people crisscrossing through Römerberg. He should have stood out, but he was gone. John walked all around the Square, looking down the side streets, but there was no sign of him. He even ventured down some of the streets trying to catch a glimpse of him, but again there was no Adrian.

Now he began to worry. They hadn't agreed what he should do if he got lost. And what's more, John wasn't sure that he knew how to get back to the hotel. He started walking in the direction he thought they had come from, but found himself at the edge of the River Main, which ran through the centre of Frankfurt. They hadn't crossed that on their way here, so he decided he'd better double back to the Square and try again. He was confident that he would be able to find that. Hopefully, his uncle would come looking.

He hadn't gone more than a few metres when he became aware of Adrian walking alongside him. John was stunned. How had he done that? As they walked back to Römerberg Square, Adrian told John that his instincts were good. A large public space, such as the Römerberg, was a good place to go to if you'd lost someone, or simply needed to get your bearings in an unfamiliar city. And if you were trying to avoid being found, a busy public area made it easier to blend in with a crowd; but you don't want to linger there, or you'll begin to stand out. Use popular civic spaces as points for orientation, but explore beyond them to get a sense of how the city spreads out from there. Look for steeples and prominent buildings, and memorize them as landmarks. A train terminal is also a good place to begin or to escape, he said. Let's have a look. With that, they walked to the Frankfurt Hauptbahnhof, the city's main railway station, a few minutes away.

He told John that a train station is a primary crossroad for anyone coming into or leaving a city. Because of that, it is an important place to locate. Find the departure board to see where the trains are headed. If you don't have a destination in mind, pick one. You want to look like you know where you are headed.

Frankfurt Hauptbahnhof, the city's main railway station.

They walked around the enormous building with its vast vaulted ceiling amidst thousands of passengers moving to and from the platforms. Adrian continued with his instructions as they moved through the swarms of travellers.

When you're in a crowd and want to blend in, he said, walk at the same speed as everyone else. Should you recognize a face that you've seen before, this is cause for concern that was known as a *'Double Sighting,'* and might mean that you were being watched or tailed. If you think someone is following you, don't look back or steal sideways glances. Try and use the reflections in shop windows to see if anyone is trailing behind. Keep moving until you are certain you aren't being followed, then at that point slow your speed as you move through the crowd, doing nothing that might draw attention. When you want to change direction, gradually drift off to one side of the main body of people, checking the reflections as you do so, and begin to move in the direction you want to go without changing pace or looking around.

Appearance is also extremely important in these situations. Adrian told John that his blue blazer with its school crest had made it easy for him to be followed. Most people don't pay as much attention to someone's face as you might think. They tend to form a general overall impression of a person's colouring and their clothing, and that's where you can make mistakes if you don't take steps to camouflage yourself. To blend in, it is essential to wear clothing you can quickly shorten, lengthen, reverse, or abandon altogether. The objective is never to appear as though there's anything about you worth remembering. You want to be as innocuous as possible.

They walked back to the hotel and stopped at an outdoor restaurant for lunch. Adrian suggested they 'people watch.' He told John to pay attention to what struck him about men and women when he really looked at them. Are their faces blank? Or are they simple-minded, bored, dull, or distracted. Do they look like they are late for something? Maybe they are upset and are trying not to show it.

John watched people passing by, and could see all sorts of things in their eyes and the twists of their mouths. There was one man wearing a red bow tie and clutching a leather case who looked out of place, for some reason. When Adrian asked if there was anyone who stood out, John said yes, there was. Adrian asked if it was the man with the case, and John said it was. The bow tie had caught his attention, but as he continued to watch, the man looked nervous and ill at ease in the crowd. Adrian agreed: that's what he had noticed about the man, too.

He spoke about how in some situations it could be advantageous to have no notice taken of you. For example, if you look like you're running late for something you don't much care about, or as though it's something that you *have* to do but are indifferent about, people tend to pay no attention. You're just somebody who's late for something. Don't try to be clever: be the opposite. Don't speak unless you have to, because when you keep your mouth shut, you can learn a lot. People might assume you're a bit dull or stupid, but that can be a good thing, too. Sometimes being unremarkable is the perfect place to be.

Over the next few days, Adrian and John continued their shadow game, always beginning in Römerberg Square. John developed an appreciation of what Adrian meant by being unremarkable. He would start following him, then watch Adrian disappear. Even though he was a distinctive-looking man, Adrian was skilled at blending into his surroundings and slipping away. If John took his eyes off him for even a moment, he would lose him. Adrian showed him some of his tricks, and John became very comfortable trying them out, managing to lose Adrian more than once.

The next variation that Adrian introduced was what he called the Contact Game. The challenge was to exchange information with someone without being seen to do so, which frequently meant avoiding meeting face to face. In certain situations, this was essential to minimize risk. The *'Dead Letter Drop'* was the most common method, which involved leaving a message or some item of importance hidden in plain sight: behind a loose brick in a wall, on the underside of a bench – anywhere accessible but not obvious. A discreet signal such as a chalk mark or a carefully offset stone would alert the recipient that a drop had been made. These were common enough tricks in the world of intelligence, but to young John they were tremendously exciting. He and Adrian even went shopping at stores that sold working men's clothes in search of simple garments that could be quickly altered in some way, just enough to change your appearance briefly and hopefully throw off anyone who might be following you.

On their last full day in the city, John and Adrian walked around Frankfurt. They revisited techniques for orienting yourself in a foreign city, and the value of finding key public places, such as train stations or central plazas or squares. Adrian stressed the importance of determining what the city's most notable points of reference are, and from that being able to create a map in your mind's eye. Memorize landmarks and their locations relative to one another to make quick movement between them easier. Determine the best ways to get in and out of any city or town, and potential safe areas where you can go to ground if necessary.

At the end of that last day in Germany, Uncle Adrian was very complimentary on how well John had done. He'd shown himself to have a strong visual memory and was able to recount much of what he had seen with precision and detail. But when they rejoined the families at the hotel, Adrian didn't mention anything about what they'd been doing; just a little sightseeing was all he said.

On the ship back to England, John frequently found Gordon and Adrian deep in conversation. Given what they had seen on this trip, both men were convinced that Germany was on a measured if covert path to aggressive expansion: possibly not against England, but certainly towards one of its neighbouring European countries. They were also concerned that the English and Canadian governments, which wanted nothing to do with any thoughts of another war, could easily be caught unprepared if the German threat was not acknowledged and scrutinized. Adrian had become aware of German agents establishing cells in England and believed that an ambitious English politician, Oswald Mosley, with strong fascist leanings, was helping to facilitate this to fuel his political vision.

After a chequered parliamentary career, Mosley had come to the conclusion that Fascism was the only way for Britain to move forward on sure footing. He united various fascist movements in England into the *British Union of Fascists* (BUF) in 1932 and promoted the importance of radical authoritarian policies as a means for England to rebuild her pre-war power. As its leader, the BUF also provided Mosley with a prominent and unique place in England's political landscape. His political campaigning was dependent on fiery rhetoric, agitation, and confrontation, drawing on tactics similar to those of Mussolini's and other fascist leaders. He was an extremely compelling orator (as were both Hitler and Mussolini), but he was unable to attract a substantial following, and by 1935 much of his influence had

Oswald Mosley, leader of the British Union of Fascists (BUF), in 1933.

The BUF flag.

faded. That did not deter him from continuing to incite confrontations between the BUF and Jewish communities in London. Adrian discreetly joined the BUF in an attempt to monitor any flow of intelligence that might exist between London and Berlin. Whatever he was able to discover, he would share with Gordon when they met. At the end of August, John and Gordon returned to Canada.

Gordon and Freda's marriage had continued to unravel, and John was now being primarily raised by his father. Gordon upheld high expectations for John's behaviour and was rigorous in maintaining disciple. On one of their European trips, John was sent to summer school in Brittany because of disparaging comments he had made about the French. Gordon told him that if he were going to pass comment on such things, then he should understand what he was talking about. Ignorance was no license for free expression. If you didn't know your facts, then you kept your mouth shut: a lesson that John observed rigorously for the rest of his life.

John's parents were each formidable in their own right, and when they were together, confrontation and argument were commonplace. Over time, John came to despise such conflict and avoided it whenever possible. Getting involved was something to be avoided if possible, he decided. Better to keep his head down, his eyes and ears open, and stay at enough of a distance to be able to see what was going on.

Chapter 5

Per Ardua Ad Astra

At his request, Adrian officially retired from the RAF in 1929 with the rank of Air Commodore and joined *Vickers Supermarine* (the manufacturer of the Spitfire) as Technical Director. He became an aviation correspondent for the BBC and served as Secretary of the *Air League of the British Empire* and the *Air Cadet Defense Corps* for many years, and was known as the Father of the *Air Training Corps* (ATC), as the League was later renamed.

On their website, the ATC offer a brief history that captures Adrian's philosophy about the significance of defensive preparedness, especially in the instance of the air force:

> In 1909, the founders of the *Air League* were concerned that Britain was falling behind other nations in the development of its aviation capability.... They foresaw the threats, both military and commercial, to the country's future wellbeing if aviation was not made central to government thinking.... History teaches that few causes, even those of vital national importance, can afford to rest on their laurels, and this has certainly been the case with our on-off love affair with aviation. The country cheered the exploits of 'The Few' during the Battle of Britain, but how many knew that they also had to thank *The Air League* for promoting the formation of the *Air Cadet Defense Corps* – later the ATC –

which provided a precious source of pilots and engineering personnel.

This was the heart of Adrian's vision and became his driving passion through the 1930s. He believed that Britain's aviation had to keep pace with the alarming (covert) growth of Nazi Germany's air force because he knew that modern war would be won or lost in the air.

In the early years of flying, most people considered aviation to be a rich man's hobby. Adrian thought making flying more accessible to amateur pilots and young people would build grass roots support for increasing Britain's aviation strength. This, to him, was a key component of a defensive strategy against the potential future threat of a well-armed and powerfully-equipped German military.

While working to further the Air League's mission, Adrian befriended a Frenchman, Henri Mignet, who had become fascinated with flying and building his own aircraft at a very young age. Mignet had been a radio engineer in the First War, but flying was where his heart lay. He built his first plane – the *HM 1* – in 1912, and by the early 1930s he was developing the *HM 14*, better known as *'The Flying Flea,'* his most intriguing and popular creation. It was an ultra-light aircraft, that looked a bit like a bathtub with a biplane's wings bolted to it. It sported a wooden propeller that was driven by a motorcycle engine that was affixed to the nose of the plywood box that was the fuselage. In 1934, he published a book, *Le Sport de L'Air*, published by the Air League as, *The Flying Flea ('Le Pou-du-Ciel'): How to Build and Fly It,* in which he included a shopping list of materials

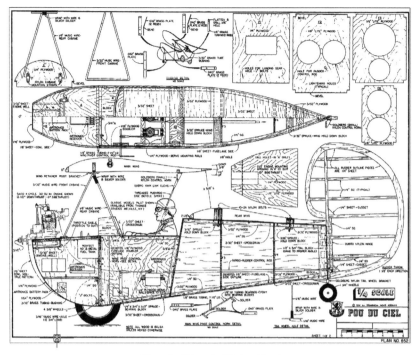

Plans for Mignet's 'Flying Flea.'

required for constructing the tiny plane.

Mignet's list included, *'2 wheels, 25 square meters of fabric, 20 liters of dope, laths and strips of planed wood, plywood, oddments of ironmongery, and a block of wood for the airscrew'.* He estimated the cost would be 1,300 francs [about $87.00]. He added that *'…a motorcycle engine of about 500 cc's is worth about 3,000 francs new, but you can often pick one up which has been overhauled as good as new for 1,000 francs [about $67.00].'* At least on paper, his creation put the dream of flight within most people's reach. Mignet dedicates the book *'To all those who dream of having wings…'* Adrian wrote the book's preface. Here are a few evocative lines from it:

> Mignet has captivated a youthful generation; he has fired them with his own enthusiasm, and he has proved that the

romance and the spirit which inspired the early pioneers of flight are still with us, only waiting for some such outlet as he has provided. I can only hope that the very many young men who speak our language [of aviation] will be encouraged to follow him in this new and exciting Sport of the Air.

In the summer of 1935, John travelled to Germany with his father, where Freda and Nancy joined them. To John, it now seemed as though the whole atmosphere of Europe had shifted, but nowhere more so than Germany. There was a much more vivid presence of the Nazi party everywhere, with huge red Nazi flags and banners brandished on buildings, lamp standards and flagpoles. Stadiums and outdoor amphitheatres were particular favourites of Hitler's for his theatrically grand rallies. Gordon told John they would make a point of attending one of them on

Freda and Nancy Weir in the foreground (family friends behind them), standing above one of Hitler's great outdoor amphitheatres in the summer of 1935. (Note the Nazi flag in the background.)

their next trip to Germany.

Back in England, the Weirs joined the Chamiers at Christchurch Airfield in Southampton. They had come to meet Henri Mignet, who was demonstrating the *Flying Flea* at an air show. Adrian had built his own *Flea* using Mignet's instructions. Now he and Mignet were going to give the Weirs an up close and personal tour. Meeting Mignet, hearing Adrian talk about it, and then seeing it fly, was one of the most profoundly eye-opening and life-changing encounters John would ever experience.

The *Flea* is a one-man aircraft, so there was no question about John being able to go up for a ride in one. But the potential for excitement that it offered was something that John never forgot. Suddenly, something quite extraordinary had fallen into the realm of possibility. Mignet added to the allure, when he wrote

> Don't think that I am exceptional. I am over forty years old, a man of routine, a typical man in the street.... It is just because I am a plain ordinary man that I write my book for normal people, that I will launch them, if they will follow me, not into danger but into the finest of sports, the sport of one's dreams.

Mignet and his plane made a powerful impression on John that afternoon at Christchurch, and flying became his irrepressible dream. Mignet was insistent that anyone could fly, and from that point forward John knew that this was be something he could do, too. This was a revelation and an inspiration. Adrian gave him a signed copy of Mignet's book, which he treasured.

The threat of war continued to simmer throughout Europe. British Prime Minister Stanley Baldwin had assured the House

Mignet standing beside his Flea in Southampton, 1935.

of Commons in 1934 that the strength of the RAF would be increased, but only if the terms of the Geneva Disarmament Conference should fail. The Conference was comprised of sixty-one nations seeking reductions in general arms. Discussions went well until Hitler came to power in 1933, and removed Germany from the conversation as well as from the League of Nations (predecessor to the United Nations). At that stage, many diplomats lost faith in the process, and most came to believe that military balance would best be achieved through treaties.

Accordingly, a major expansion of the RAF followed. By the end of the 1930s, the number of first-line strength squadrons had been increased significantly, from a few dozens to a total of one hundred and twenty-eight. Despite this, not to mention the debut of the iconic Supermarine Spitfire in 1936, the majority of the RAF's aircraft were seriously underpowered and outdated. As Germany's rearmament continued unabated, Adrian's repeated warnings to the British government in 1935 and 1936 continued to fall on deaf ears. Gordon confided to Adrian that he had received a similar reception from the Canadian government.

The two men had one long final meeting before the Weirs returned to Canada that summer. John wasn't a part of their talk, but he remembered how serious they had been. Adrian had always been so approachable and welcoming of John's company, and Gordon was more relaxed when he and Adrian spent time together. But there was not enough time in that summer of 1935. John could see that something very worrying loomed and darkened both men's spirits. John remembered fragments of conversation he'd overheard: *'German rearmament... growing threat... Britain's failure to acknowledge...'* that stuck with him for years afterwards. The prospect of war had become a reality for him, something of which he could not yet make sense.

By the fall of 1935, he was in Grade Eleven at Upper Canada College (UCC), a short walk from the Weir home. He always had solid grades, was very active in sports, and also served as a sergeant in the college battalion. (Military training was a common part of the high school education system in Canada in the 1930s.)

UCC is a preparatory school that offered boarding for students. One such student was Hugh Constant Godefroy – Hughie, to his friends – the son of a Dutch mining engineer, Constant Godefroy. Hughie had been born in the Dutch East

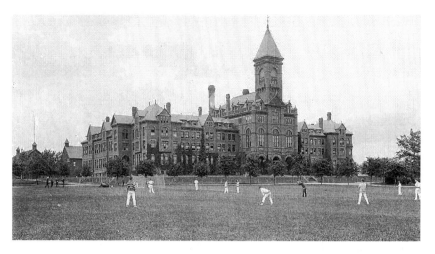

Upper Canada College in the 1930s.

Indies, but his Canadian mother, Maude McLachlin, wanted him to have a Canadian education, which ultimately brought him to UCC.

Constant Godefroy much like Gordon Weir, in that he firmly believed that the burden of responsibility for one's future rested on each individual's shoulders. There were no shortcuts to a purposeful and productive life. You had to earn your place in the world, and work for the betterment of others. To even *have* the opportunity of obtaining an education was a privilege, and one must never abuse such a privilege. It's not surprising then, when visiting from the Far East, Constant Godefroy was extremely disappointed to discover that his youngest son had '...*a handful of first team cups and a boxing mug,*' but lamentable grades. The Godefroy family was descended from Dutch Huguenots, with a distinguished lineage that could be traced back to the Crusades. But this was not a subject that Constant spoke of with Hughie. When his grandmother raised the topic of their

65

ancestry, his father quickly put things back into perspective. He made it clear that while their ancestors may have done great things, that did not make either him or Hughie exceptional. What was important was what Hughie made of himself, and most significantly, what he contributed to the world. The rest was nonsense. Gordon Weir could not have put it better.

When John and Hughie crossed paths at school, each discovered a kindred spirit in the other, and a friendship immediately took root. Both had strong-willed and resolute parents, and both had developed senses of humour that helped carry them through the more stressful parts of life. Both were very athletic, albeit quite dissimilar in physique: John was trim and compact, whereas Hughie was almost a half a foot taller, with broad shoulders and strong arms. They naturally gravitated toward similar likes and dislikes, and within weeks

Hughie Godefroy.

of meeting one another an enduring bond was formed. This is no idle phrase. John's affection and respect for Hughie never diminished. When asked about his experience as a pilot sixty years later, he would typically say, *'You should really talk to Hughie. He's the one with the terrific war record and all the medals; he could tell you what it was like to be a real fighter pilot.'* Hughie was equally enthusiastic about John.

Mary McCormack, an attractive seventeen-year-old who attended the Bishop Strachan School, a neighboring all-girls prep school, remembers John as a well-known character around their neighbourhood. She described him as a high-spirited and well-liked fifteen-year-old 'kid' (she was two years older). As she crossed the field at UCC one afternoon, John dropped unexpectedly down in front of her out of a tree, then started chattering away as though his entrance had been the most natural thing in the world.

By his own description, John was like a 'fox terrier' in those days, darting around the fields playing football, soccer, or rugby, or dashing off to catch a streetcar at 5:30 in the morning to play hockey at one of the city's many rinks. He was an extremely good right wing. Until war broke out, he played for the *Toronto St. Patrick's (St. Pat's) Hockey Club*, a precursor of the Toronto Maple Leafs, and proudly kept his St. Pat's shoulder insignia for the rest of his life as one of his treasures. Hughie was right there in the thick of it with him, even being offered a position with a professional team just weeks before war was declared.

The two of them created a featured place for themselves on the gymnastics team at UCC. (John acknowledged that the team was possibly a little thin in terms of numbers and depth of talent.) He and Hughie both had a knack for the sport, and together they developed several two-man combinations that they performed in competitions around Toronto. They had a signature routine for which they became well known. John was 'top' man, being more slight of frame, and Hughie was 'bottom' man. Hughie stood in the middle of the gym floor, and John backed off about twenty feet or so. When they were ready, John ran straight towards Hughie. When he reached him, John grabbed Hughie's outstretched hands, and with his help, vaulted up on Hughie's shoulders. Still gripping each other's hands, Hughie extended extend his arms straight up, and John would curl up into a handstand and balance there, both of their arms straight out. They'd hold that for a few seconds, and then John somersaulted back to the gym floor. It always got a great reaction.

Hughie's father worked overseas in the Dutch East Indies managing mines manned by Javanese prison labourers, and only occasionally returned to Canada. By the early 1930s, with his parents' marriage fragmenting, Hughie and his older brother were being shifted from relatives to family friends, and then into boarding at UCC. After he and Hughie had become close, John, in his delightful and very direct way, told Hughie he thought to live at school was foolishness, and so he was to pack his kit and come live in a spare bedroom at the Weir house on Forest Hill Road straight away. And that's precisely what he did, with John and Hughie living together there like brothers until they were separated by the outbreak of war four years later.

John practising his routine with Gordon in 1935 in Muskoka.

In the summer of 1936, John turned seventeen. Hughie had gone to Java for a summer visit with his father, and John was expected to find summer employment to earn university tuition and pocket money. Gordon said that the important thing was the work itself. Nepotism was against company policy at McLeod Young Weir, so something there wasn't an option. When Gordon asked John what jobs he'd considered, he admitted that he hadn't given much thought to what he would like to do. Gordon made it clear that he did not care if John didn't know what he wanted to do. What was important was to figure out what he *didn't* want to do. And if that meant trying something different every year, so be it. Getting comfortable with uncertainty was an important part of that.

With this in mind, John tried many different jobs – messenger for an advertising agency, copyboy at a newspaper, working as a clerk in Simpson's (a large Toronto department store). He hated them all, and what was worse, Hughie wasn't around as a companion for a weekend at friends' cottages on Georgian Bay and in Muskoka. Trips to Algonquin had all but ceased, with Fiji having disappeared forever back into the forest. Despite these disappointments, there was one special event that redeemed that gloomy summer of 1936 and remained one of John's fondest memories of his teenage years.

UCC organized a six-week packhorse trip in the Rockies for the students. They would be accompanied by teachers, and have experienced native guides leading them. One of the chaperones was a teacher, Nick Ignatieff, who was a particular favourite of John's. For John, Ignatieff exemplified what a great teacher could be: someone who'd had an interesting life, and went out of his way to help the boys better understand the world they were stepping into, and taught their students how to see the world for all it was.

Nick Ignatieff's father, Pavel, had been the last Minister of Education for Tsar Nicholas II in Russia. Ignatieff and his family had escaped the fate of the Tsar and other senior Russian officials through the good graces of sympathetic guards. The Ignatieffs fled to France, and then to Canada. Nick took tremendous pride in his adopted country and placed great value on the trips to the mountains with his students. He explained why in a speech to the *Empire Club* in 1937:

> Last year we took thirty-two boys to the Peace River country where we crossed the Rockies into the Fraser Valley and then descended along the route made famous by Sir Alexander MacKenzie and Simon Fraser down the Peace River through the Rockies back into the Peace River Country. I believe this sort of thing has a three-fold educational value. First, it opens up the eyes of young Canadians to the romance, the grandeur, the immensity of Canada and its vast problems as nothing else can. It may teach them to think in terms of national development and inspire them with the idea of national service. Secondly, it challenges them to meet hardships unflinchingly, when hardships are but an adventure, and thus may help to revive the spirit and courage of the old pioneers. Thirdly, a hard long journey of this kind teaches the value of voluntary coöperation and comradeship – the very foundations of all democracy – in a way that cannot be taught in the classroom, playing field or by preaching.

That echoed everything that Gordon believed in. It was almost as though all the major influences in John's life had agreed on common terms of reference for his education and upbringing. For John, the trip was not only a welcome break from the tedium of a summer job; it was an opportunity to refine skills he'd been taught by Fiji, and to be challenged intellectually by Ignatieff and other chaperones. This was a learning experience that Gordon heartily endorsed, and was a fair alternative to a summer job that year.

They rode west on a Colonist Car, something of a relic even in 1936. These dinosaurs were the most basic means of transportation, not much more than a step up from a boxcar. The Colonists were old wooden rail cars that had been re-built at an absolute minimum of cost to provide cheap transportation for the masses that were heading west in the first decades of the century. They had cement floors with wooden seats that faced one another. Their backs could be folded down to form a kind of sleeping pallet, with a second pallet that could be folded down from above. At one end of the car, there was a toilet, and at the opposite end a pot-bellied stove. Gas lanterns hanging from the ceiling provided lighting, but as the windows were painted shut, there was little in the way of ventilation. Any sour smells would linger to be shared by all until the clerestories in the roof were opened, which in turn would let in a whirling draft of wind laden with cinders blowing back off the coal-burning locomotive's smoke stack. It was about as basic a ride as there was.

On the ride west, John did something so typical of the boy and the man. He explored the train, from stem to stern, and took enormous interest when the locomotive was serviced at the occasional stop, watching the railway men adjust valve 'A' and realign lever 'B'. He especially enjoyed watching locomotives be switched to different rail lines using an enormous turntable that rotated the 200-ton machines on a dime. He loved the mechanics of it all.

The group travelled west where they were met by their

native guides and picked up their packhorses for the trip. The lead guide, Bill, was Cherokee, a quiet, well-spoken man who kept to himself. To John, Bill seemed like a kindred spirit and reminded him of his friend Fiji. Keen to make a connection, John spotted a porcupine up a tree and said to him, *'That's good eating.'*

Bill looked at John somewhat doubtfully, then asked him how you would cook such a thing. John explained what his friend Fiji had taught him: you wrapped the porcupine in clay and placed it directly in the fire, then let it cook for about four hours. The clay would turn hard as a brick, and when the time was up, you'd break it open and the clay would pull all the skin and quills off. This surprised Bill, who was by nature wary of these young people from the city. But John's enthusiasm and lack of guile bridged the gap between them, especially as he made clear that he was primed to soak up any knowledge Bill was willing to toss his way.

One night, unable to sleep, John climbed out of his bedroll and eased away from camp to visit the group's horses. They were a hundred or so yards away from the camp and hobbled with ropes to keep them from wandering. He moved silently towards them, just as Fiji had taught him, and through the shadows he could see several elk mixing with the horses. It was magical. Then a hand touched his shoulder, giving him a start. It was Bill.

Before John could find words, Bill put a finger to his lips and pointed. When John's eyes had adjusted to the dark, he saw a grizzly bear moving through the darkness a few dozen yards away, stalking the elk and the horses. On Bill's signal, they edged away and went back to camp. When they were safely by the fire, Bill said to John, *'The thing to remember is that your Grizzly will outrun you every time going uphill. Downhill's a different matter; sometimes you can beat him running down as long as you don't fall. You fall, and he'll have you. You got to learn how to turn when you run so you don't stumble.'*

John listened to this without comment. Bill suggested that he not come out again at night by himself, as it could be dangerous. John thought this to be a very fine idea. Bill returned to the horses to deal with the bear, while John slipped into his bedroll, still shaken but very thankful for Fiji's gift of walking silently in the forest and Bill's gentle common sense. Nick Ignatieff and Bill were worlds apart in many ways, and yet they shared a conviction in the inestimable value of challenging yourself in life. And nowhere better to do so than in the wild. There you could also learn what coöperation and comradeship meant.

For years, John had listened to his father and Uncle Adrian talking about the growing threat of Nazi Germany. From 1935 onward, John was very conscious of Gordon's frequent trips to Ottawa, and the heated political discussions held in the Weir home, and at the Granite Club and Badminton & Racquet Club with friends and business associates of his father. Gordon's common theme was that war was coming, and to ignore the signs was foolish and irresponsible.

It wasn't surprising, then, that when a Talent Night was

announced for the boys at UCC, John and Hughie (who shared John's views) put together a satiric sketch about Hitler and Mussolini, which they performed on the appointed night in the gymnasium. John swung from the ropes and bars in the gym doing a baboon impersonation, dressed to look like Hitler or Mussolini or maybe a bit of both, while Hughie strutted and gesticulated madly, bellowing a sort of mad Teutonic gibberish, goose-stepping, and vainly attempting to lift very small barbells.

It did not go over well with the staff. After the performance, the headmaster called the boys into his office and reprimanded them for what he felt was their flagrant attempt to provoke the students into enthusiastic support for war. He told John and Hughie that his generation had fought and suffered in the Great War, and because of that, and what so many around the world had died for, no sane nation would ever allow war to erupt again. Furthermore, anyone who thought otherwise was a warmonger, and there was no place for any such agitators at his school.

Far from feeling reprimanded, both John and Hughie became more resolute in their convictions about the coming of war. John had great admiration and respect for so many of his teachers at UCC. There had been those, such as Nick Ignatieff, who had done remarkable things in their lives, and been a positive influence on their students. He and Hughie were simply saddened by the Headmaster's dismissal of what they had been trying to say about the menace that Fascist leaders in Europe posed. It would not be long before they were vindicated.

Over the next four years, many European friends of Gordon's

came to the Weir house, stayed for an afternoon or occasionally a few days, and then moved on. It puzzled John. They were all extremely gracious, albeit very reserved. He judged from their accents that they were mostly German and Dutch, and typically had only a modest familiarity with English. They were certainly different from his father's usual circle of friends and business associates, not the least reason being how cultured and yet shy they were. He would politely introduce himself, but none of them spoke at any length with him. When he asked his father, he was told that they were clients visiting from overseas, and nothing more.

Hughie and John got to talking about it one day, how mysterious these guests were, and how private they seemed. But they were obviously very appreciative towards Gordon and his kindnesses. After watching one family leave, profusely thanking Gordon as they went, John said to Hughie, *'I think they might be Jewish.'*

Chapter 6

The Turning of the Tide

In June 1937, John had a summer job that he hated (clerical work), but he put in the hours without grumbling. Thankfully, Gordon invited him to come on another trip to Germany – likely the last such trip before things began to erupt over there, his father said. The Spanish Civil War had broken out, and Hitler's Germany had insinuated themselves, supporting Franco's nationalist troops with powerful air and armoured units. The skirmishes provided the Germans with invaluable combat experience and a testing ground for their advanced military technologies, but Hitler saw the danger of the conflict escalating into a world war. This was something he was not prepared for, so he limited the extent of German involvement. Nevertheless, Germany's meddling in another country's civil war demonstrated that the Nazis had no compunction about their disregard for the restrictions of the Versailles Peace Treaty. Hitler would rebuild his great country on his terms.

That same month, Canadian Prime Minister Mackenzie King visited Hitler in Berlin. In his diary, he wrote,

> [Hitler's] face is much more prepossessing than his pictures would give the impression of. It is not that of a fiery, over-strained nature, but of a calm, passive man, deeply and thoughtfully in earnest. His skin was smooth; his face did

Mackenzie King receiving Nazi salute in Berlin, June 1937.

not present lines of fatigue or wariness; his eyes impressed me most of all. There was a liquid quality about them which indicate keen perception and profound sympathy.

Mackenzie King was by no means alone among international leaders in his positive impressions of the Führer.

John and his father first travelled to Frankfurt, where the atmosphere seemed unusually charged and edgy to them. There was a pronounced military presence that scrutinized visitors as unwelcome and suspicious. The German people, however, were ebullient and in the grip of a zealous nationalism. They were enthralled with Hitler and felt newly empowered by all that he promised for them and their country. John found their fervour unsettling.

When Gordon finished his client meetings, he and John went to the *Waldstadion*, a fifty thousand seat stadium, to get a first-hand view of the magic with which Hitler enraptured them. A massive rally was getting underway as they arrived.

The stadium was packed with tens of thousands of Nazi party faithful, and the crowd was charged with adrenaline at the prospect of seeing the great man in person, whose arrival was imminent. Nazi flags and banners snapped in the wind, and the noise in the stadium was deafening, with trumpet fanfares and the crowd chanting and singing patriotic songs. John was overwhelmed with it all, even becoming caught up in the excitement.

He had a half-frame Leica, which he took out of its case to take some snapshots of the incredible scene exploding around them. As he raised the camera to his eye, Gordon quickly put his hand on John's shoulder and told him to put it away immediately; he was not to take a single picture. John did as

Hitler at a Nazi Party Rally in Buckeberg, 1934.

he was told. Only then did he notice the people around them staring and whispering darkly to one another. What alarmed him most was how his father had become so clearly unnerved. Gordon grabbed John's arm, and they left as quickly as possible. They took a taxi directly to the railway station and boarded a train to Cologne.

They had tickets for a First Class compartment, but once onboard, there was open hostility towards them. They were foreigners, and if you weren't German, you weren't welcome, and you had no rights. They were elbowed out of their compartment and forced to stand outside in the passageway for the duration of the trip while Germans took their places. The experience shook them both, and the rest of their train ride was spent in silence.

When they were settled in their hotel in Cologne, Gordon, looking very serious, sat John down: he needed John's help. As a teenager, John had frequently run errands for Gordon on their European trips. These were simple enough – typically delivering messages or collecting letters and bringing them back for his father. Now Gordon had a more challenging assignment. He had a note that needed special vigilance in delivery. He told John to tuck it into his shoe beneath the leather insole, and then go to a hotel a few blocks away. He should not stop or talk to anyone on the way, and should try to be aware if anyone appeared to be following him. If there was, he was to come back immediately.

When he got to the hotel, he was to bypass the front desk and head directly upstairs to a particular room. He was to knock on the door, then go in if someone answered. At that point, he should hand over the hidden note, and he would be given a note in response. That was to be hidden in his shoe the same way, and then he was to come directly back to their hotel. Again, no stopping or talking to anyone on the way.

John did as he was instructed, and the notes were successfully exchanged. Gordon said nothing more about it, but John had become very keyed up and alert. This was very different from anything he was used to.

Two days later, they boarded a boat heading down the Rhine for Holland. Along the way, the boat stopped to take on supplies. While they were docked, Gordon took John aside and told him to wander up to the bow, and look for a ginger-haired, middle-aged man. If he was there, Gordon said he wanted John to ask the man a question; something about the weather and what the forecast was over the next few days. Gordon told him to pay close attention to what the man said in response. He was to remember it precisely, word for word, then come back immediately and tell Gordon what he had said. John found the man and exchanged messages without difficulty

Once they were underway, Gordon explained that this had been to establish if it was safe to meet a certain person in Amsterdam. He said that many European cities – German ones, in particular – had, for many people, become increasingly dangerous places in which to live. He was working to help his clients protect their assets, and when possible, facilitate their emigration to Canada. John was unclear why they couldn't just leave on their own, and Gordon told him that it was complicated. But he had determined that helping these families was something that he had the resources to do. That meant he had a moral duty to assist them in any way possible. If you *could* help, then you *had* to get involved, even when it was costly or dangerous.

John asked if Uncle Adrian and he were working together. Gordon chose his words carefully, telling John they agreed that their governments weren't taking appropriate defensive preparations and that people's lives had been endangered as a result. That was all he had to say about it, and told John not to talk about any of it with anyone.

Back in London, they stayed with the Chamiers. One morning when Gordon was out at a meeting, Adrian sat down with John. He said that Gordon had mentioned the talk he'd had with him, and he was pleased to hear how he'd been able to help his father. But there was something else he wanted to discuss. As John had recently turned eighteen, Adrian wanted him to consider doing what he referred to as *'field work.'* He went on to explain what that meant.

He began by saying that for many years, German agents had been embedded throughout England. Given the current political situation in Germany, this had become a serious threat to national security. Adrian had submitted numerous reports to key government departments, warning them of the situation that was brewing, and the threats it posed. He had met with various cabinet members – as had Gordon – and submitted briefs to MI5 and MI6. (Military Intelligence Section 5 and 6.)

But the politicians remained resolutely pacifist and unmoved. They wanted no talk of war.

Adrian decided that something had to be done. By 1930, he had retired from RAF intelligence. Drawing on that experience, he began building an intelligence network that would operate below the official spectrum of MI5 and MI6, and without their bureaucratic and procedural inefficiencies. Departmental infighting compounded their frequent ineptitude in information gathering, which in turn created serious vulnerabilities for national security. The focus of Adrian's network was the surveillance and tracking of enemy agents, and the flow of top-secret material out of England.

He told John that the exercises and games they had shared over the previous eight years had demonstrated his natural aptitude for observation and field work. He explained that the best defence against plots and attacks was to be informed about them in advance, and that was a matter of gathering good intelligence. Adrian would like him to consider volunteering for the network. John readily accepted, but Adrian cautioned him about what getting involved meant. If he accepted, he could never discuss any assignments. He could never mention the Network to anyone but Adrian. If no one was aware of him or his work, then he had succeeded. In that regard, the work was the definition of thankless.

The network's greatest strength was the facelessness of its objectives and agents. Communication would always be covert, and it was highly unlikely that he would ever meet another agent face to face. Anonymity was its hallmark. Most assignments would be mundane, being minor parts of larger plans. At some point, there would come a time when John would be asked to take on an assignment that he did not want. However, as with anything in the military, refusing orders was not an option. Volunteering meant that he would be bound by the *Official Secrets Act* in perpetuity. There would be no turning back.

He challenged John to think very seriously about it. If it was more than he was able to commit to, there was no disgrace in declining. John asked if his father was a part of the network. Adrian avoided giving a direct answer, but said that they shared a conviction that there were few in government who were responsibly assessing the dangers of Hitler's Germany. He and Gordon had resolved to accomplish what they could with their own ways and means. In short, they could not rely on any official sanction or protection.

The last thing that Adrian told John was the name of the network: *Acquisitor*. When John was ready to make a decision, he was to get in touch and make reference to that name, without revealing any other purpose or meaning behind it.

On their return trip to Canada, Gordon talked about summer employment. John had completed his 'senior matric' (high school) that spring, and been accepted at Queen's University in Kingston for the fall term. Now he had to earn his tuition.

John hadn't liked any of the businesses he had worked in over the past summers. The *Flying Flea* and flying in general, however, had made a big impression on him. He thought that working at the Toronto Island Airport would be a great solution.

Gordon had another idea. He had found an opening for John to work 'mucking' – digging and excavating underground – in a gold mine near Timmins in Northern Ontario. Timmins had been founded during the Porcupine Gold Rush in the early 20th century, and in 1938 still had a rough atmosphere about it; a workingman's town. John was not happy about the prospect of spending the remainder of the summer in such a place, but there were few jobs for someone his age that paid better, and his father had already arranged it.

His expectations were low when he headed north, but he was unprepared for the harsh reception he got when he arrived at the Augite Mine. The Depression had made the mineworkers protective of their jobs and income, and as such they deeply resented the kid from Toronto, who effectively stole a position that might have gone to one of their sons. For the six weeks he worked with the miners, they never let him forget their resentment, relentlessly bullying, chivvying, and pushing him around.

On his first morning, John climbed on the railway skiff that transported the miners down into the mine. Cradling his lunch pail in front of him, the other miners piled on and pushed up against him until they squashed him and his lunch. John said nothing; he knew he had to work with them for the next six weeks, and so he had better keep his mouth shut and put up with it.

His first serious challenge was fetching water in twenty-gallon pails. This involved hauling two full pails from a stream up fifty yards of steep ground. At first, he could barely lift a single pail, struggling uphill to the waiting truck, stumbling and spilling water the whole way. But he was determined and pushed himself a step at a time. After a week, he had built up some strength, and after two weeks, he found that he could manage without too much difficulty. That was the easy part. Life was much harsher underground in the mine.

There his job was filling a wheelbarrow with damp earth and rock, which was then wheeled up a ramp, and dumped into a skiff that was hauled up to the surface. Even though he went about the backbreaking labour without complaint, some of the miners still got a charge out of finding ways to make him work even harder. There was an obnoxious Englishman by the name of Harold, who had taken an instant dislike to John. His favourite prank was to load a wheelbarrow in such a way that when John went to lift it, it toppled over. Every time this happened there were gales of laughter from the miners, which John silently endured as he refilled the barrow.

Amongst this flinty lot there was an exception: Gunnar, a Swede, who was a hardened veteran of the mines. He had a son back in Sweden around John's age, which inclined him to look on John with something like a paternal eye. He shared tips on how to handle a shovel properly, how to dig gravel for hours without exhausting yourself, and how to pace yourself through the long underground shifts. Gunnar quietly watched Harold bully John for the better part of his first week, then decided to step in. Gunnar suggested John swap places with Harold for a shift, which meant John would be doing most of the heavy lifting. Harold was all too pleased to have the kid to do the shovelling. That meant he could relax with a cigarette until his time came to wheel the barrow up the ramp and dump it. Gunnar gave John a hand with the shovelling, showing him how to properly load the wheelbarrow. When it was full, Harold stubbed out his cigarette and picked up the barrow, whereupon it flipped over backwards and knocked Harold off his feet. John said nothing, but Gunnar and the others enjoyed him being the butt of the joke for a change, the general attitude being *'Serves you right, you little shit.'* As ever, John kept his thoughts to himself.

The work underground was not only grueling but dangerous, too. Accident rates in hard rock mining were high, with about a third of the miners sustaining injuries each year. This was no place for the faint of heart: it demanded a strength of character to survive in a place that was so primitive, both above and below ground. The miners lived close to where they worked, and living conditions on every front were spartan at best. Surviving that was an education unto itself.

The strange thing is, after the first couple of weeks, John came to like it. He had to learn everything the hard way, and in the 1930s, everything in mining was hard. Gunnar continued teaching John some of the skills he had acquired from years working mines. These included how to *'read'* the rock, danger signs to watch for, and techniques of rebuilding and shoring up the framing of tunnels.

At the end of John's first two weeks, Gunnar came to him with a proposition. If they worked as a team, they could earn more by not taking an hourly wage, but by being paid for *'piece'* work. If they met or exceeded a weekly quota, they stood to earn about four times as much money. John was quick to agree. One of his strengths was recognizing the value of working as a team.

Their partnership was a great success financially, as well as making the time fly. With Gunnar's experience and direction, and John's single-mindedness and drive, they became an extremely productive combination. Week after week, they surpassed their quotas. By the end of August, Gunnar had earned his return passage to Sweden, and John had made more than enough to cover his tuition for Queen's. Physically, the work had an enormous impact as well. John filled out, increasing in weight from 118 pounds to 155, all of it muscle. He put on so much bulk that when he returned to Toronto, most of his clothes no longer fit, and he was in the best shape of his life.

He started at Queen's in September, pursuing a degree in Chemical Engineering. At first, that had seemed as good a choice as anything. But after a month of it, he found that he had no interest in the subject. He finished off the term, then arranged to transfer to the University of Toronto, where Hughie had enrolled. At *Varsity*, as it was known, John decided to study Aeronautical Engineering, which for him meant more than the physics of aerodynamics. It would be his way of earning a university degree, with the very attractive side benefit of learning how to fly.

Ever since he'd seen the *Flying Flea* in action, met Henri

Mignet, and heard Uncle Adrian enthusing about flying, he knew it was something he wanted. If war did come, he would enlist, but not in the army. After the stories he had heard from Gordon, photos of WWI trenches and battlefields with bodies scattered across No Man's Land, the misery of mud and disease, and the mutilations from shrapnel and machine gun fire, he'd made up his mind. He was not going to be one of the *'Brown Jobs'* stuck on the ground being shot at. If war came, Aeronautical Engineering would give him a head start, and he would be at the head of the line to join the air force.

He was going to fly.

Chapter 7

War

John and Hughie shared the dream of flying. But both knew their fathers expected them to complete university and start earning a living and building a respectable life, so they resigned themselves to the grind of earning degrees and waiting for something exciting to happen. They didn't have to wait long.

War was declared between England and Germany on Sunday, September 3rd, 1939. That was not a great surprise to John or Hughie, and they were keen to sign up. But an unexpected event spurred them to join much faster than they might have done otherwise.

That weekend – Labour Day Weekend in North America – Hughie's girlfriend, Peggy Hodge, was returning to Canada from England with her sister and mother onboard the *S.S. Athenia*. A few hours after the official declaration on September 3rd, a German U-Boat mistook the *Athenia* for an armed merchantman (a supply ship equipped with guns for defensive purposes) and torpedoed it without warning. In doing so, the Germans defied the *'Prize Rules'* of war. Also known as *Cruiser Rules*, these were internationally recognized treaties that had been signed by both countries many years before. Technically, this obligated the Germans to force the *Athenia* to stop, and

S.S. Athenia at anchor.

allow her passengers and crew to abandon ship before she was sunk. But the Germans were waging a war unlike anything the world had known before, and such treaties and rules – while not wholly abandoned – were rarely honoured.

In the commotion of the torpedo hitting the ship and the subsequent explosions, there was panic and confusion among the passengers and crew. Even though there were sufficient lifeboats, evacuation plans had been informal at best. Peggy and her sister managed to find their way to their boats but lost track of their mother. She jumped or was accidentally pushed off the stern, and was lost along with one hundred and eleven other passengers. Peggy was left adrift in a lifeboat for fifteen hours on the Atlantic before being rescued and returned to Liverpool, where she managed to reconnect with her sister.

The next morning, September 4th, Hughie received a telegram from her confirming she was safe. John and Hughie enlisted that same day, driven in part by a desire to strike back at the new enemy in light of Peggy's loss. But equally compelling was the tremendous excitement at the prospect of someone paying them to learn how to fly. Five friends – John, Hughie, Jimmy Jordan, Paul Phelan, and Jim Scott – went down to York Street in Toronto, around the corner from the Royal York Hotel, and enlisted in the nascent and poorly equipped *Royal Canadian Air Force (RCAF)*. It wasn't until they were on their way back to the Weir house that Hughie said, '*John, what is your father going to say about this?'*

John had been troubled about that. In most military families, it was tradition that the son serve in his father's regiment. In John's case, that would mean joining the ranks of the *Governor General's Horse Guards* (Gordon's regiment). His father was not going to be pleased when he heard about the air force.

Hughie, on the other hand, had a different if equally daunting challenge. His father despised how Europe had been turned into a battleground in the Great War. He believed this could happen again. Constant was Dutch, and they were a peaceful people. He was not about to allow his son to run off to war just to be killed. Hughie knew his father would be extremely angry at what he had done, but hoped that if he first broke the news to Gordon, it might in some way make things easier.

That evening, John and Hughie were at the Weir house, telling Freda about having signed up, and trying to sort out the best way to tell Gordon without too many fireworks. Gordon arrived home unexpectedly early from a trip to Ottawa. He asked the boys to join him in the library for a talk. John and Hughie were sure he must have got wind of them enlisting

Lt. Colonel Gordon Weir, DSO, MC (and Bar), at his Toronto home, September 1939.

in the 'wrong' branch of service, and before Canada had even declared war.

That wasn't it. He announced that he had pulled several official strings, and managed to arrange commissions for them both in the *Horse Guards*. This was greeted with silence, and he could see that something was up. He told John to tell know what was going on, *'...and to do so without any dressing.'*

John got to his feet and stammered out that they had signed up for the air force that morning. Gordon frowned. As Hughie and John remembered it, Gordon turned towards the fireplace without a word and stared into it for a long time. Then he turned back to them and said, *'We thought the last one was sure to be enough. God help you.'*

Gordon would have been thinking about Adrian and his experiences in the Great War. Pilots had been extremely vulnerable. Anyone with a rifle had a reasonable chance of hitting an aircraft flying overhead, and the casualty rate for fliers had been extremely high.

When Hughie finally spoke to his father several days later, Constant reacted just as expected. *'Monumental stupidity,'* he called what they had done, especially for Hughie with his peaceful ancestry. Constant made it clear it was not *their* fight. Holland would remain neutral, and in any event, Germany would never invade Holland. It had no military value.

The day after enlisting, John and Hughie decamped to a family friend's cottage on Georgian Bay, where they waited to be called up into active service. Both were delighted to set aside their studies at the university, and to have the prospect of now learning how to fly. Canada declared war a week later, but it would be months before they would see any part of it.

The war took the better part of a year before it evolved into something that seemed 'real.' Apart from a few minor skirmishes, neither Britain nor Germany launched major military operations against the other for the next uneasy nine months. This curious period of waiting was referred to as the *Twilight War*, the *Phoney War*, and *Sitzkrieg*. German generals later acknowledged that had Britain and France struck decisively against the German army in September 1939, their combined one hundred and ten divisions would have been able to suppress the twenty-three German divisions within a couple of weeks, and the war would have been over. But no one wanted to believe that any war whatsoever was an option. Better to sit tight and see what happened, and put one's faith in treaties and peace accords.

As a result, few countries prepared. Germany, however,

had been organizing and re-equipping for years. While the Canadian army was well established and ready for mobilization, that was far from the case for the RCAF, which was comprised of a handful of aging aircraft and a couple of *Hurricane* fighters (precursor to the iconic *Spitfire*). There were no training facilities or formal pilot training. There was a need to create a coördinated plan across the Commonwealth to train men for a unified air force. By contrast, Germany had been rebuilding its military for almost a decade. They had tested their tactics and equipment in the Spanish Civil War and had developed high-efficiency production facilities that were up and operating at nearly full capacity. And they had been for years.

An unexpected obstacle arose for Hughie. He received notice that as he had been born in Java – even though he had spent most of his life in Canada and had a Canadian mother – he was considered to be a Javanese national. He would have to wait for the Canadian government to grant approval of an 'Alien's Enlistment.' Once they realized the RCAF was nowhere near ready for them, John and Hughie reluctantly returned to their classes at U of T. It would likely be months before they would be called up, by which time they suspected the war might over. Very disappointing.

Two days before Christmas, John was invited by a friend, Peter Hart, to join him and his girlfriend, Betty McMaster for a night of dancing at the Palais Royale on Toronto's lakefront. He liked dancing, so he said yes, but became horrified when he overheard Betty on the phone asking her friend Fran

McCormack to join them as his date. John tried to wave Betty off, but she ignored him. He had been seeing another girl for a while – not a girl*friend*, but someone who liked to dance and see a movie once in a while. John's worry was that he was very innocent and a little awkward with girls when it came to romance. Going on a blind date was something he did not want to do. He dreaded the coming night, especially knowing he would be relegated to the rumble seat of Pete's Model A roadster. Once they picked up Fran, she would have to tuck in close beside him.

When they picked her up, and Fran squeezed in, she was pretty, bright, and had a sense of humour about it all, making everything much easier for John. But what eventually made the date a success was the dancing at the Palais Royale. She was a terrific dancer, and everything was easy and second nature, almost as if they had been dance partners for years. At the end of the night, they drove Fran home. John hopped out of the rumble seat, helped her get down, and then shook her hand warmly. He told her he'd had a really good time but then stumbled. He couldn't remember her name.

She didn't miss a beat and said she'd had a good time, too. She said that her name was Frances McCormack. She added that her older sister, Mary, knew John. Mary had been the girl who he'd dropped down out of a tree to chat with at UCC four years earlier.

John was smitten. Here was someone he could be himself with, and who liked the same things. He later made note of the date in a journal he started during basic training. For years to come, that date was a special anniversary for him. Fran and John didn't go on a real first date until the middle of January, but when they did it was every bit as much fun. They started seeing each other every day, and he recognized she was something special, and pursued her accordingly.

His formal call-up came towards the end of the month. He received notice that he was to report to the Winnipeg Flying Club on the morning of Monday, January 29th. Even though this is what he'd waited months for, his imminent departure brought about strong mixed emotions. He'd fallen head over heels for Fran, and never having had feelings like that before for anyone, those feelings knocked him completely off balance. In the week before he left, the two of them spent a lot of time together. On one of their last nights out together, she had encouraged him to buy a journal to keep a running account of his training. He had never done that kind of thing before, but the idea stuck with him because of her; he'd keep one for her.

Being the first to be called up of the five friends who had enlisted together, Hughie, Jimmy Jordan, Paul Phelan, and Jim Scott came down to Union Station to see John off on January 27th. They brought him a piglet as a going away gift (which John narrowly escaped having to take with him). But there was no Fran on the platform, which was awful. Maybe she didn't have that much interest after all. He had bought a journal as she had suggested, and he began writing in it two days before heading out. For the next two years, he faithfully kept track of what happened every day; it made him feel like he was talking to her, and unintentionally became a remarkable record of his evolution into a frontline fighting man.

The war was sufficiently distant that travelling across Canada to learn how to fly seemed more of an adventure than preparing to go into battle. During those first months of the war, there was no established flight training program for the RCAF. Instead, the first wave of young men who enlisted were sent to civilian airstrips across Canada to be trained by local instructors. There was little in the way of equipment, uniforms, or even accommodations, so John was billeted at the YMCA during his first weeks in Winnipeg.

Their *Initial Training Session (ITS)* lasted twelve weeks, and was a combination of flying lessons and classroom lectures. New airmen were taught to fly in biplanes, *Trainers*, which were very stable, flew around a comfortable 60 miles per hour, and were all but pilot-proof. John and the others learned on three iconic

John standing in front of a Fleet Finch at the Winnipeg Flying Club, February 1940.

aircraft, or *'kites'* as the boys called them: the Fleet *Finch*, and the de Havilland *Tiger Moth* and *Gypsy Moth* (named in recognition of founder Geoffrey de Havilland's renown as a lepidopterist). Because it was winter, the trainers had skis on them instead of wheels, which added to the challenges when landing. John discovered that his *Tiger Moth* had a tendency to slide for quite a distance when he touched down, especially with a tail wind. The implications of this didn't completely sink in until he came in and landed at sixty miles per hour on a frozen field. His plane slid a couple of hundred yards further than he'd anticipated, and headed directly toward the hangar, finally nosing up against the hangar door with a gentle *'thump.'*

But such close calls never fazed him. You learned by getting your kite up into the air, circling around, and then getting it down again, constantly correcting the mistakes you made as you repeated the cycle over and over again. In his journal, John

Coming in to land on skis.

never mentioned any fear. Rather, he worried about passing tests, expressed frustrated at bad weather (which cut down valuable flying time), boring lectures, and always sounding restless for what was coming next. Getting comfortable with the unknown was an important facet of this learning process.

It was his feelings for Fran that struck fear into his heart; more specifically, his worry that she might not share his feelings. If this war was, in fact, a phoney one, he hoped it would wrap up soon and allow him to get back to Fran. But he wanted to finish his flight training first.

Like many neophyte pilots, John suffered from airsickness. Apart from the obvious discomfort, this was a potential disaster, because to get airsick meant that you could be washed out as a pilot, and sent back to be re-trained for some lowly trade.

On February 11th, he wrote,

> I flew this afternoon and was so close to being airsick that it wasn't funny. I've been seasick like a dog before, but onboard ship at least I have somewhere to be sick. But up in the air in a small plane there is no room to be sick, and when you can see the airport is 10 minutes away, and it's a bumpy ride, well it's just a toss-up. Literally. So either you win or you toss up all you have.

He had been flying for less than a week, and the prospect of getting airsick started to haunt him. His instructors were a mixture of brusque and tolerant, and thankfully one of the more understanding men took John aside and gave him a tip. *'Bring something up with you to be sick in. Should you forget to do so, scrub your plane clean once you're down and before you turn her back over to the ground crew.'* Once he knew he had ways to manage the problem, he never felt sick again.

Those twelve weeks in Manitoba didn't feel like they were preparing for war. John's class of five pilots were having too much fun. They ate well, slept in comfortable beds with clean sheets, went to the movies a couple of times a week, had parties and dances, and were regularly invited for home-cooked dinners by the locals. During the days, they followed a routine of classroom lectures and practical flying time with their five instructors. They needed to keep accruing flying hours because prospective pilots had to have 50 hours in the air to pass the course. Every flight was recorded in detail in each man's log. Those hours were spent doing endless basic take offs and landings, which are always the most challenging and dangerous aspects of flying for any pilot. They gradually added aerobatic skills such as steep turns, spins, and loops. One of the most hair-raising manoeuvres a pilot had to master was to put his plane into a dead stall, let it spiral down, and then pull out of that before crashing. John was particularly fond of the adrenaline rush which that particular stunt delivered.

In his journal entries – there are over 600 of them between January 1940 and November 1941 –John slowly evolves from a lovesick young man to an experienced combat pilot. At the outset, he is in love, bursting with the adventure of learning to fly, earning a salary doing what he would have happily paid someone to do, and living with a group of like-minded young men. Life was wonderfully exciting.

Gradually, his journal reveals his growing maturity. During his first week in Winnipeg, he sounds young and impatient:

A Fleet Finch.

Sunday February 6th

It seems we only get to fly every other day. Today was a rotten windy one, so we had lectures all day and plenty of them too. Tonight I played stud poker. I liked it and it gave me something to put on this page.

Twelve days later, he's more matter of fact:

Sunday February 18th

Today was a half-day. The weather was useless so they let us off. If it's clear tomorrow, then we fly. Lectures in the morning.

And a week after that, he's flying solo and driven to reach his objective of earning his wings:

Saturday February 24th

Boy, today was a day! I flew solo, exactly 4 weeks since I left Toronto. The instructor and me flew around three times, and after our third landing he said, and I quote: *'How'd you like to take it up yourself?'* End of quote. Naturally I said yes. Who doesn't want to solo? So out he got and away I went. Now I have eleven hours and a bit more. Thirty-eight to go.

The age of his instructors was surprising, as some were only a couple of years older than John.

> February has been a good month all in all; the instructors are all darn nice. Cliff, the head instructor, is a bit snappy, but I like him. Archie is a regular fellow. Bill is only 23 or so but he's darned nice and tries very hard to put across his lectures to us. Herb of course is a peach of a guy and has all patience in the world (or else he's awfully good at keeping his feelings to himself). How any man living or dead could endure teaching five guys like us to fly is beyond me.

But his feelings for Fran never diminish; they are there on every page. He had given her the nickname 'Robin,' which he'd dreamed up because she was perky and spritely and full of life – just like in the popular song, 'When the Red, Red Robin Comes Bob, Bob, Bobbin' Along.'

She was always on his mind when he sat down to write in his journal about what happened each day. And although he kept the journal to himself, and *for* himself, it was his way of talking to her. Nearing the halfway mark of the course, he wrote about how much he missed her, and how the Phony War was beginning to frustrate him:

Thursday February 29ᵗʰ

> Still having heart trouble over Robin… but she'll never find out unless this crazy war stops soon This book should be called Robin's Book – after its inspiration. I'd never keep it if it wasn't for her.

He wrote to her about his close calls:

Sunday March 3ʳᵈ

> Well, today I was (pretty nearly) a dead pigeon. I almost fell

asleep in the plane three or four times. Luckily it was all bumpy and every time we hit one it woke me up. I was up an hour in the afternoon. I've now got 15 hours and 30 minutes. All's well except with my heart. How's yours?

As the weeks pass, his determination to succeed in his new profession is clear:

Friday March 8th

Lectures this morning, then flying this afternoon for about an hour. Practicing spins, steep turns, and stuff. 17 hours and 30 minutes, and not enough time to make up those last few hours before our 20-hour test, maybe on Sunday.

Tuesday March 19th

Today we started aerobatics! Loops and slow roles – more fun, most fun yet. We had news today that we might be stationed at the Eglinton Hunt Club in Toronto!

This was a major development. The Eglinton Hunt Club was then located on the east side of Avenue Road just north of Eglinton Avenue – only a few blocks away from his house and Fran's, too.

Tuesday April 16th

After an hour's flying this morning, through three layers of clouds, we took our tests and all passed!! Tomorrow we fly by instruments, and then we're finished!

Wednesday April 17th

We finished up the [instruments] tests and all of us passed. Just back now from a party at the Flying Club and another at the Royal Alex Hotel. We fly home to Toronto tomorrow!! Yeeeah Hooo!!!

John was home the next day, and four days later he reported

to *No. 1 ITS* at the Hunt Club, the first school of the budding *British Commonwealth Air Training Plan (BCATP)*.

The Plan was a massive air-training program involving Britain, Canada, Australia, New Zealand, and Southern Rhodesia during World War II, and remains the single largest aviation-training program in history. It was responsible for training nearly half the pilots, navigators, bomb aimers, gunners, wireless operators, and flight engineers of the Commonwealth Air Forces during the Second World War. Canada was chosen as its primary location due to her ample supplies of fuel, wide open spaces suitable for pilot and navigation training, industrial facilities for the production of training aircraft, parts, and supplies, and its proximity to both the European and Pacific theatres of war. Over 167,000 students, including over 50,000 pilots, trained in Canada under the program from May 1940 to March 1945, more than half of whom were Canadian.

The spacious grounds around the buildings at the Hunt Club were a key asset for training, as they provided generous space for drills and parades. There was also a gym, a bowling alley, a ballroom, stables for a hundred and fifty horses, an indoor riding ring, and a swimming pool. But the young airmen were not allowed to make use of these. They did little but march.

John and the other *Pilot Officer Provisionals (POPs)* – commonly referred to as *P.O. Prunes* – were there for basic training, which meant having as much of their individuality drilled out of them as possible. They were under the command of a permanent force RAF veteran, Warrant Officer First Class Firby, whose rough, working-class accent and sarcastic turn of phrase were ideal complements to his hard-nosed style of instructing.

Firby marched his young charges relentlessly back and forth across the Hunt Club's grounds, attempting to marshal them into some kind of synchronized formation. Firby wore a large nickel-plated whistle around his neck and used it to signal pattern changes in close order drills. After two days of frustration trying to get the boys marching together as a unit, no one could bear its shrill shriek. On the morning of the third day, Firby lined his section up alongside the swimming pool, barking at them that they could use the pool's edge as a guide by which they could recognize what a straight line looked like. In no uncertain terms, he outlined what his plans were. He was going to march them and drill them until their feet were bleeding and, through sheer brute force if nothing else, they had become the best-trained prunes their superior officers had ever seen.

There was an upcoming Close Order Drill competition at the *Canadian National Exhibition (CNE)* grounds in two weeks' time, pitting army, navy, and air force units against one another. Firby had entered them, and he intended on having them '... *jumping around the grounds like a bunch of monkeys fucking a bag of tacks!'* He made it very clear that they had bloody well better win, or they would repeat their four weeks in basic training.

A career soldier, Firby had been raised on army discipline. With not much war on yet, drilling was an excellent means of toughening up the boys and cutting short their daydreaming. One of the young pilots was offended by Firby's harsh treatment of them. He stammered that his father was a very important person in government and that this was no way to talk to provisional officers. Firby listened, nodding his head with understanding, and then walked over to the boy and toppled him backwards into the swimming pool. When he came spluttering up for air, Firby stared down hard at him. He told the young man that they would continue their talk in his office in twenty minutes in a dry set of clothes, or he would be grounded permanently. Firby asked if there was anyone else who wanted to talk about his dad. There wasn't.

Early in their first week, uniforms arrived. For the previous three and a half months, the boys had only their own civilian clothes to wear. Getting uniforms meant they would look the part of pilots, which would give a much-desired boost to their social status. When the tunics were distributed, however, they left something to be desired. The waists were inches too large, and the legs were inches too short. Most of the boys wasted no time in tracking down a tailor to have appropriate alterations made. Since they were having things adjusted in any event, there was an irresistible temptation to add padding to the shoulders, which gave the tunic a more dramatic and dashing silhouette.

Inspections were a part of the daily discipline routine. Belts, buckles, buttons, and shoes all had to be brightly polished, and trousers crisply pressed, with no show of individuality. Everything had to be 'just so,' or God help you. When the new and improved uniforms appeared on morning inspection, complete with impressive shoulder widths, Firby was not pleased. He wasted neither time nor words. Taking a straight razor from his pocket, he sliced open the shoulder pads of one boy's tunic and pulled out the superfluous stuffing, silently dropping it at the boy's feet. He noted acidly that when the rest of the misguided matinée idols had also removed their stuffing and returned their tunics to regulation form, they would then reassemble in formation and inspection would be resumed. Furthermore, they would remain on parade, standing at attention, until he was completely satisfied that order had been restored.

John and his friend Paul Phelan had both had their shoulders extended inches on either side. They did their best to slouch at attention in hopes of minimizing their oversized shoulders hope and escaping Firby's scathing eye. They got lucky. Firby

John in 1940.

turned on his heel and dismissed them all, at which point Paul and John hustled off and had their uniforms restored.

At inspection the next morning, Firby moved up and down the line and made no comment about the uniforms. Instead, he tugged on the fringes of hair on the backs of their heads. He called them a lovely bunch of chorus girls with flowing tresses, and that they had better get to a barber and get a proper cut, regulation short, by inspection the next morning. If they didn't, the corporal would see to it that any non-regulation hair left on their heads would be removed with a straight razor. He assured the boys that none of their boyfriends would like the results.

Over and over again, they practiced their drill patterns on the parade ground, with Firby's whistle signalling each change. To everyone's surprise, it worked, and Firby's *No. 1 ITS* section won the Close Order Drill competition. That was a bright spot during those early months when the training seemed to go on and on into the distant future. The young pilots were impatient to get into the fight before it was all over. News reports of the European war, as it was often thought of in the early months, made it seem like a bit of a charade to some, John among them. They all wanted real action.

John and his fellow provisional pilots were reassigned to *Service Flying Training School* (SFTS) at Camp Borden near Barrie, an hour north of Toronto, to become combat pilots. They spent the next four months there being trained in the fundamentals of flying modern combat aircraft, or as modern as the RCAF could get. (The Canadian air crews were always last in line to get new equipment.) At Borden, the boys flew over a much broader range of country: urban areas, hills, valleys, and large bodies of water. This entailed learning *Visual Flight Rules (VFR)*, which are the guidelines used to fly around visible objects, such as trees, buildings, and other aircraft, without colliding. As basic as that might seem, the inability to understand and incorporate those rules into a pilot's skill set was one of the major causes of accidents during training. New pilots had to internalize all of this, so their actions and reactions became reflexive and automatic in simultaneously managing pedals, stick, airspeed, altitude, flaps, rudder, and issues of prevailing winds and visibility. There was a daunting amount of memory work in the course, quite apart from additional considerations such as the proper use of navigational aids, armaments, and tactical skills.

Anyone who can drive a car can probably steer a small standard trainer. But flying a fighter was like driving in a fourth dimension. Just getting off the ground and get back down again in a high-powered fighter or bomber separated the living from the dead. The close calls, the unpredictable winds, and the bad landings were, for John, all part of the excitement. His first time soloing at Borden gave him an ecstatic high that he never lost; in fact, it became an addiction:

> I soloed today for 40 minutes! The first time I have even flown one alone. The Kite didn't have breaks or steerable tail wheel, so it was a bit hectic on the ground... I was up for one hour and five minutes in a Fleet Finch and had a pretty good session – mostly trying to learn about the aircraft – I did my first roll off of a loop today, more accidental than anything else. But it rolls beautifully!

John felt as though he became a part of the plane once he'd left the ground. From the start he believed he was one of the best, and that kind of absolute faith in yourself is what often kept good pilots alive.

By the spring of 1940, those at Base Borden who hadn't been washed out or killed were sent for intermediate training as bomber pilots at Trenton RCAF base, an hour and a half east of Toronto. This was a much more demanding kind of flying because the planes were larger and less forgiving. But for John, a bomber pilot meant you were responsible for the men on your crew, which made him realize he would be gambling with other men's lives. He hated that thought.

The boys started on the *Fairey Battle,* an aging three-man British bomber that had already been pulled out of frontline action. It was slow, limited in range, and highly vulnerable to attack, making it an unnerving and challenging airplane to go to war in. The *Battle* was frequently unpredictable and unreliable in the air, as John discovered during his months at Trenton. All pilots have their bumpy landings, and John had one of his worst while flying a *Battle.* His friend Paul Phelan was onboard as an observer. John attempted to touch down on the landing strip from a greater height than he was aware. At around forty feet off the ground, he cut back his throttle, which abruptly brought the plane down to earth with an impact akin to driving a large American sedan off the roof of a two-storey house. A ton of whining metal and Perspex hit the runway with a bone-jarring *'whirrrrr-BANGGGGG,'* bouncing Paul around like a gumball. When the plane came to a shuddering stop, John glanced back at Paul's bloodied nose and bugged-out eyes. He scrambled out

A Fairey Battle.

of the cockpit and beat a hasty retreat to the barracks, where he lay low until Paul eventually cooled down.

Such close calls never fazed John. He wanted to fly, and imperfect landings weren't going to keep him out of the air. They were a part of the whole experience. Over the following weeks, he flew endless solo hours working to smooth out the rough edges of his technique, and to add more hours to his flight log in the never-ending hope of being reassigned to flying something faster and more lethal.

In his third week, he was completing another *'review the essentials'* flight, and as he came in to land, his engine caught fire, which apparently was an all too common quirk of the

Battle. He got his plane back on the ground just as the engine seized, and then sprayed engine-cooling glycol back into the cockpit and over John. Reeking of anti-freeze, he scrambled out of the plane before the fire spread, looking like an unholy mess, but otherwise no worse for wear.

The next day, a dress parade was called for the POPs to be inspected by a visiting English RAF Group Captain. POPs were only issued one uniform, so John had no choice but to go on parade in his stained and battered tunic. The glycol had bleached it into a strikingly mottled amalgam of greens and greys. Also, he had put on some weight, which made the jacket strain at its seams and required him to cinch his tunic's belt tight and with the buckle off to one side.

The Group Captain moved down the lines of smartly turned out airmen standing to attention when John caught his eye. He paused, then strode over to John, looked him up and down, and said, *'And who might you be?'*

John gave his name and saluted. The Group Captain acknowledged this, then turned to the base's commanding officer (CO) with a quizzical expression, as though he was missing a private joke, but received no clarification. He looked John up and down again, and turned back to the CO and said, *'Rather a scruffy looking individual, wouldn't you say?'* He then carried on with the inspection. There was a ripple of chuckles from John's friends down the line, but the name stuck.

From that moment on, to the boys he flew with, he was known on the squadron as *Scruffy.*

Chapter 8

Circuits and Bumps

By that summer of 1941, John had been transferred to a training stream headed for Bomber Command, which depressed him. He wanted to fly fighters. But it didn't matter what you wanted; you went where you were sent. Hughie had finally been called up at the end of April 1940 and was now stationed at *No. 2 ITS* in Regina.

There came a point in *ITS* when some were informed that they hadn't made the grade as pilots. Hughie had been one of the fortunate few; if he hadn't been chosen, it would have devastated him. Both John and Hughie had seen how that disappointment of not being chosen could be utterly demoralizing to those who'd dreamed of little else.

Out in Regina, one of Hughie's fellow POPs received the good news that he was moving forward in the pilot stream. He ran back to his barracks, shouting, *'I'm going to be a pilot! I'm going to be a pilot!'* The barracks were full of boys who had just been told they hadn't made the grade, which meant they would have to learn another trade. Unable to endure his self-centred enthusiasm, they pounced on him and dragged him to the window. *'Okay, fly boy,'* they shouted, *'Let's see you fly!'* And tossed him out the third-storey window. Hughie's *No. 2 ITS* section suffered their first casualty.

John was still a provisional pilot, for which he was thankful. He accepted the regrettable shift away from fighters and transferred from Trenton back to Camp Borden to begin his *Advanced Training School (ATS)*, the final stage of training, flying newer two-man bombers, *Oxfords*, and the docile and forgiving *Ansons*, dubbed *'Faithful Annies'* by those who flew them. It was still anyone's guess what kind of aircraft would have the most impact in this war, which meant all options were being explored and pilots trained accordingly. Training consisted of lectures, cross-country flights, night flying, combat tactics and aerobatics, and endless *'Circuits and Bumps,'* as the relentless practice of taking off, circling around, touching down, then taking off again was known. This was repeated until a pilot could do it in his sleep, and it all contributed to the flying hours necessary to earn his wings.

John still loved flying, whatever the aircraft. But the great thing about being back at Borden was that he was only an hour's drive away from Fran, at least if you drove fast. Despite

An Avro Anson.

115

strict regulations forbidding airmen leaving the base while in training, John would dash down to the city to see her in the late evening hours (when no one at Borden's front gate paid too much attention). But some days when he couldn't get away, he managed to stay in touch. When he knew he'd be flying cross-country sorties, John would write Fran a love note, bundle it up in a small weighted bag with an improvised handkerchief parachute, then fly down over her house and drop the notes from his plane. His aim was pretty good, but even when he was a few houses or streets off, the neighbours came to know that it was John and would deliver the errant messages to Fran. When she vacationed on Georgian Bay, he found out what cottage she was at, then came flying in fast and low across the lake in a *Harvard*, its engine roaring as he swooped in twenty feet off the

Harvard Trainers flying in formation.

water. That made a definite impression.

John and Paul Phelan roomed in the same barracks at Borden and had worked out a plan to skirt regulations so they could slip away on Saturday nights and drive down to Toronto to see their girls. When it was Paul's turn, John would stuff Paul's bunk to make it look like he was sound asleep under a tangle of bedclothes. And when it was John's turn, Paul returned the favour. It worked quite well for a few weeks.

One warm June night in 1940, John was down in the city, and very late heading back. He didn't leave Fran's until around 4:30 am, which meant it would be nip and tuck to make it back to Borden for 6:00 am roll call. Being *AWOL* (*Absent Without Leave*) was an extremely serious infraction, especially for provisional pilots.

He went tearing north through the towns scattered between Toronto and the base in his car. The roads were quiet, which was a blessing. On the outskirts of Barrie, just south of the base, he passed a sedan heading in the same direction. John caught a glimpse of the driver out of the corner of his eye and saw that it was his flight instructor. He slumped down in his seat, stepped on the gas, and managed to put some distance between them. He skidded up to the base's front gate with no one in his rear view mirror. The guards knew John from his frequent after-hours excursions and waved him through. He dumped his car behind the barracks, ran inside, and jumped into bed fully dressed, burying himself beneath blankets to blend in with the other sleeping bodies.

Ten minutes later the lights snapped on, and the instructor

strode in, barking that roll call was in fifteen minutes. Heads stirred, and the boys rolled out of bed. He added that there was no need for Mr. Weir to feel the need to dress if he didn't want to, as he was damned sure that he was dressed already. John got up and mumbled an explanation, which the instructor cut short. He'd heard enough of John's excuses. As the other men filed out for morning parade, the officer informed John that his hooligan behaviour not only showed disregard for regulations, but an equal disrespect for the men he was flying with. He was forthwith being transferred out of the section.

John was shattered. This meant he'd *'washed out,'* and would likely be sent to *No. 1 Composite Training School (KTS)* at Trenton. This was the demoralizing final destination for any unfortunate airman who didn't make the grade. Every recruit wanted to be a pilot, but only a few had the requisite skills. The other options were to retrain to become an air observer (navigator), a bomb aimer, a wireless operator, or an air gunner. Each was a good and challenging trade with its specific set of skills.

However, being sent to *KTS* meant these options had been withdrawn as well. Not only would you never pilot an aircraft: you would now be stuck indefinitely with a bunch of other boys who had washed out, too. At *KTS*, psychologists interviewed and evaluated you, then hopefully gave you a passing grade. If they did, flight instructors made a final decision about whether there was any prosaic role you could fill in the service as a third-stringer. In short, you were officially a failure. The boys who underwent this demoting never lost their profound sense of shame about it.

John and Fran in the backyard of the Weir home, June 1940.

John struggled with how he was going to break the news to his father, to Hughie, and worst of all, to Fran. What would he tell them? When he found the nerve to approach his flight instructor, he asked when he would have to report to *KTS*. With enough time, he hoped he might come up with a good story for his family.

The Flight Instructor dismissed the question with a shake of his head. He said it wasn't time for *KTS* yet. Instead, he had arranged a transfer for John to singles – fighters – where he felt John's independent spirit and aggressive flying style might be put to better use. He cut short the burgeoning smile on John's face by saying the transfer was intended to be a punishment.

But for the record, he added that it had been John's skill and confidence in the air that made this move an obvious one. John saluted, thanked him and went to collect his gear.

That transfer may well have saved his life. At that point in the war, Bombers Command's casualties were high. Fighters were principally doing reconnaissance and patrols, and as of yet weren't in the thick of the fight. However, that was about to change.

Two months later, at the end of August 1940, John had earned his wings and shipped overseas to England to join the first Canadian fighter squadron, *RCAF No. 1 Squadron* (later, *RAF No. 401*). John and a few hundred other newly minted airmen arrived in England onboard the *RMS Duchess of Athol*, an aging Canadian Pacific steamer; or as some of the boys called her, the *'Duchess of Asshole,'* because of her decrepitude. She was

John receives his wings, June 1940.

also known as 'The Drunken Duchess,' due to her flat-bottom and a lack of stabilizers, which made the ship simultaneously pitch and roll crossing the North Atlantic.

From the second day at sea, John had been sick as a dog; hard *not* to be seasick on a flat-bottomed ship like that in heavy weather. Even the huge Cunard liners, the *Queen Mary* and the *Queen Elizabeth,* would sway back and forth as they zigzagged their way at high speed across the ocean dodging U-boats.

The issue of seasickness was of concern because of the unofficial RAF policy to ground you if you were inclined to upchuck while flying. There were too many other would-be pilots with cast iron stomachs waiting in line behind you to take your place. John was looking forward to getting his feet back on solid ground.

France had fallen to the Germans in June 1940, and the vague threat of German invasion had become a very real danger. *Operation Sea Lion*, the Nazi plan for the invasion of England, was well underway, and the Battle to save Britain had begun.

Sea Lion was an orchestrated series of aggressive raids that the Germans directed against Britain in preparation for a full-scale invasion. The first objective was to cripple shipping; next, radio transmission towers would then be knocked out; finally, the Luftwaffe would destroy all RAF fighter bases across the south coast of England. At that juncture, Nazi forces would flood across the Channel and occupy the country. This had quickly become the very worst of times to be sent into combat. The largest, most professional and heavily armed military force in the world – in history – was sweeping across Europe and conquering it. And while most did not want to admit it, Britain was on the brink of defeat.

It took the better part of a year to train a pilot, and by the time that John and the other Canadian POPs were on their way to England, they were champing at the bit to get some experience flying a real combat aircraft. Those who had made it this far loved flying. The idea of sliding sideways through the air strapped into a ton of metal awash with lighter fluid was their idea of fun. Instructors kept an eye out for new pilots who demonstrated a sure hand on the controls, especially in the trickier situations. John was one of them.

There were about seven times as many German fighters flying as there were Allied fighters at that time. What was worse, the German planes were almost all newer, faster, and more deadly. Thankfully, the newly-arrived Canadian pilots were largely unaware of this. Even if they had been, every one of them was eager to jump into the thick of things. They wanted to fight. There was so much that was startlingly new, both in terms of warfare, equipment, living conditions, and where the next battle front would open up, that most simply put the lousy odds of survival out of mind.

The *Duchess* chugged into Liverpool Harbour in the middle of an air raid. The raid had left much of the city on fire, and so it wasn't until the next morning that the ship could approach the docks and have the passengers disembark. In his journal, John wrote about their arrival:

Friday October 25ᵗʰ

Here we be at Liverpool. Arrived about 3:30 in the afternoon and sat in the river all day. At 8:45 pm the air raid sirens were sounded and nothing happened for about an hour. Then we had some crashes of guns and stuff, but no bombs have been dropped as yet (10:25 pm). One thing is certain though – when they say blackout they mean blackout – gosh, it's black – not a light showing anywhere.

In the morning, they were herded on to small, slow-moving trains and transferred to aircrew Manning Pools outside of London. These were transit camps where new aircrew were billeted for a week or two before being shipped off to the various bases around England and Scotland, where they would be trained to fly combat aircraft in battle.

Saturday October 26ᵗʰ

We started for Salisbury Plains, and have been on the train for over 12 hours. The blackout is really black, and since I'm damn tired I think I'll just tell you about it tomorrow. There's the air raid siren now. No signs of bombing. Got here and there were no quarters for us. Slept on the floor in the Officers' Mess. Tomorrow we move into tents.

Sunday October 27ᵗʰ

Cold? Wow!!! A dreary day with nothing doing to speak of. We were allotted our tents today. Our beds consist of a bunch of hay in the form of a mattress wrapped in blankets. The running water we get is when it rains, or else we do the running. It's really quite fun, 'cept it would be a lot more fun to be here together. Wish you were here!

Monday October 28ᵗʰ

Got tin helmets, but did nothing else except freeze this

John standing in front of his tent on Salisbury Plain, October 1941.

morning when we got up.

Tuesday October 29th

We were paid! £20 and got leave to go to London. I'm staying at the Regent Palace Hotel. You can really see the effects of the bombing – one whole block knocked out alongside our place.

They could see the vapour trails of German Junkers 88s and Messerschmitt 109s over the English Channel, and see the RAF fighters that chased after them. On a clear day there would be hundreds of them crisscrossing the sky, the short skirmishes

Vapour trails from a dogfight over the English Channel.

usually ending with one of the planes spiraling down in a plume of smoke and extinguishing like a lit match as it crashed into the ocean. It was all a little unreal to someone just off the boat from Canada.

London was a short train ride away, so when the boys had some leave, they took advantage of the chance to visit the city as accidental tourists. For most of them, it was far and away the largest city they had ever seen. Even though London was being hammered by nightly air raids, that didn't deter the airmen from flooding into town to experience all that was on offer.

John had a standing invitation to stay with Uncle Adrian and Auntie Ted when he was in town, an offer he gratefully accepted (after discovering how hard hotel rooms were to come by at short notice). He liked London. When he and his friends went out on the town, they would see shows and have drinks, often staying out well into the night. What startled him was the social life. Sex, to be more specific. An astonishing number of professional girls offered their services, but it seemed to John that pretty much *everybody* was happy to hop into bed with anybody at the drop of a hat. This was not a situation he'd ever had any experience with, and it rattled him a bit. In his journal, he wrote,

> The same ones are all after the same stuff which is all well and good, especially as they are so frank about it. But I don't like it much. I guess I'm just a stuffed shirt. The more I see of it, the more certain I am I'll stay faithful.

He was known on the squadron for having no interest in any wartime romances or flings. He was committed to Fran. But he found himself caught in an awkward situation one night when he was out at the pub with the other pilots. An attractive blonde came over to John and made obvious advances. He had no interest in talking to her, but found himself at a loss as to how to politely ask her to leave him alone. Jeep Neal rescued him by stepping in and telling John it was time to rejoin their friends. As they walked away, John said, *'Thanks for saving me from that girl. She wouldn't take 'no' for an answer.'*

Jeep said, *'John, that wasn't a girl, that was a man. So finish your drink and let's get out of here.*

London also offered a peaceful respite for many servicemen. One Royal Canadian Naval Intelligence Officer, Don Sutherland, loved being in London during the war because, he said, *'It was so quiet.'* There were free concerts in the parks, few trucks and cars on the roads, and it was safe to walk everywhere. It was a peaceful, beautiful city. As regards the air raids and the bombs, he said you got used to it. *'Apart from those* [bombing raids], *it was a wonderful place to be during the war.'*

Air raids were indeed a part of every day life, but failed to bring the city to a standstill as German High Command had predicted. As posters displayed around the city advised, *'Your Courage, Your Cheerfulness, Your Resolution Will Bring Us Victory.'* A person simply had to exercise common sense. When the air raid sirens started, Civil Defense instructed you to get to a shelter as soon as possible. If there wasn't one close by, a next best option was to stand flat inside the doorway of a solidly constructed building. That would provide some protection. The important thing was not to get caught out in the open.

On leave in London in early November 1940, John was walking up Regent Street when the sirens started wailing. Seeing no shelter signs, he quickly ducked into a doorway and stood back from the street, pressing himself against the stone.

A man who had been walking near John looked around for shelter, then panicked and started running. John yelled at him to find cover, but he showed no signs of having heard. Bombs started falling and exploding, and one hit high up on one of the buildings, sending shards of stone and concrete raining down. John watched as a fragment hit the man and clipped off his head as neatly as a blade of grass. He was the first person John saw killed in front of him.

Moments like these turned the abstraction of war into a real if impersonal threat for the newly arrived servicemen and servicewomen. There had been the occasional training accident back in Canada, but no one among John's bunch had been killed. However, within the next few weeks of training, three of the boys that had shipped over with John died in accidents. In a journal entry in November, he wrote, *'Bill killed today. A really nice guy.'* Death was becoming commonplace.

On November 5th, John reported to *Operational Training Unit* (*OTU*) *Sutton Bridge*, an RAF fighter base two hundred miles northeast of London, for the final stages of his training. At long last he would be flying the aircraft that he would be taking into action in a couple of months.

Ten days later, John received a letter from Auntie Ted and made this heartbreaking entry in his journal:

> Today I got the worst news I've had for some time. Pat Chamier [Ted and Adrian's youngest son] was killed doing a cross country [flying exercise] in southern Rhodesia. He had just got his wings, too. Gad, it seems impossible but it's true. Auntie Ted must be almost crazy over it. I vow I won't rest until at least 4 Huns pay for it.

His dramatic statement of wanting to even the score was, in fact, a cold-blooded affirmation of purpose. Pat's death was the first of many such wartime tragedies that forged his hatred of the Germans. To John, they had drawn first blood, and he was single-minded in his determination to even the score. He was ready to fight.

Pat Chamier (centre) in 1935.

Chapter 9

Battle Orders

At Sutton Bridge, John learned that he was going to complete his training flying the *Hurricane*, a robust single-wing fighter that was the foundation of the RAF in the early years of the war. Long overshadowed by the more romantic Spitfire, Hurricanes had provided the lion's share of Britain's air defense during the Battle of Britain, seeing more action and making more enemy kills than any other aircraft. Like most large machines, the plane had a very distinctive personality to which you had acclimate yourself.

The Hurricane was vastly more powerful than the trainers the boys had earned their wings on in Canada, so everything the new pilots had learned about flying had to be rethought. It was like having driven an old VW for years, then buckling up in a souped-up sports car that was ten times as fast, and being given freedom of the road. It was intoxicating. The Hurricane was built like a truck, and yet was highly manoeuvrable. John loved the fact that they could have the hell kicked out of them, and would still keep flying. It was a terrific plane to go to war in.

Transferring to these high-octane fighters was also when the boys started having many more close calls and hair-raising

John in front of his Hawker Hurricane.

accidents. Eugene *'Jeep'* Neal was in the same squadron as John and became a lifelong friend. John wrote,

November 25th

> Jeep's undercarriage collapsed while he was landing, and he ploughed in nose first – unhurt. That boy is lucky. It's the 4th plane he's racked up since we've been here.

November 30th

> Had my first crash this month. The clouds had closed in right down to the ground, and I was forced to land because of bad weather in a farmer's field the size of a peanut. Couldn't see much of anything. The wet grass made my brakes useless, and after some bad judgement by me, I ended up in a hedge on my nose. That will be my last! [It wasn't.]

After the pilots had gained confidence in the basics of flying the Hurricane, they learned to fly in *'flight'* formation. A flight

A 'Flight' of three Spitfires from 401 Squadron.

was three planes that flew together at slightly different altitudes from one another, with a leader and two wing men. Each pilot provided cover for the others: one watched forward, the second watched the rear, and the third watched the periphery. Formation flying was a constantly evolving strategy used for confronting the enemy in air and ground attacks.

During the six-week training period, the *sprog* (new) pilots were constantly flying formation exercises. Typical assignments included *Cross Countries*, which were reconnaissance flights at around 5,000 feet, during which the pilots sharpened their observation skills by identifying specific villages, rivers, and railways, and any landmarks that could be used as points of reference. The objective of cross-countries was to give the pilots as much flight time in as variable a range of conditions as possible, to hopefully prepare them for whatever situation they would eventually be thrown into.

Once the pilots had passed these final hurdles, they were

transferred to *'operational'* status and assigned to squadrons to be eased into action. An active fighter squadron's day-to-day work entailed several types of missions. The most straightforward was a *Sector Reccie* (short for reconnaissance), where the pilot flew from one aerodrome to another, touched down, then took off again and flew around to identify key landmarks and characteristics of the base so that when he returned, he would be able to get his bearings. Reccies were also flown at night, so the pilot had to develop very clear points of reference to keep himself oriented in the dark.

Combat Sorties, also known as *Shoot-ups*, *Beat Ups*, and *Rhubarbs*, were more interesting. A flight would be dispatched across the Channel to attack *'Targets of Opportunity'* – shipping, trains, convoys, trucks, or airfields. The pilots in the Flight would fly low to the water across the Channel to avoid being spotted. When they reached the coast, they would pull up sharply to avoid anti-aircraft fire (known as *'ack-ack'*). Once clear of the coastal ack-ack, they would swoop down again to see what trouble could be stirred up. If a line of trucks or a train were spotted, they might attack and try to *'give them some squirts,'* which was slang for bursts of machine gun fire. Firing machine guns in the air while flying at high speed was more like aiming a hose than a rifle. All things being well, they would then dash back home across the Channel.

On such operations, a pilot was rarely in the air for more than an hour. If he got into a skirmish, he went full bore when attacking or taking evasive action, which burned a lot of fuel. Then the problem became making it back across the Channel.

Most experienced pilots tried to be conservative in their fuel usage, because once they got into a dust-up with the enemy, they wouldn't have time to watch their gauges. A lot of guys ran out of gas and had to ditch in the sea. Many of those who went down couldn't be rescued in time, as their parachutes tended to drag them underwater, despite wearing their *Mae West* floatation vests. It boiled down to a matter of being able to unbuckle your harness quickly enough, and whether or not luck was on your side.

There were also reconnaissance missions, known as *Sweeps*, which were flown to get a picture of the enemy's positions in Northern France. If the planes spotted an aerodrome, they might swing down and attack. But they'd have to make sure they could get in and out quickly. Learning how to interpret what you saw on these sweeps provided key tactical information for squadron intelligence. In those early years, the air war was the only offensive arm that the Allies had against what had become Fortress Europe, and fighter sweeps were invaluable in learning where the Germans were dug in, what their strength was, and sometimes even providing clues as to what their objectives might be.

The war encouraged a rich cornucopia of acronyms, nicknames, shorthand, slang, and jargon, all arising out of the need to say a lot with a little. John's nickname, Scruffy, is a good example, capturing something of his story as well as a bit of the spirit of the man himself. In the air, pilots couldn't chatter on *R/T – Radiotelephony*, their radios – when they were flying. The RAF had a strict R/T procedure. If and when there was talk, everything had to be boiled down and reduced to the minimum language and code words.

Scruffy was flying a reccie in Lincolnshire, and as he came up over the brow of a hill, he was greeted by a panorama of military confusion. A bunch of Brown Jobs – Army types – were thrashing about in the throes of one of the innumerable training schemes that the army conducted to train the soldiers in tactics, as well as to keep the troops sharp. (They also helped stave off the boredom of waiting to get into the war.) It was a *'Red Army attacks the Blue Army'* exercise. Thousands of men and vehicles had come to a dead stop at a crossroads, and no one was willing to step back and admit responsibility or defeat. Scruffy, who had to report on any such situation he encountered, radioed in a one-word report to describe what was happening: *FUBAR*. Made famous in Steven Spielberg's *Saving Private Ryan*, this was an acronym for *'Fucked Up Beyond All Recognition.'*

The other two acronyms pilots commonly used on R/T were *SNAFU* – *'Situation Normal, All Fucked Up'* – and the most delightful, which he used the next day on his follow-up report for the army mess he'd come across, *SABU*, which translates to *'Self-Adjusting Balls Up,'* indicating that the *FUBAR* situation had resolved itself without intervention. (The acronym designating the worst state of affairs was *TUIFU* – *'Tooey-Foo'* – meaning, *'The Ultimate in Fuck Ups.'*)

The exception to talking over the radio was if you were in action engaging the enemy. Should a man on your flight spot an enemy plane threatening your tail, he could break in with an abrupt, *'Yellow Leader, mind your ass!'* At which point, if you were on your toes and still alive, you'd punch your throttle, flip the aircraft over to the left and into a dive, and quite likely pray. Things happened extremely fast in the air, flying 350 miles an hour (or more) directly at your enemy.

John completed his operational training at Sutton Bridge in December 1940 and was posted to *No. 1 'City of Westmount' Squadron RCAF*, which had distinguished itself flying with the RAF during the Battle of Britain from August through October of that year. The Squadron had suffered substantial losses in equipment and men, and in October 1940 it had been withdrawn to Prestwick, Scotland, to re-man and re-arm. On December 7th, the Squadron was transferred to Castletown, the most northerly RAF station in Scotland.

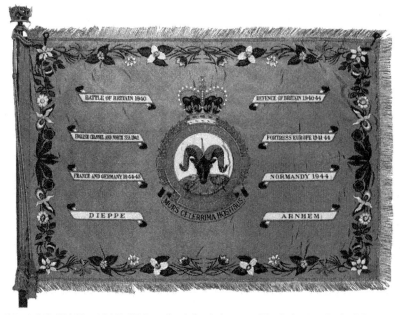

No. 1 RCAF/ No. 401 RAF Squadron's battle honours. The badge is a Rocky Mountain sheep; the Squadron's motto is, "Terribly Swift Death to the Enemy." The Squadron was the highest-scoring RCAF fighter squadron in WWII with 195 ½ enemy planes destroyed.

Before his arrival in Castletown, John met with Adrian. It was time to talk about *Acquisitor*. Now that his training was complete and he was operational, he was ready to volunteer. Adrian accepted, simply and decisively. He gave John his code name (the unexpected *'Collette';* Adrian's was *'Aerial'*), and then established the standard protocols of communication.

Adrian's office was at *Adastral House*, the Air Ministry's headquarters in London, which was ideal for monitoring the ebb and flow of the flow of RAF intelligence during the war. His relationship with the Air Ministry facilitated how John would receive his instructions for *Acquisitor*. Orders would be sent from Adastral, and be issued to the CO of John's squadron specifically requesting him. The CO would know nothing about the objectives, only its essential logistics: vectors, time frames, and so forth. If the orders included certain key words or phrases, John was to find a neutral telephone and call Adrian, who would provide additional and sensitive information. John's standing orders were simple and direct: keep his eyes open and report if anything caught his attention. After giving his report, he was to forget any knowledge of it.

The principal intelligence services in England were *MI5* and *MI6*, which operated under the auspices of the War Office in England. *'MI'* was an acronym for *Military Intelligence Section*, and there were nineteen *'M'* sections in all, each operating under separate and distinct mandates. They were ostensibly secret departments, but they were also government, which meant that there were inherent weaknesses and flaws.

Adrian created *Acquisitor* so that it could operate below the spectrum of those agencies, free of conference rooms, paper trails, and political jealousies. The *MI* departments' operations would effectively conceal *Acquisitor's* work. And as there were no distinguishable threads linking *Acquisitor's* agents or their movements, *Acquisitor's* operatives were able to pursue their objectives without attention. The network was, by design, effectively non-existent. It was invisible.

The *Abwehr* was the German Intelligence Ministry that posed the greatest threat to English national security. As the

Abwehr radio operations regional headquarters.

CIA was to the *FBI*, and *MI6* was to *MI5*, the *Abwehr* was German international intelligence, and the *SS* and *Gestapo* controlled German home fronts.

The majority of German agents who had managed to embed themselves in England in the 1930s (and during the war) were not crack professionals. There may have been die-hard Nazis among them, but most were questionable characters living on the fringes of society. Often they were borderline criminals who recognized a once in a lifetime opportunity to peddle their assets in a seller's market. If their superiors in Berlin or Paris were desperate for information, these agents were in a unique position to provide reports on everything from troop movements to the food served in RAF messes. Early on, nothing was too small or insignificant to flip into a moneymaking opportunity. These wartime spies were men and women who had discovered leaks in the flow of information between London and Berlin, and capitalized on them. It was a profession that dealt in cash, which satisfied the instant gratification that drove many such agents into that dangerous line of work.

Most were amateurs so guileless that they were willing to wander into a city, town, or village and just assume that they would blend into the crowd. Which, of course, by the very nature of their nonchalance, often proved to be a very effective method of slipping through the cracks of English security.

Adrian had been aware of such weaknesses in security, but he was not alone. Churchill had long shared this view. When he was elected Prime Minister in May 1940, he was able to act. With Hugh Dalton, one of his Cabinet ministers, Churchill created the *Special Operations Executive (SOE)*. With the admonition to *'...Set Europe ablaze!,'* its objectives were to encourage and create sabotage and espionage behind enemy lines. It would also serve as the core of resistance in England in the event of invasion, a very real prospect at that point in the war.

Adrian was aware of these plans, and worked in coöperation with the SOE in refining how to best implement field strategies. The SOE came to have a great impact in the European theatre of war, but in its early years it could be painfully inept, sabotaged by bureaucratic logistics and departmental infighting, as Adrian had feared. He intentionally kept *Acquisitor's* operations in an autonomous orbit, working towards common objectives with the SOE, but at a remove from its vulnerabilities.

By way of example: one of the Abwehr's most significant successes was the infiltration of a Dutch resistance circuit in 1941. Circuits were cells, or networks (much like *Acquisitor*) of resistance agents that were supplied and facilitated by SOE's London office and its field agents. SOE agents were known as *'Baker Street Irregulars'* (their offices were located at 64 Baker Street, near Sherlock's fictional stomping grounds), and they had devised a simple and seemingly foolproof system to confirm the identity and status of field agents in their wireless transmissions from occupied countries. When an agent established radio contact with England via Morse code, they were to *'key'* in two acknowledgments of their identity. The first was a *'bluff'* (false) identity codename, and the second was the *'true'* (confirming) codename. If an agent had been captured and was being forced to transmit, only their first bluff identity would be sent, thereby alerting HQ in London that the agent had been compromised. Bad luck for the agent, but it ensured the integrity of the resistance circuit.

Unfortunately, a keen but inexperienced officer at SOE headquarters had been placed in charge of receiving these communications in the early months of the SOE's penetration of occupied France and Holland. On one terrible occasion, upon receiving only the first bluff check from a compromised agent, and ignoring the implicit message conveyed by the single 'bluff' transmission, the SOE office sent a return signal to the captured agent,

> *My dear fellow, you only left us a week ago. On your first message you go and forget to put your 'true' check.*

The Gestapo had arrested the agent when this message was

An SOE radio set, hidden in an attaché case.

received from London HQ. (He was later executed.)

One can only begin to imagine the rapacious delight of the German interrogators to have discovered such a gaping hole in the armour of British Intelligence, through which they could now confidently extract key information from captured agents. Once they had coerced the captured men and women into coughing up their true identity key codes, it was a simple matter of regularly sending false communications back to England, with assurances that the resistance network was secure. From that point on the Germans held all the cards, as London was unaware that resistance circuits had been infiltrated and broken. This afforded the Abwehr the opportunity to send an endless stream of false reports back to London, allowing the Gestapo to arrive early at secret drop zones to wait and arrest new agents as they parachuted in. The result was the capture, torture, and execution of dozens of agents and hundreds of members of the resistance, and the near destruction of the majority of resistance circuits in France and Holland.

According to the few SOE agents who were caught and managed to still be alive by the end of the war, the Abwehr's interrogation centre in Paris had wall charts detailing the SOE chain of command from the head man and woman, right down to the names of the various resistance circuit leaders and their contacts. It is small consolation to know that both sides suffered from such lapses in judgment and security. But it is a vivid illustration of how it was often the small things at the sharp edge of war that determined how you lived and how you died.

MI5 did not intrude on MI6's areas of operations, nor did

MI5 have any sovereignty over police matters, which were Scotland Yard's concern. The SOE worked in both domestic (MI5) and foreign (MI6) theatres of war, but there were innumerable conflicts of interest and refusals to cooperate and share information. *Acquisitor* was able to achieve its success and remain invisible because of its ability to operate outside of formal channels of procedure. Adrian had devised his network with an understanding of what a shoddy and dangerous business wartime espionage was.

The Squadron's main purpose was to protect Scapa Flow, the primary base for the Royal Navy, situated near the Orkney Islands. John arrived in Thurso, the town nearest to Castletown, on December 17th. He wrote,

Arrived here at 9:40 this morning. Thurso is a very small

The runway at the Castletown RAF base.

town in the very north of Scotland – just on the coast opposite the Orkneys. Gads what a place – quiet is putting it mildly. The rumour is that the Germans are planning to 'pay us back' for the Royal Navy's attack on Taranto [an Italian naval base] and give Scapa 'what for.' The English are still pretty scared of an attempt to raid the Isles by an invasion on Scotland, which is very vulnerable at this point. It's going to be very interesting here if things start to happen – they'll be happening fast and furious!!!

His CO on the squadron was Deane Nesbitt. Deane was a highly decorated pilot and greatly respected officer. Coincidentally, he was the son of Arthur Nesbitt, who co-founded *Nesbitt Thomson* (later *Nesbitt Burns*), a Canadian stock brokerage firm and Montreal-based contemporary of McLeod Young Weir. John came to admire him immensely.

The Squadron's principal day to day duties entailed flying cover for ships entering and leaving the port, as well as intercepting any German aircraft flying reconnaissance or

401 Squadron CO Deane Nesbitt.

threatening an attack. In his first weeks there, John logged dozens of hours of flight time. He also flew several missions on behalf of the army along the east coast of Britain to determine whether their camouflage was effective or not. After a couple of such trips, he made a recommendation that the Army use colour-blind spotters: it stood to reason that they would be less likely to miss oddities in camouflage. It was an extremely effective technique that the army immediately adopted.

Scapa was always a prime target because of the presence of the Royal Naval fleet. One of John's regular missions was being *'scrambled'* (called into action at a moment's notice) to intercept *'Weather Willy.'* This was a Luftwaffe pilot who flew his *JU-88* fighter over Scapa to report weather conditions and troop movements back to German command. He flew at 10,000 feet, and always at the same time: you could literally set your watch by him. John had been trying to catch him for weeks, but he was flying a Hurricane, and the JU–88 was faster and could outrun anything flying at Scapa. But as frustrating as it was, John liked the challenge. He devised a plan where he would fly up to an altitude of 16,000 feet and wait for Willy to show up at his usual time. He would then dive down very fast from high and above, and open fire before Willy knew what had hit him.

A good day arrived, with clear skies and minimal wind. He took his Hurricane up to 16,000 and marked time until Willy showed up on schedule. John watched from a distance, then opened up his throttle, and went into a steep dive. Gravity helped push the Hurricane past its top speed as he lined up Willy in his sights. Just as he came into firing range, his radio

A JU-88.

crackled and a German-accented voice said, *'OK, Yellow Leader, you may pancake now'* (pancake = land). Then the JU-88 spat out a couple of puffs of black smoke, flipped over, and disappeared into the horizon.

John was stunned. Willy had not only anticipated him being there, but he had also used the RAF term *'pancake'* as well as John's 'call colours' – *Yellow Leader* – which was highly secret information. There must be someone at the base who was transmitting this to German HQ. He landed, baffled and angry, but determined to do something about it.

RAF Castletown was a small, isolated, and rather primitive air force station. That winter of 1940–41 was one of the coldest that Scotland had seen for many years. The men lived in draughty Nissen huts with concrete floors and a small stove for heat. On such remote air force stations, the *Navy, Army and Air Force*

Institutes (*NAAFI*), a British government-run organization, provided modest catering services to servicemen from boxy vans that became a familiar sight all over Britain during the war. At Castletown, these *NAAFI* mobile canteens were driven directly onto the grounds adjacent to the runways. The van's side would lift up, creating a small canopy and revealing a service window from which the person manning the van sold rationed sweets, soap, and cigarettes, and handed out cups of tea and warm buns.

The vans were staffed by *NAAFI* enlisted men and women (members of the *Royal Army Service Corps* and *Auxiliary Territorial Services*), with the occasional volunteer at remote bases such as Castletown. One of these was a grey-haired vicar in his 60s, who was never without his dog collar and well-worn tweeds.

Like most of the pilots, after landing John would stop at the van and get a cup of tea, and then be debriefed by Herb Norris, the squadron's *Intelligence Officer* (*IO*). A few days after John's

Nissen huts at Castletown.

A NAAFI food services van.

encounter with Weather Willy, he returned from a routine patrol and stopped at the NAAFI van for his tea, but the counter was closed, and no one was around. As he walked away, he thought he heard a muffled voice speaking German. He approached the van, thinking it must have been his imagination, fueled by his encounter with Willy. He walked backed to the mess and got his tea there.

He then headed out to give his report to Herb and saw that the van was operational again, with the vicar working the counter. He bought a couple of chocolate bars and went to give his report.

In their meeting, Herb remarked on how serious John looked. Given what had happened a few days earlier with Weather Willy, John said he was sure that someone was leaking information on the base. Herb wanted to know if he had any idea of who it might be. John wondered if there was someone new on the base: possibly a tradesman, or somebody on the ground crew. Herb said there were only the usual faces. No one new.

After the debriefing, John left the base and walked into Castletown, where he placed a call to Adrian and explained what he had seen and heard, and what his suspicious were.

A week later, Deane called him into his office and told him there were orders from Adastral House for John to report to London for 48 hours, and he should set out immediately. When he arrived for his appointment, Adrian got right to the point. The vicar from the van had been picked up, and there was no question he was the source of the leak. They had managed to extract a good deal of information from the man. Afterwards, Adrian told John that the vicar had had an *'unfortunate accident,'* and that was the end of that.

John was very pleased with himself at having caught his first spy, but Adrian cautioned him. What he'd done was very useful, but also extremely dangerous. He had made himself a potential target by talking so openly to Herb at Scapa about the leak and suspicious new faces on at the Station. Herb was completely trustworthy, but reports would have been filed and notice taken. Adrian suggested techniques for reporting threats like the vicar in future without John making himself vulnerable. He then asked if there had been others that he had come across who he thought were suspicious. John mentioned two men he'd noticed at other bases. Again, there was nothing specific, just something about them that didn't fit: an arrogance that John had seen so much of in Germany during the 1930s. Adrian thanked him with a warning to be more circumspect.

John returned to his squadron the next morning, feeling a curious combination of satisfaction and unease.

Chapter 10

The End of the Beginning

John increasingly found himself singled out on the squadron for special duty. Requests would come in for a volunteer to go on a sortie, and he repeatedly found himself being assigned. He had flown a wide range of aircraft (20 different types by the war's end) and was considered to be a very experienced pilot capable of handling any flying condition. He had a talent for observation and recognition and a reputation for reports that were accurate and uncoloured.

His flying orders came through the Squadron, but covert orders were issued directly from Uncle Adrian and *Acquisitor.* On occasion, there were anonymous contacts that came by telephone. An unfamiliar voice on the other end would recite a string of numbers. He had been instructed to disregard certain number patterns, and the remaining numbers would indicate a phone number that he was to call, which rang a neutral call box located in London. Another unfamiliar voice would answer would give him his orders. When required, dead drops were used to exchange written reports or materials. However, Adrian was the only contact that John ever knew.

A typical mission would unfold like this one of April 1941. Adrian told him over the phone, *'You're going to be invited to a party, and the party is private.'* This meant that he could speak to no one about what he saw on the mission, and he would be flying alone. No more than an hour after that call, Deane called John into his office and gave him orders to fly cover for the English aircraft carrier, HMS *Ark Royal*. She was one of England's premier aircraft carriers, and an essential defense in providing air cover for the vulnerable merchant convoys transporting supplies to England. She was, therefore, an extremely valuable target for the German Navy because of her size and the number of aircraft (around sixty) that she carried at any given time.

John approached the vector coordinates he'd been given and spotted the ship from 2,000 feet. He quickly realized it wasn't the *Ark Royal*, but an old rusty tanker that had been given a makeshift stage dressing to make her appear like the *Ark Royal,* at least from a distance. The use of that kind of theatrical 'slight

HMS Ark Royal escorted by Swordfish torpedo bombers.

of hand' was very common during the war, especially around D-Day. The objective in this instance was to use the tanker as bait to draw out U-Boats and *E-Boats* (fast motor torpedo boats) from discreet ports on the French and Norwegian coasts. Having John flying top cover was to add credence to the whole pantomime.

The Germans attacked, the tanker was sunk, and an RAF fighter squadron attacked the deluded Germans with resounding success. The day after the mission, with MI5 having already leaked false intelligence to the Germans, the British newspapers reported the *Ark Royal's* sinking. (An interesting exception to the newspaper industry helping with matters of national security was *The Times*, who politely declined to publish a single paragraph that would help support such deceptions, because the publisher refused to insert any items of news that it did not believe to be true.)

John was happy flying, regardless of what the missions were. Sometimes his work for Adrian made him feel conspicuous among his friends because he was so frequently requested for special duty. That made him distinctly uncomfortable. But as the squadron rebuilt and saw more action, the focus at Castletown was on what was happening, not on John's occasional absences.

Furthermore, there was no regularity to these assignments, which were scheduled erratically to avoid any discernible pattern. John told Adrian that he occasionally got funny looks during his frequent disappearances. Adrian's response was short and to the point: *'You know how to handle it. You are the dumbest fellow I know. Just carry on and play your part.'*

So John continued to fly special operations and polished his routine as the happy-go-lucky guy who wasn't the sharpest tool in the shed. He was volunteered for test missions, flying Hurricanes up to 40,000 feet, higher than they'd been built to fly. He flew wearing a gas mask and other extraneous gear to test the feasibility of flying under those conditions. He flew aerobatic drills demonstrations – Flying Circuses – all the while fulfilling his duties on the squadron.

During several of his leaves, he undertook commando training at Arisaig in the west Highlands of Scotland, and took courses at *Beaulieu* in Hampshire, on of the highly secret training centres of the SOE. There he was taught security and

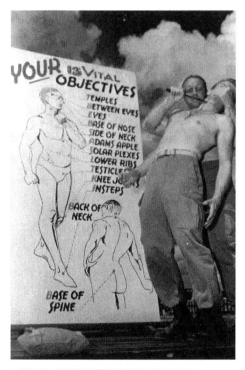

SOE hand to hand combat training exercise, highlighting vital objectives for disabling and killing an enemy.

Beaulieu Palace House in Hampshire, a training centre for the SOE during the war.

'tradecraft' by professionals (often ex-cons) in such skills as lock-picking, breaking and entering, interrogation, and hiding in plain sight. This involved tricks of disguise and evasion, and such as how to quickly rearrange clothing to change your appearance, or making use of limp, which could be a disguise in itself and could be simply produced by tucking a small stone into your shoe.

Agents were drilled in how to move through cities and towns without attracting attention. The cardinal rule was never to glance behind yourself, *'...which would make even the Archbishop of Canterbury look shifty,'* one instructor said. Never speak to strangers, never get drunk, and if you were stupid enough to pick up a girl (or a man) in an occupied country, then you were on your own and deserved to be caught.

An agent who was arrested wearing civilian clothing could be treated as a spy, which meant interrogation, torture, and probable execution. With this in mind, the young women and men, all of whom were volunteers, were never in doubt as to the inherent risks. To prepare them for what they might face in the case of arrest, they would be dragged out of their rooms from a dead sleep, tossed into a cell, and then aggressively interrogated by two SS officers (played by instructors). They were taught that under such questioning, they should stick as close as possible to the truth. They were given cover stories that had been developed to closely mirror the lives of the agents and the experiences and places they had come to know. In this way, under interrogation, an agent could answer with as much ingenuous confidence as possible, buying some much needed time.

Under interrogation, the agents were taught to speak slowly. As they took time choosing their words, they would try to anticipate what questions might be coming next. They were instructed to be vague in their answers, but never to tell an unnecessary lie. The objective was to assume an air of befuddled innocence and maintain a consistent story, so the interrogators were unable to trip them up with simple details. If the questioning became more brutal, there was nothing to be gained by being brave. It was best to reveal inconsequential information, so the interrogators felt they were getting something. If the pain levels increased substantially, then make some noise; let them hear you scream. It helped deal with the pain while convincing the interrogators that they were getting results. The most important skill of all was to be ordinary and blend in.

Much of this was familiar ground for John, skills he had acquired from Adrian, his father, and even Fiji. As a boy, John had learned how to walk and breathe silently; he had learned to control his breathing so as to avoid snoring, a serious vulnerability when sleeping out in the open. Nothing was left behind when you were on the move; any trace of fire, paper, or food had to be buried. When dealing with the enemy, never underestimate them, and never try to short-change or cheat anyone that you might be fortunate enough to befriend. The essential common sense of the SOE training was that amateurs brainstormed schemes, but professionals studied logistics. Surviving was about knowing where you were, knowing how to get what you needed, and knowing what had to be done next.

Being so isolated, Castletown had few visitors. When an RAF officer from Adastral House appeared at the office asking for 'Scruffy' Weir, '...just to say hello,' John's guard went up. The men on the squadron called him by that nickname, but no one else did. Certainly not his family or any officer he'd ever met outside of the squadron. More significantly, no officer would ever be so informal, let alone travel 700 miles, to drop in and say hello. Something was wrong.

He went looking for the man and found him in the mess. He was an unremarkable middle-aged RAF officer, who had nothing that set him apart except his misplaced sense of self-importance. He greeted John, shook his hand, and called him Scruffy. He congratulated him on identifying the vicar, and other characters that he had drawn to Adrian's attention. John listened carefully, responded with calculated deflection, and said he had no idea what the man was talking about. The officer said it had come to their attention that 'Scruffy' might be quite useful to them. John said that some mistake had been made and started to walk away. The officer stopped him and told him it was all right. He understood that Scruffy received his instructions from a special source. *'You take your orders from Aerial.'*

John smiled politely, repeated that he had no idea what he was talking about, and asked the officer who he was.

'Who you *are is the question,'* the man said.

John was shaken because this stranger had used Adrian's code name, *Aerial,* a serious breach of security regardless of who he was. No legitimate intelligence officer would dare drop such a thing as casually as this man had. John left him there and found a call box on the outskirts of the base. He called Adrian, who told him in no uncertain terms that he had neither sent this man nor knew anything about him. He instructed John to have nothing more to do with him. He asked where the man was, then concluded the conversation by saying he would be taken care of.

By the time John returned to the mess, the stranger was gone. John never heard another word about him. But now he was aware of how vulnerable he had become.

By March 1941, the squadron had been renumbered as *401 Squadron RAF*. It was back at strength and had moved south to Digby in Lincolnshire. Here, they were thrust back into the thick of the action, flying sorties day and night. John caught up with Hughie Godefroy in June. He saw a posting of Hughie's transfer to *401* and got permission from Deane to fly down to Sutton Bridge where Hughie was completing his OTU stint.

John strolled into the OTU mess just as the men were sitting down to lunch, and shouted, *'Is there a P.O. Prune Godefroy here?'* Hughie turned around and couldn't believe his eyes. It was a most welcome reunion. John told Hughie that they were

Hughie with his new puppy in a peaceful moment.

in the same squadron and would be on the same flight. Hughie transferred to Digby four days later, where John said from that point on they would only fly together. He wasn't about to trust anyone else as his wingman.

At that time in the war, the life expectancy for new fighter pilots hovered at around six combat hours. Yet for the majority of pilots, the idea of being shot down never entered their heads. No one thought about dying. When Hughie arrived at Digby, John greeted him and showed him to his room, number thirteen, across the hall from John's. He explained that the room had previously belonged to Paul Henderson, who they both had known and liked at UCC. Hughie asked where he'd been transferred, and John said off-handedly, *'He pranged himself the other day. Too bad. He was a nice guy. See you in the mess, Hughie.'* (To prang meant to crash, likely killing the pilot.)

Hughie knew John well and was startled by how casually he had passed along the information about their friend's death. But the general thinking on the squadron – and for most that were active on the front lines – was that if someone *'bought'* it, it was best just to keep moving and not look back.

It helped both of them that Hughie and John flew together through the summer of 1941, with Hughie flying as Wing Man to John's Leader. Hughie had sharp eyes, and John had six months more experience flying ops, and together they became an extremely effective team. Both enjoyed the exhilarating atmosphere of an operational squadron's fraternal day-to-day life, where your job was to skate the fine line between skill and the dangerous side of luck at 350 miles per hour in the air.

Scrambling into action.

They shared some unforgettable experiences. One memorable morning, John and Hughie were on stand-by to fly cover for a convoy off the east coast of England. They dragged themselves out of bed, threw on their damp clothes (everything was always damp), splashed water on their faces, and stumbled in to breakfast. The Flight Commander announced that Weir and Godefroy were on *First Readiness*.

That brought them both to life, as it meant they had to be ready to scramble if a signal came in. They taxied their planes into position, left their helmets on their control sticks, laid their parachutes on the leading edges of the port wings of their aircraft, then dashed back to the dispersal hut to try and grab a bit more sleep.

They had only just laid down again, when the Tannoy speakers announced, '*401 Squadron Red Section scramble!*' John and Hughie bolted up and out again, cursing the controller, and a minute later they were airborne. The controller radioed them their vectors, and off they went with the sky to themselves.

It was the responsibility of the Flight Leader – John, in this instance – to get the *'Letters of the Day'* before taking off. This was a code used by pilots to identify themselves as friendly aircraft if challenged by ground or sea forces. The Flight Leader would tap out the Letters of the Day in Morse code, which the identification light on the belly of his aircraft flashed to the ships and troops below, and all would be well. They were changed daily and top secret, so they could not be sent by radio signal. Most significantly, they had to be collected in person at the Dispersal Hut before taking off.

The vectors took John and Hughie straight out to the east coast and out over the sea. They'd flown about sixty miles when the shapes of a huge convoy began to be visible. Circling around the ships were ever-vigilant destroyers, which began training their guns on John and Hughie.

John looked over at Hughie, and said, *'Have you got them?'* [the Letters of the Day]. Hughie shook his head, and John raised his eyes to heaven. At that moment, they got a challenging series of flashes from the Aldis signal lamps from the lead escort vessel. John did a gentle turn away and gave them a belly view of his aircraft to show that they were friendly, then tapped out a random series of dots and dashes on his light key, hoping he might get lucky.

He then raised his hands to his ears and ducked his head. Every armed ship in the convoy opened up, and in an instant the sky was full of black puffs and curving tracers of Bofors anti-aircraft shells. The convoy escort leader was taking no chances. John and Hughie turned tail and got out of there as fast as they could. They had no recourse but to turn around and fly back to Digby for John to get the codes.

They both loved to scramble – racing into action, then the mad dash to your aircraft when the siren sounded. Pilots on *First Readiness* were required to wait in the dispersal hut, dressed in full uniform, tunic, tie, flying boots, and Mae Wests, playing chess or bridge or darts, or napping if there were a bed available.

The ground crew started the aircraft, the men slipped on their chutes, clambered into their cockpits with the ground crew buckling them in, and off they went. Possibly because *401 Squadron* was the first wholly Canadian squadron, they

401 Squadron pilots on First Readiness. John is centre, looking at the camera.

prided themselves on having the fastest scrambles in England, an honour they held for a long time. They also had the cleanest planes with the fewest service problems. The ground crew loved their work every bit as much as the pilots, and took immense personal pride in what they considered to be 'their' aircraft, immediately fixing anything that was amiss.

A few months after Hughie was posted to 401, John encountered another old friend from Toronto. He was in the mess when someone shouted out, *'Johnny!'* No one on the squadron called him Johnny, but he recognized the voice. A lanky figure approached him, and he saw it was his pal Wally Floody, who he had known years before at Sunday School. Wally had been born in Chatham, Ontario, and moved with his parents to Toronto. In 1936, he headed north to Timmins

Wally Floody (left) shortly after his arrival on 401 Squadron.

to work in the mines as a mucker, just as John had.

There were new friends on the Squadron as well. Ian (*'Ormie'*) Ormston connected with John in the early months of 1941. Another was Eugene *'Jeep'* Neal, who had a tendency, when he got excited, to flip back and forth between French and English (his father was Anglophone, and his mother was Francophone). Jeep was shot down a half dozen times but never captured, and made it through the war with only a couple of broken bones. Ormie crashed landed, somersaulting his plane down the runway, breaking his back. (After a couple of months in traction, he became extremely frustrated that he wasn't being sent back into action.) These were resilient individuals, who became steadfast friends.

Wartime friendships are unlike any other. These young men had been 'blooded' together, which meant they'd shared life and death experiences. There was no closer bond.

'Ormie' (at left) on First Readiness.

'Jeep' Neal.

John was still like a fox terrier, always in the middle of the fun, and quick to make friends with new arrivals. Ironically, this was one aspect of squadron life that worried some of the senior officers. Some veteran pilots were too friendly and too connected with the new guys. Deane Nesbitt was nine years older than John, and had seen hundreds of pilots come and go. That summer, he pulled John aside and warned him it was time to stop making so many friends. This surprised John, as he was naturally outgoing, and the squadron was their only social outlet. Deane said that if he kept buddying up to all the new men, only to watch them get killed, it would eventually kill something inside John as well. Hughie, Ormie, Jeep, Wally fair enough, those guys were his friends already. But he should ease up on making new ones if he knew what was good for him.

John thought about the dozens of men whose names and faces he could now barely remember, who had joined the squadron and now were dead. He had trained himself not to think about those who'd bought it, but Deane's mentioning of it hit home. From then on, he followed the advice. With each new wave of replacements, he would make a point of connecting with a simple, 'Hi, nice to meet you,' then go on his way. It stood him in good stead through the summer and the fall of that year. He focussed on honing his flying and stopped trying to be everyone's pal. The war was starting to feel like a game of last man standing.

In the following months, John continued flying special duty. Hughie was his Wing Man, never questioning what the mission was. The amount of combat flying was slowly increasing, day and night, as was the exhaustion. The more hours the pilots flew in battle, the more the odds became stacked against them surviving. The pressure could be crippling.

There were a few who cracked, and were transferred to a 'Glass House' for LMF – Lack of Moral Fibre. This was a terrifying threat to the pilots. It was worse than washing out: to be designated as LMF meant being branded a coward. Those labeled LMF became pariahs in their squadrons. The other men wanted nothing to do with you – you had become a liability and a curse. You sometimes were given two choices: to be returned to Canada in disgrace (but not discharged), or to be sent to a Glass House and have it drilled out of you.

RAF Command played on this notion as an intentional deterrent to pilots contemplating pulling back from active duty without incontestable grounds. There was an unspoken but widespread belief among aircrew that LMF was contagious and could eat through the heart of a squadron if left unchecked.

Glass Houses were anonymous bases that dealt with airmen who had repeatedly choked in combat. The routine was one of rigorous discipline. The men were awakened at five in the morning, run to the latrine to do what was necessary, then run to the mess for breakfast where they had five minutes to eat their meal. Immediately afterwards, they were hustled out for a 10-mile run carrying a full pack. On their return, they had to run to lunch, run to the latrine again (whether they needed to or not), drilled with full packs in the afternoon for two hours of marching, run to dinner, and then finally run to their barracks and bed, knowing the whole routine would be repeated the next morning, and for weeks on end. The objective was to drill the consciousness of fear out of the men who had seized up in action.

This grueling routine sounds sadistic, but it served an essential purpose in maintaining the structure of the flights within a combat squadron. At the beginning of the war, the RAF deployed flights of three aircraft, while the Germans were using Flights of two. *401 Squadron* came to the conclusion that the Germans were right: flying in 'twos,' with a leader and a wing man, each man's role was clear. Flying in 'threes' is a tight formation, whereas flying in 'twos' is loose, and makes it possible to break free and roam the sky.

But this put a great deal of pressure on pilots, know
survival depended on their flight partner. As their frie:
shot down and the death rates increased, some you: ⌣ ,
panicked, which could grow into blind terror. After taking off,
a pilot who had lost his nerve would rattle off any excuse he
could come up with, such as, '*My oil reservoir was zero,*' '*I ran out
of gas,*' or '*My gun panel was loose.*' Then they'd drop out of the
formation and return to base, leaving their flight partner alone
and exposed to attack. If a pilot pulled this more than a couple
of times, he would be designated LMF and shipped off to a
Glass House.

The location of these re-training bases was secret, partially
in order to remove any potential contact with their squadrons.
John discovered there was a Glass House not far from one of the
bases that *401 Squadron* had been stationed at. He knew some
boys who had been sent to one, and was curious to see what
they were like. He found the base and approached the Officer of
the Day on duty at the gate, who duly gave him hell for nosing
around. He warned John that if he didn't get lost, he would
report him as being sympathetic, which meant he would be
grounded immediately.

John beat a hasty retreat. But he was reported, and received
a call from Uncle Adrian. He tore a strip off John with the
warning that it was none of his business what went on at the
Glass Houses, or with the men who were afraid to fly, and that
if he didn't have anything better to do with his time, he would
make a point of finding something that would fully occupy his
attention.

The day you join the service, discipline is hammered into you. You learn to do what has to be done without asking questions. At each turn, you are taught to suppress your sense of self for the good of the whole. And while fear is hard-wired into everyone as a survival mechanism, the military seeks to short-circuit that wiring to focus on objectives and not emotions. That doesn't mean that men and women in the line of fire weren't fearful; they simply learned how to do what they had to do *in spite* of their feelings. Youthful bravado and ignorance are the most common balm against fear. Most soldiers and airmen simply thought they would never be the ones who would get hit; it was always going to be the other guy.

Some men psyched themselves up to deal with their nerves before heading into action. One Spitfire pilot worked himself into a lather of hate for Germans before taking to the air, in the same manner he had worked himself up before football games at McGill. After the war, an accomplished group of Luftwaffe pilots admitted that they rarely went up into battle in their fighters without a few drinks in them. The pure oxygen they breathed in their aircraft sobered them up fast enough, and once in the air they were swept up in the exhilaration of the fight. But while on the ground, waiting to go into action, they spent much of their war with a pleasant *'buzz'* on. That made it possible for many of them to treat going into combat as a game, and not the daily life and death struggle that it really was. Self-delusion can be an important instinct for survival.

And then there were the rare few who were without fear. These curious beings weren't reckless and theatrically brave, but were simply unable to recognize or sense danger, in much the same way a colour blind person can't see colour in a normal way. A young Canadian soldier from Kamloops, Robert Laroux, was just such a young man. He was a private with the *Princess Patricia's Canadian Light Infantry* (the *PPCLI*, or *Princess Pat's*), and was happy soldiering with never any interest in winning medals or moving up in the ranks. He was tough, uncomplaining, and lacked any sense of fear. His sergeant tried to dig out of him why this was, but it was beyond Laroux to explain. He simply didn't know what fear meant or what it felt like. On patrols or in combat zones, when his platoon was being shelled and shot at, he was aware of the danger but felt no sense of anxiety or self-preservation.

While moving up the line in Italy, Laroux's platoon came to a river that they had to cross by wading or swimming. Like the other men, Laroux was carrying about ninety pounds of equipment when he went in. It was pouring rain and the river was swollen above its banks. Even though he didn't know how to swim, Laroux walked straight into the water with no sense of the danger that the river presented. That was the last anyone saw of him until a few days later when his body washed up downstream. It had no wounds on it; it looked like he'd simply fallen asleep in the water. He had drowned because of his dedication to duty and his inability to experience fear.

When John returned from a mission, he was typically drenched with sweat from the stress. He felt the fear, but he didn't try to avoid it or to numb it. It was just something that was part of the work, and that gave him detachment from it consuming him. His point of view was that if his ticket had been punched, there wasn't anything he could do about it, so there was no point worrying. Youth certainly played a part in his ability to disregard what his autonomic nerves were doing, but there was more to it than that. In the hundreds and hundreds of hours of flying time that he had logged, he had come to respect the speed at which things happen when you're flying. He never stopped developing his skills; he wanted flying to become as automatic as breathing. As soon as he started worrying about what might happen when you were in action, he (and Hughie, too) had decided that it was probably already too late. This management of fear was something he shared with Gordon.

It was the personal losses, like Pat Chamier, that came close to undoing him.

Uncle Adrian's official wartime duties as an Air Commodore included two that were less onerous. One was overseeing the *British Balloon Command* (barrage balloon) defenses. The second duty was one in which he took great pride: his work with the Air Cadets. That helped balance the stress of his more official work.

In the summer of 1941, the cadets had gathered for an annual fête at Spalding, Lincolnshire, not far from where 401 Squadron was stationed. Adrian was to visit them, give a welcoming talk, and inspect their ranks on parade. He planned to visit John at *401 Squadron's* base, but early in the afternoon of the first day, John received a phone call and a string of numbers. He called back and Adrian answered, and said *'You're going to be given an appointment tonight, but you are not to complete the rendezvous.'* John understood.

That evening, a flight of German bombers came on an attack of targets on the east coast of England. John was the only pilot scrambled, but his orders from Adrian were to observe but not engage. He flew up to 16,000 feet and watched from a distance as the Germans came in. As instructed, he did not attack, even though the Germans appeared to have little opposition. They dropped their bombs on their targets and returned to the continent unmolested.

Uncle Adrian in 1941.

The next morning, Uncle Adrian came to the base to speak with John. Adrian was uncharacteristically quiet. John gave him a report of what had happened the night before, and how frustrating it had been to remain at a distance. Adrian said that about four hundred of the cadets had been killed in the raid. He said that there was nothing that John could have done to prevent it, and was glad that John had understood his message not to get involved. British Intelligence had intercepted and cracked German coded messages about the raid, and so the RAF knew when and approximately where it would happen. Had the bombing raid been intercepted, it would have tipped off German Intelligence that their communications had been breached. It was essential to keep the transmission of coded messages flowing, even when it meant putting lives at risk. No one had anticipated the Air Cadet's fête being in harm's way; and it was improbable that a single fighter could have done anything in their defense.

Having information such as the advance notice of the German raid, without the ability to act on it, haunted John. He wept for much of the day just thinking about what had happened. He came close to breaking, and considered requesting a transfer from the squadron to the Merchant Marine, which was recruiting pilots to fly Hurricanes off catapults mounted on supply ships. John thought his piloting skills might be useful, and as he would be shipping back and forth between Canada and Britain every few weeks, Fran might come down and visit. But by this point, John was a senior pilot with *401* and badly needed there. He decided he had to stay where the need was

A pilot prepares for an early morning 'reccie' in his Spitfire..

greatest.

By September, the squadron had been re-equipped with Spitfires, which had come into their own as the premier combat aircraft of the RAF. They were much faster than the Hurricanes, and almost equal in speed to the Messerschmitt. But a Spit could almost always out-turn a ME-109, which usually flipped when it tried to match the Spit's aerobatic agility. The Spitfire could fly up to 30,000 feet, but John and Hughie usually flew between 24,000 and 25,000 feet. The Messerschmitt had a two stage turbo-charged engine that kicked in between 24,000 and 25,000 feet, which made them faster when they were flying at heights where there was less oxygen. John and Hughie figured out that this offered an advantage. When the Messerschmitt's supercharger engaged, there was a telltale puff of black smoke and a momentary loss of power, which made them vulnerable for a couple of seconds. So between 24,000 and 25,000 feet, a Spitfire could force the 109s into stalling for a precious moment or two when they could strike. This meant the Spits got more ME-109s than the Germans got in return.

John, Hughie, Jeep, Ormie and their friends on the squadron had become veteran combat pilots by the simple virtue of having survived. The downside to that was that the more experienced pilots were moved into separate Flights to break in the new arrivals, which had the result of weakening the teamwork that had developed among the men. The losses were mounting, and at times the squadron seemed barely to be holding its own. The reality was that they were living a charmed existence in the face of the high casualty rate that was the lot of fighter pilots. It was no longer a question of *if* you might get it; it was a matter of *when*.

Acquiring experience flying in combat at that time in the war depended a great deal on blind luck. The RAF was so short of pilots that young, inexperienced men were constantly being brought on to the squadron as replacements to keep manpower at strength. Many had never flown in formation with the veterans, let alone in combat, the first time they scrambled. All that could be done was to tell them, '*Keep an eye on your tail and keep an eye on my tail.*' Experienced pilots like John and Hughie knew that most of the newbies didn't stand a chance, being so desperately inexperienced. The irony was that the longer you flew unscathed, the steeper the odds were against you: your clock was running down.

John had accumulated almost a thousand hours of flight time by October 1941, and flown over a hundred special operations. RAF HQ in the person of Uncle Adrian felt that he'd been too lucky – which in fact was the case – and that the odds were against him. Adrian summoned John to London for a talk.

He told John it was time to transfer out of 401 Squadron, and as it happened he had a special assignment he wanted John to take on. Nine agents were to be parachuted into North Africa, each in their own sector but working together. John would be briefed with his assignment once he had met with the handlers. The target date was two weeks away.

John refused, the one thing he'd sworn never to do. His argument was that the squadron needed him now, as they were desperately short handed. He was Flight Leader; Hughie had been transferred to a different flight, and the squadron was having to spread its ranks extremely thin to cover their losses and fully man all the aircraft. The RAF was beginning to get a foothold against the Luftwaffe that fall, but 401 Squadron was still getting badly hammered, flying daily missions out of Biggin Hill airfield southeast of London, where they were now stationed.

Adrian listened, but was unmoved. He explained to John that it wasn't just his unreasonable number of flight hours. He was also the common thread linking him to five German agents who had been arrested. These were men that John had identified, and sooner or later someone would connect the dots and John would have his own 'unfortunate accident.' He had been too busy and wrapped up in the work of the squadron to be thinking about the repercussions of his spy catching work. Still, John was reluctant.

Adrian challenged him, asking if he felt he was irreplaceable, and more significantly, was he was actually refusing. There would be consequences. John acknowledged that if Adrian ordered him, he would transfer. And that was the end of the discussion. Adrian ordered John to report for assessment pending reassignment.

With deep regret, John left 401 Squadron and went to London. His French and German were reasonably good, which he would need for the new assignment. Furthermore, he had extensive training in special operations, making him an ideal candidate for re-deployment.

He was subjected to a battery of tests. His field skills were evaluated, as were his fitness level, ability to survive interrogation, and fluency with languages. At the end of five days, he received outstanding reports in all areas apart from his languages. Both the French and German assessors reported that he was comfortably proficient in their respective tongues, but that his accent(s) were pronounced, and the odds were that he would be arrested if he tried to pass himself off as a local in any non-English country. Two days later, John received a curt message from Adrian: 'The party's off.'

The mission went forward, and within the month all the other eight agents were dead. Their circuit hadn't been broken. There was just something about the way they dressed, walked, or acted that caught the Germans' attention. In the early years of the intelligence war, it was the small telltale errors in judgement that got an agent killed. Agents from North America were particularly vulnerable, as were the well-fed outdoorsmen typically recruited by Camp X and the SOE. They lacked the pale, drawn look of someone in the occupied, food-scarce countries of Europe. John was confident in his survival skills, but was acutely aware that he likely would not have fared any better than the unfortunate eight.

With this chapter behind him, John was very happy to return to 401 Squadron and getting back to doing what he knew best. The squadron was off balance, though. Ormie and Jeep were on leave when he rejoined, Wally Floody had been shot down a couple of days earlier, and Hughie was leading another Flight.

Scruffy pleased to be back at 401 Squadron.

This meant that John found himself flying with replacements with a fraction of the combat experience he had. In that first week of November 1941, the squadron lost ten pilots out of twelve, and was losing new pilots as fast as they could replace them. The squadron was practically all newcomers, and it made John nervous.

Chapter 11

Stranger in a Strange Land

Hughie, now leading 'B' Flight, returned from an exhausting dogfight over the Thames Estuary. Discouraged and weary, he reported to the IO for debriefing, who informed him that John had gone missing. Hughie was devastated.

> I never worried about John. He was always there, always had been there since school. He had spent a good part of his life trying to keep me out of trouble. I thought of how we used to meet at 5:30 every Saturday morning at the streetcar stop with our hockey sticks and skates over our shoulder on our way to play hockey. Half the time, he would forget his shin pads, but would play anyway. Tough as nails and a perpetual clown. I can see him catching that pass I was supposed to throw to somebody else in a football game against St. Andrew's, and how he ran zigzag all around the field with half the St. Andrew's football team after him while he avoided their tackles with little bursts of speed. It seemed impossible. He was too fast; they couldn't have got him.

He pictured John's mother Freda, and Fran, now John's fiancée, reading the telegram they would be getting in a day or so, expressing regret that Flying Officer John Weir had been reported missing in action over enemy territory.

Hughie wrote the Weirs a letter, even though he couldn't think of anything useful to say. He kept hearing Colonel Weir's voice in his head: *'Okay, Hughie, just give us the facts and forget the trimming.'* He drifted through the next few days in a fog. Later that week, Adrian invited Hughie to come up to London to have dinner and spend the night. Hughie went through the unhappy task of pulling John's things together to ship home. He took these to London with him, as he thought the more personal correspondence might make it past the censors if it was sent with Uncle Adrian's assistance.

Adrian met Hughie at Victoria Station, and they rode in a cab back to the Chamier flat in silence. Once inside, with a large whisky in hand, Hughie blurted out what little he knew about what had happened. Adrian listened in silence. Spotting the bag with *'F/O JOHN. G. WEIR'* printed on the side, Adrian asked, 'Would you like me to take care of that?' Hughie gratefully passed it to him, glad that he wouldn't have the painful task of sending it home to Toronto.

On Saturday, November 8th, John had taken off to fly a Sweep over Abbeville in Normandy with a new pilot, Gardner, freshly attached to the squadron. This was a dangerous mission. Abbeville was one of the main Luftwaffe bases along the northern coast of France, with as many as a thousand fighters stationed there. John was trying to keep an eye on his Wing Man who was new to flying in *'twos'* – two planes flying as a fighting unit – and this was worrying him. Would he know what to do when they were attacked? Fifty hours of training wasn't worth an hour of combat. It's the Wing Man's responsibility to watch his Flight Leader's back as well as his own, and as Flight Leader, John's responsibility was to keep his eyes peeled for enemy aircraft in the sky ahead. In RAF parlance, John was 'nurse-maiding' his new partner instead of focussing on the attack.

As they crossed the coast and flew inland, a group of ME–109s appeared out of nowhere, and with the sun behind them, swept down in an ambush. Instead of keeping his eyes on them, John glanced back yet again to see if Gardner was in position. That was a mistake. In the split second that John glanced away, he lost track of the Germans. They swung around behind him and out of sight, and by the time he looked forward again it was too late. He and Gardner were trapped. John flipped his Spitfire over hard to the left and down, his best hope to shake off a pursuer. At that same moment, he heard Gardner shout over the

ME-109s (Messerschmitts).

wireless, followed by a scream; dead before his Spitfire began to tumble out of the sky.

Everything happened fast; John didn't have time to think. A Messerschmitt attacked him from behind. Its 20mm cannons blew the left wing off his Spitfire, and machine gun fire raked his instrument panel and upper fuel tank. The tank was full, so it didn't explode, but gas sprayed back over him. The instrument panel began showering sparks. Those ignited the gas and the raw oxygen from his oxygen supply, which caused the cockpit to erupt in flames. What was left of his aircraft began to spin and disintegrate in mid-air. Now engulfed in flames, he yanked open the plane's canopy and tumbled out.

He and Hughie had talked through what would happen if there was a fire in the cockpit. If you gasped for air, you would breathe raw oxygen and gas into your lungs, and would be dead in seconds. They decided the best option was to hold their breath and bail out as fast as possible. So although his tunic, gloves, and helmet were on fire, he concentrated for a precious few seconds on his breathing.

He cracked his head against the Spitfire's tail fin as he fell out. A pistol that he had tucked into his left boot was lost when his parachute snapped open, and the slipstream and sudden jolt ripped both his boots off.

At 26,000 feet, the air is extremely thin, and pilots jumping at such heights died more often than not, asphyxiated from hypoxia. This is the state in which the body is deprived of adequate oxygen supply, causing unconsciousness and eventually death. John had gone through special operations training, including numerous high-altitude parachute jumps. During those tests it was determined that he had a slow heart rate and low metabolic rate and required less oxygen than was typical. He managed to remain conscious, holding his breath until he was clear of the flames.

It was a long way down. Descending from that height took a long time, which in itself was disorienting. Being blown out of the sky at heights of 15,000 feet or more, the experience was hallucinatory for most airmen, largely due to oxygen deficit. It was also freezing at that altitude, which may have helped anesthetize any pain. In combat, engine noise blots out everything else, so a dogfight could often seem to happen in a blanket of white noise. Being abruptly launched into the air would have been like diving into a pool and suddenly having all familiar sounds disappear.

Which is perhaps why John thought he was hearing things, when at about a thousand feet he began to perceive sounds that had no place at that height: a rooster crowing, then a dog barking. At around five hundred feet, he could hear two men talking in a field below, and he saw them watching him. He wasn't hallucinating after all.

As he came down, he tried to picture where he had been when he was hit. He thought it was about 30 kilometres miles southwest of Caen, so maybe with some luck he could evade capture, and head west to his old summer school in Brittany.

He landed hard, bootless, battered, and badly burned, with his uniform in tatters. He set about burying his parachute as he knew the Germans would have seen him coming down, and would already be on the hunt for him. If he had any hope of escaping capture, he had to get moving as soon as possible.

Airmen had been warned that, if shot down behind enemy lines, they should not approach groups of people. If you needed help, find someone on their own, and stay away from main roads and villages. The two men he had heard talking in the field walked towards him. They looked harmless enough, but he decided to keep his distance. As they approached he murmured a simple, *'bonjour,'* and started walking in what he thought was the right direction.

As he walked, he checked himself over. He knew he had been burned in the cockpit fire, but didn't feel much pain; it felt more like a sunburn. His eyes itched as though they had dust in them, and he had to squint to see anything in the bright sun. His hands were sore as if he had scraped them down a brick wall. But he was in one piece, and so he kept moving.

A lone figure appeared on the road walking towards him. He was about forty years old, with a friendly face, and John decided to take a chance. Each morning while on operations, John received Maquis *'call words'* for the day, via *Acquisitor.* The Maquis were French resistance fighters in rural France, and the call words were seemingly innocent phrases used to identify members to one another. That day, the phrase he'd been give was, *'Where is the British captain?'* He saw recognition register in the man's eyes, which meant they could trust one another.

In his Québécois accented French, he explained who he was and where he was headed. The man agreed to help. He told John to keep heading on the road he was on, and not to stop for anything or let anyone see him if he could avoid it. He would come to a crossroads, and should wait there until he returned with some clothes.

John headed off, and in due course found the spot. As he waited, a brisk November breeze stung his face. His eyes were watering, and the sun seemed unusually harsh, making it difficult for him to see. His hands were red and blistered, and clenching his fingers into fists was painful.

He began to feel uneasy sitting out in the open. But after a few minutes, the stranger reappeared on a bicycle with the clothes and a bottle of water. John removed the remains of his uniform and gave them to the man, who said he would dispose of them. He dressed quickly and downed the bottle of water.

The man looked at John, touched his face in several places, then shook his head. He said he was sorry, but could do nothing more. He told John what he saw. His face, neck, and hands were severely burned, and his hair had been singed to blackened wisps. His scorched eyelids were virtually fused shut. John could make out shadows and shapes if he tilted his head back and peered out through the slits, but he was effectively blind.

He told John to wait for the Germans, as they would be able to give him the medical help he needed. Then he said he had to get moving, or he would be arrested, too; more likely shot on the spot for having given aid to an enemy.

Minutes after he had gone, Germans arrived with tracking dogs. 'For you, the war is over,' a sergeant said. He was bundled him into a truck and driven to a nearby Luftwaffe base for interrogation. The soldiers smoked and talked as they bounced along, ignoring him.

So far, adrenaline and shock had kept the worst of his pain at bay. He kept very still and quiet, which made it possible for him to listen to what the soldiers were saying. He was reasonably fluent in German and memorized anything he thought might come in useful.

He was escorted to a nearby Luftwaffe squadron barracks for interrogation. This was brief, due in large part to his unsettling appearance. There were ghoulishly blackened slits where his eyelids had once been, his facial hair had been reduced to charred wisps, and the skin on his face and neck was red and puckered from the flames. These were the kinds of injuries that airmen feared most, and they undoubtedly induced some professional sympathy from the Germans.

He was sent to a hospital in the small city of Saint-Omer in Nord-Pas-de-Calais for treatment. The hospital was spartan and ill-equipped, and the resources for dealing with injuries like John's were minimal at best. Without anesthetic, disinfectant, or antibiotics such as penicillin, John began to comprehend just how serious his injuries were. A pilot from his squadron, Brian Hodgkinson, had been shot down at the end of October (the same day as Wally Floody), and was in the same hospital with serious burns to his groin.

When John had the dressing on his head removed for examination, Hodgkinson didn't recognize him. Parts of John's head had swollen to what looked like twice their normal size. His cheeks and forehead were bloated with pus and protruded beyond the tip of his nose, and his eyes were barely visible slits. His mouth was a flexible gash but looked unable to form words or sounds. John recognized Hodgkinson's voice and called out, *'Hodge! It's Scruffy! Don't you recognize me?'* Hodgkinson was deeply shaken for months afterward seeing the condition John was in.

The German doctors had few supplies to work with. They improvised a burn salve by mixing boric acid with petroleum jelly. First thing each morning, they smeared the mixture over his face, neck, and hands, and then replaced the dressings. Having this applied was painful, but once on it was cooling and provided some relief. However, when the bandages were removed, and air hit the raw flesh, the pain was excruciating. Dead skin peeled off like tissue paper. Without so much as an aspirin to alleviate the pain, it felt like he was being flayed alive. This rudimentary treatment went on for two months until new skin began to regenerate, and the danger of infection had passed.

For those months, John was blind. But he was able to get around using sound and his sense of touch to guide him. Hodgkinson had been badly burned in his groin and couldn't walk. So the two of them would occasionally team up, with Scruffy carrying 'Hodge' on his back providing their eyes, and Scruffy transporting them providing their legs.

Shortly after New Year 1942, the doctors cut open his eyelids – the lids had healed shut – to see what condition his eyes were. His pupils moved slightly, so they were satisfied that he hadn't gone permanently blind. Over the next few days, John's eyes became used to the light, and he could make out the blurred shapes of people and objects around him. He had developed strong impressions of what the doctors, nurses, and orderlies looked like while he had been unable to see and was often startled by how wrong his impressions had been.

In the second week of January, the Germans transferred John to Dulag Luft, a transit camp for Allied PoWs where virtually all captured airmen were sent for processing and interrogation before being assigned to a PoW camp. Dulag Luft was located just outside Frankfurt and was a collection centre for the massive amounts of information extracted from those prisoners in seemingly innocuous fragments.

Skilled interrogators would meet all new arrivals, gently and obliquely extracting bits and pieces from them, often in the context of friendly and casual conversations. Off-handed details of the planes their squadrons were flying, radio frequencies being used, maybe a useful name or two were drawn out, but rarely by threat and intimidation. The best interrogators

Dulag Luft, the main Luftwaffe Interrogation Centre.

had no accents; their chats were indiscernible from something you might have with a friend over lunch back home. Nothing personal, nothing sensitive. In this way, the Germans gathered a staggering amount of information that they assembled into a very clear picture of the Allied air war effort.

One RCAF Spitfire pilot, Jack Fleming, had such an interview with an interrogator. The German mentioned that the pilot's squadron was being moved to Sutton Bridge, and named the new CO. Jack smiled at this awkward attempt to draw him out, shook his head, and said, *'I don't know where you heard that stuff, but it's wrong.'* The interrogator said, *'No, it's all quite true,'* and produced a copy of the previous day's *Toronto Star* that confirmed this in one of its pages of war news.

The interrogator then went on to give Jack a verbal travelogue of his movements from the day he enlisted two years before, to the day he was shot down. The stunned pilot later told friends, *'He knew more about me than my mother.'*

Dulag Luft's appearance was unremarkable. There were a dozen or so single-storey wooden buildings, with barbed wire fences surrounding the grounds. The Germans knew the Allies would never bomb the camp as long as it could be identified as housing PoWs, so there were large white rocks that spread across the yard, spelling out, *'Prisoner of War Camp.'* The same words were painted in white letters across the roofs of most buildings, thus ensuring that the Germans' interrogations could continue without fear of disruption.

The welcoming committee at Dulag Luft was a combination of Gestapo and Abwehr Intelligence officers. The captured airmen would first be submitted to basic questioning – name, rank, and serial number – after which they were placed in solitary confinement, typically for one to two weeks. While the Geneva Convention forbade torture, the Germans had ways of softening up the men that deftly avoided falling under the negative label of 'torture.'

One of the most effective techniques was to confine a man to his cell, a space about five by seven feet. It had nothing in it but a narrow bed, a small sealed window, and a large radiator. Simple food and water were slid in through a trap in the door twice a day. Dinner consisted of a mushy vegetable soup, with an occasional piece of black bread (normally padded out with sawdust), and ersatz coffee made from burnt barley, acorns, and other such odds and ends. It tasted terrible, but it was warm and provided much-needed water. You were escorted to the toilet twice a day.

The softening up process began subtly. The radiator was gradually turned down. As the temperature dropped, the prisoner was left shivering beneath a single thin blanket. Then, the rad would be cranked up again, and the cell would heat up like a sauna. This cycle would be repeated again and again – off, on, off, on – every day, and all day. When challenged about this, the Germans argued this was merely a side effect of an inefficient climate control system. Many PoWs found themselves wondering if they were going to spend the rest of the war wracked between freezing and baking in their tiny cells.

During this softening up period, each prisoner was carefully observed to discover his habits, likes and dislikes, and ability and inclination to resist intimidation and inducements. Accordingly, a suitable method of interrogation was planned, and the system was set in motion to gradually break down the prisoner's mental resistance in the shortest possible time.

If he showed signs of fright or nervousness, he was threatened with all kinds of physical torture. Others were bribed with the offer of simple luxuries: clean clothes, a warm bed, edible food, and plenty of cigarettes, all of which would be exchanged for answers to specific questions. Those who could neither be swayed nor bribed were treated with respect, but were made to suffer long miserable hours of solitary confinement in their confining cells.

The interrogators were curious about John but did not manhandle him as much as they might have. Possibly this was because of how dreadful he looked. He gave them his name, rank, and serial number; but they already knew who he was.

No mention was made of his spy catching work in England with Adrian, for which he was thankful. He remembered Adrian's admonition about having drawn attention to himself by openly identifying the German spy at Castletown. He knew there was a possibility they were aware of this and were simply biding their time until he slipped up. He resolved to follow Adrian's advice and to keep his mouth shut and act dumb.

Having visited Frankfurt several times before the war and being familiar with the city, he thought seriously about trying to escape. If he had been able to see properly or had full use of his hands, it might have been possible. But he was in no shape to do anything of the kind.

Chapter 12

Evading

A fter a week at Dulag Luft, John was taken from his cell and herded onto a truck with no information about where he was going. He and a few dozen other prisoners were driven to a train station and escorted onto railway cars. Their destination was Stalag Luft I, a PoW camp outside of Barth, Pomerania, on the Baltic Sea in the north of Germany. By January 1942, there were about a thousand men in the camp, half officers and half non-coms. (A *'non-com'* is a non-commissioned officer, someone with the rank of sergeant or below.) John was assigned *'Kriegie'* number *'7-1-5,' Kriegie* being the nickname the prisoners gave themselves instead of the German *'Kriegsgefangener'* – literally, war-prisoner. The prisoners called the German guards as *'Goons,'* which puzzled them. When asked, some PoWs explained that this was an acronym for *'German Officer or Non-Com',* which they apparently believed and happily accepted, even occasionally referring to themselves as goons, to the delight of the PoWs.

Hermann Göring, Hitler's Deputy and the head of the Luftwaffe, had been an ace in WWI. He was an arrogant man and believed in a tradition of dignity in the air force, and that he was its natural leader. He decreed that PoW camps for airmen should not be under the command of the SS or the Gestapo,

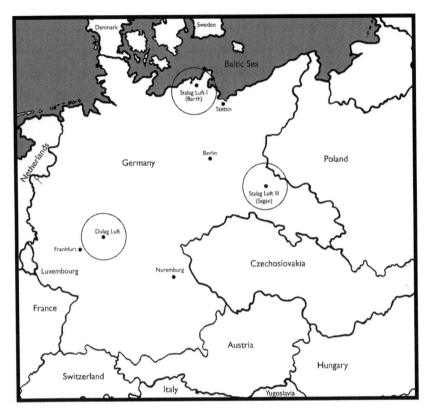

whom he considered little more than thugs. This led him to create camps specifically for air force personnel. These were named '*Stalag Luft*' (air force camp) and '*Oflag Luft*' (air force officer camp) and administrated under his direct authority.

Stalag Luft 1 was the first. Like most such camps, the buildings had been constructed roughly and cheaply. They were cottage-like buildings that were raised off the ground so the Germans could search underneath for signs of escape. The huts had fifteen to twenty rooms in them, with each room able to accommodate nine men in three triple-decker bunks. (As the war progressed, the Germans squeezed in as many as twelve men in a room.) Heat was provided by a small pot bellied stove, and

John in Stalag Luft I, shortly after his arrival. His 'raccoon' eyes are a result of his burns.

the prisoners were given a small amount of crushed powdered coal each day, but it was never enough.

For the early arrivals, rooms weren't as crowded as they would soon become. John was assigned to a nine-bunk room with four other flyers. To his great delight, his old friend Wally Floody was one of them. This was the first he knew that Wally was still alive and breathing after having been shot down in late October. The others were Hank Birkland from Calgary, 'Pop' Collett from New Zealand, and Zbischek Gotowski, a Polish air force officer. A couple of weeks later they were joined by

Jens Müller, a Norwegian pilot who had trained in Canada at Little Norway, a Royal Norwegian Air Force training camp then located on Toronto's waterfront (which later relocated to Gravenhurst, Ontario).

Barth was potato country, and so the diet at Stalag Luft I relied heavily on starch for every meal, supplemented by watery turnip soup, black bread, and a dab of a margarine-like fat. There was also a drink called *'surface beer,'* which was skimmed from the top of commercial brewing vats and given to pigs and other livestock – and to the men in Stalag Luft I. Surface beer contained very little alcohol – between 1 and 2 percent – and the Englishmen wouldn't touch it. But it contained small amounts of yeast and malt, and the men in John's room knew the value of anything that offered some protein. They happily took the whole block's ration. You couldn't get drunk on it, and it tasted rather sour, but it gave one's system a healthy flushing and provided a minute infusion of nutrition.

The guards also gave the men German newspapers, which John read in an attempt to improve his German. Once the boys

Stalag Luft I in Barth, Northern Germany.

had finished with them, they were collected and burned for heat. It was cold in Northern Germany, and the huts had no insulation. John had an idea. He made a starchy paste from potatoes that had gone bad and used this to wallpaper the bare wooden walls with the newspaper. Their room was soon the warmest in the hut, and it didn't take long for the rest of the prisoners to follow suit.

Escape committees at Stalag Luft I were in full swing in early 1942, and they were a source of hope for the frustrated prisoners. Barth was a promising location from which to attempt a break, being on the Baltic Sea. If escapers could find a boat, it would be possible to sail it the hundred or so miles across the Baltic to Denmark. But first they would have to escape. That was no simple matter, as there was a double perimeter of high fencing that enclosed bales of tangled barbed wire spread out on the ground between them. There were guard towers every hundred metres, and guards with dogs patrolled the grounds day and night.

The committee had determined that tunnelling was the only feasible way to escape. The problem was that the tunnels were collapsing as fast as they were dug. Being so close to the sea, the water table was only six feet down, and the soil was predominantly sand. There was constant flooding in the tunnels, leaving the boys frequently trying to tunnel through mud. Wally, Hank Birkland, and John had all worked in mines in Northern Ontario, and they talked about how tunnelling could be improved using techniques they had picked up.

At escape committee meetings, the PoWs exchanged

information and provided suggestions, supplies, and support if someone had a plan that had potential. There were several accomplished escape artists among them, and their collective experience was invaluable. But the bitterly cold weather of that winter, and the unstable wet and sandy soil, provided serious challenges. Wally, Hank, and John thought they might have some solutions.

John's badly burned hands hadn't fully healed, and he was unable to dig or grip tools with any strength. Although he was in no shape to dig, John was invited to attend a meeting. Typically, such secret meetings were only for familiar faces. It was unusual for a newcomer such as John to be extended that level of trust. Wally and Hank vouched for him, and perhaps that was enough.

The discussion focussed on rumours that they were about to be moved to another camp, and the challenges that presented. Stalag Luft I had opened in November 1941 as a British officer PoW camp but had quickly become overcrowded. Most of the RAF PoWs were young and from the ambitious middle and working classes, and were not afraid of challenging authority. The Luftwaffe's decision to intern these daring young men together created an extremely bright and spirited 'talent pool,' boys who saw their capture as an opportunity to turn escape into purposeful acts of resistance. The brightest and most resourceful PoWs had already made an impact. In turn, their German captors recognized a need to build camps that would be virtually escape-proof. The new camp, rumoured to be located near the Polish border on the Eastern frontier, was the first of these. Its isolated location alone would be a prime factor in discouraging escapers.

Escapes had all but stopped at Stalag Luft I. At the beginning of the war, there was an almost casual atmosphere in many camps. Some even relied on a Trust system to keep the prisoners behind the wire. But now that the war had intensified with the entry of the United States, and Russia no longer an ally of the Germans, security had become much more rigorous. These were discouraging days for the PoWs.

The consensus was that in the coming days they would be shipped by train southeast from Barth to the port of Stettin (now Szczecin, Poland), and then to the new camp. This would further limit opportunities for escape.

In the escape committee meeting, the boys pored over a map of Stettin and its surrounding area. This was a port city with its harbour on the Baltic, and an obvious choice to find safe passage to Denmark or Sweden. What's more, all railways heading south passed through Stettin, which meant any train headed for the Eastern Front would pass through there, too.

Everyone contributed ideas and information. Someone familiar with the rail lines described how, at the first station south of Stettin, the train had to climb a rise, forcing it to slow down. This would be the place to jump. However, no one knew how much security would be on the train, or how difficult it would be to get down to Stettin Harbour and find a welcoming boat, especially in winter, when things were so much more quiet. John listened to all of this and memorized the details of the map and the other useful fragments of information.

The move came the next day, sooner than anyone had anticipated. Hundreds of RAF and Fleet Air Arm officers were told to collect their belongings, and then marched to the train station on the outskirts of Barth. In the haste to collect their kits and dress against the winter cold, talk of escape was set aside. By nightfall, the boys had been loaded onto railway cars, and a couple of hours later the train set off. The few guards posted onboard were preoccupied with their own discomfort on the long ride, and the uncertainty of where they would be when they reached their destination.

Wally and John's other friends were on separate cars, so he was alone with his thoughts. Once the train started moving, he examined the windows. They hadn't been secured with nails or screws, merely held shut by two wooden wedges between the window and the frame. That started him thinking.

With no guards at his end of the car, he patiently worked away at one of the wedges, and after about 15 minutes was able to work one free. He loosened a second one, then switched seats with the boys sitting opposite and started working on another window. About an hour out of Barth, he had freed up two windows.

Three boys sitting nearby had watched him with interest. Michael Sextus Wood, who John knew slightly from Stalag Luft I, asked what he was doing. He said he was going to escape. He was planning to jump out the window as the train slowed down just south of Stettin and then head for the harbour and a ship. Michael asked if he could come, and John said certainly, happy to have the company. The other two were more cautious.

One of them was a Red Cross representative, who'd been unfortunately detained by the Germans despite the neutrality of his work. He was wary, not the least reason being that he was a civilian. But he didn't want to spend the rest of the war in a camp, either. The other fellow decided he'd chance it, too.

John reviewed the specifics of his plan. As the train slowed coming up the rise into the station south of Stettin, they would slide open the windows and dive out, then lie flat in the snow until the train had passed. Then they would follow the train tracks back into Stettin, and find their way down to the harbour. He assured them he had a clear picture of the city's layout, and would get them there.

Michael asked about food. John said he'd canvas the other guys on the train for contributions, pack that into a bag, and one of them would toss that out after John had jumped so he could keep his hands free. No one had any questions.

John foraged up and down the length of the car and managed to pull together a good collection of chocolate, bread, and other odds and ends sufficient to hold the four of them for a couple of days. Most thought John was out of his mind to try, but they humoured him. He packed the supplies into a bag and gave it to the Red Cross man. John and Michael would jump first, then the bag of food would be tossed, and the other two would follow close behind.

The train slowed as it passed through the Stettin station without stopping. It continued heading south and began to climb a small hill, just as predicted. Outside were dark, snow-covered fields with no lights and no signs of activity, which was good. John reminded the others to roll away from the tracks when they jumped, and then to lie flat on the ground until the train was out of sight.

As the train slowed almost to a stop, John gave the other three a nod, then opened his window and dove out, tumbling down the embankment that ran alongside the tracks. He lay there until he was sure the train hadn't slowed or stopped. He stood up to see where the others were. He saw Michael right away because of a luminous white belt he was wearing, which he told him to get rid of before they were spotted. But where were the other two?

John and Michael looked up and down the icy embankment, and it soon became clear that neither of the others had jumped. And although they searched, there was no bag of food, either.

Now it was just the two of them standing alone in a snow-covered field at midnight in April somewhere in northern Germany.

Chapter 13

An Education

John and Michael ran north from the tracks until the train was out of sight, then started the walk back to Stettin. It was just after midnight. The sky was clear with a full moon, so John was able to get his bearings. It was bitter cold, and after no more than an hour, they were desperate for shelter. Drawing on his memory of the map he'd seen back at Stalag Luft I, John headed for a residential section of the city to look for someplace they could rest and hide.

They came across a large public garden, where John spotted a tool shed at the far side. He tested the door, and it wasn't locked. It was about the same size as the cells back at Dulag Luft. It had a cast iron stove with a small supply of wood; there were even some matches. John knew the smoke wouldn't be noticed at night, so he built a fire, and the shed began to warm up. He found two thick glasses, gave them a wipe, then put them on the stove. He'd stuffed two chocolate bars in his pocket back on the train, which was all they had now to keep them going. He broke off two cubes and put one into each of the glasses with some snow to melt. It wasn't much, but the watery chocolate was hot, and put something in their stomachs to fall asleep with.

They woke at daylight. The fire was out, and once again they were shivering and hungry. Michael was in particular distress with hunger pangs. John told him to tighten his belt, as tight as it would go, because that would help suppress the stomach ache, an old but effective trick. They couldn't re-light the fire for fear of smoke being spotted, and they would have to hide out for at least another day because the Germans were likely searching for them. It was going to be a long, cold day.

John cautiously peered out of a grimy window, and as he did, a thin teenaged girl walked by leading two children. She looked in directly at John, which startled him, but she showed no reaction. She continued down to the bottom of the garden, dropped the children off at what was presumably a school, then walked back past the shed again without showing interest in who he was or what he was doing. She wore a distinctive blue triangular patch sewn on to her coat, which meant she was likely a Pole or Russian working as forced labour for the Germans. It was unlikely that she would give them any trouble, but it was only a matter of time until someone else did. John decided that they had to move that night.

They huddled in the shed for the rest of that day, fighting off the gnawing cold and hunger, restlessly marketing time until it was dark enough to light the fire. The small supply of wood had been used up, so they snapped the wooden handles off the garden tools to get the fire going.

About one o'clock in the morning, with the fire once again slowly dying, they each ate a last cube of chocolate and melted what was left of the chocolate mixed with snow in their stubby glasses on the stove. When they were finished, they tightened their belts and headed out. Everyone would be asleep at that time of night, or at the very least dozy, which John knew would give them the best chance of getting down to the harbour without being stopped.

They had to cross a bridge over the Oder River that separated the greater city from the lower harbour where they were headed. Finding a ship and crew who were sympathetic to Allied evaders was a gamble, but their only hope. As Michael could speak nothing but English, John told him to play deaf and dumb if they met anyone. He would do the talking.

Michael had on a heavy greatcoat, and John wore a battered French army uniform he'd been given when he left the hospital. They looked like any one of the tens of thousands of PoWs scattered across Germany working as forced labour, and should pass muster at night if they were stopped.

They had to run and hide from a soldier riding a bicycle who shouted after them, then found their way to the bridge that led to the harbour. There were soldiers posted at either end. John told Michael to hang back while he and the soldier exchanged a few words about how cold it was and the miserable army life. He let them pass without question. At the other end, the soldier was asleep.

They headed for the waterfront, steering clear of main streets. John told Michael to walk beside him and look straight ahead; no nervous glancing around. He kept an eye on the reflections in windows to see if they were being followed. They were looking for a Scandinavian ship moored in port for the winter. Surely a captain from Sweden or Denmark would hide them until the ice broke in a month or so and then take them back to a neutral country. By 2.00 am, they had found the harbour; but there were only two ships at the wharf.

Clouds now obscured the moon, which made it difficult to see any markings on the ships. Neither had gangways lowered, but both had mooring lines down to the quay. Michael had to clamber up and try to make contact with someone onboard, as John's hands weren't healed, and he still couldn't grip anything tightly. He hoped Michael would be able to bluff his way past anyone he encountered.

Michael shinned up the rope of the larger of the two ships. As John's eyes adjusted to the light, he noticed barbed wire running along the ship's gunnels. A soldier appeared, patrolling the deck, at which point John realized what the ship was and started hissing up to Michael.

'Come back... Michael! For Chrissakes, it's a prison ship...!' Michael looked back at John, unable to hear what he was saying. The guard looked over the side of the ship, then started to laugh at the two tramps trying to sneak into his jail.

Michael slid back down as fast as he could, and the two of them ran across the quay and ducked into an open warehouse. They hid there in the darkness, listening for footsteps or voices, but all was quiet.

John stared down the length of the warehouse, its far end open to the harbour. Peering through the gloom, he could see a large silhouette bobbing gently in the water, but couldn't make sense of what it was. A soldier with a machine gun came in to view just as a hollow metallic 'clank' from the hull of the vessel in the water caught his attention. He raised his weapon in the direction the sound had come from and swung a flashlight beam across the boat he was guarding. John grasped that they had stumbled into a secret U-Boat berth in the middle of this harbour, and had better get out of there immediately. He grabbed Michael's sleeve and whispered to him to stay quiet and keep moving.

They slipped out of the warehouse without being seen and ran into the streets of the lower city. At the Escape Committee meeting, John had heard someone talk about a whorehouse down near the harbour. It was staffed by daughters of Polish families who had not coöperated with the Nazis, and had subsequently been forced to work there as punishment. These girls deeply resented the Germans and were sympathetic to Allied airmen. They would hide them for a day or two.

After much searching, they found a three-storey house with its lights on and watched as a couple of men scuttled out. As it

Stettin in 1941.

was the middle of the night, John felt this must be the place. He quickly sketched out a scheme for Michael.

Small European hotels like this often had a common floor plan, with a large main room off the entrance, then a long hallway that ran the length of the house to the back, where there was a staircase to the upper floors. He told Michael that he would go in first, walk straight through, and then up to the second floor. Michael was to wait a minute or two and then follow. Their story was that they were there to find a girl, so no looking around when they entered: stare directly ahead and head for the stairs. And not a sound: if anyone spoke to them, Michael was deaf and dumb.

John tried the door, and it was unlocked, so in he went. Inside, the layout was just as he'd expected, and he walked briskly to the back. As he passed, he thought there were a couple of people standing at what looked like a bar. But he didn't hesitate or look around. He found the stairs and started up. A minute later, he heard the front door open and close. Then there was a loud, *'Halt!'*, and the sound of a pistol being cocked. He froze, and then a voice called out in German, *'And you.'*

He came back to the bar. Michael stood there with his hands up, and a Gestapo officer was levelling a gun at him. The bartender was visibly shaken. Michael hadn't been able to resist peeking into the bar when he came in. Scruff appeared, and the officer pointed the gun at him and said, *'Who are you, and what are you doing here?'*

In a mixture of French and German, John said that they were French PoWs on the run. He told the officer about trying to climb the mooring line of the prison ship, and the Gestapo officer started to laugh. Then he asked where they were trying to get to. John said they were just trying to get home to see their families.

The officer shook his head and said that wasn't going to happen. He bought them each a beer and asked a few more questions, some directed at Michael. John explained that he was shell-shocked, and couldn't speak or hear. The officer asked questions about where they had been working, and where John's family was from. Then, offhandedly, the officer turned to Michael, and in perfect English said, *'And where are you from?'* Michael said, *'Surrey.'*

Then they all laughed. With no apparent irony or threat, the officer said that they would spend the next few days in the Gestapo's custody, and it wouldn't be very pleasant. But there was nothing to be done. John glanced at the bartender, who was intently polishing glasses and tidying. He had remained silent, but now caught John's eye and looked directly at him. John felt certain that he was trying to communicate something. Then he turned away and made himself busy at the sink.

The officer took them to a jail the Gestapo used as their headquarters in Stettin. Michael and John had a few hours to get warm and dry and catch up on some sleep. Interrogations began the following morning.

The standard Gestapo interrogation process began with inducing a psychological regression in the prisoner, removing all sense of autonomy of judgement and action. The guards dictated everything that was to be done, and the prisoners had to respond precisely. They were escorted to their cells. Each had a bunk folded up on the wall, and it remained there until permission was given to lower it. They were issued a chamber pot. Twice a day each prisoner's cell door was opened, one at a time, and the prisoners had to run to a trough on the far side of the room, empty his pot, then run back to the cell. If you didn't run fast enough, you were hit with the butt of a rifle. If you talked, you were hit. If you disobeyed the guards in any way, you were hit.

Michael didn't understand a word of German and was regularly beaten for moving at the wrong time, or for not following the proper sequence of the various routines. When John tried to whisper to him what to do, they were both beaten.

John had never been in jail, and so he focussed on understanding what its procedures were. Like most things German, he found them to be systematic and fixed, which made it easier for him to hold himself emotionally detached. Even in their cruelty, the Gestapo were methodical about it. He watched to see what patterns there were; this helped him stay calm.

The basic comforts of water, shelter, and a bit of food also helped him get comfortable enough to put up with the harsh treatment. Perhaps he was less abused than some of the other prisoners because of his unnerving appearance. Without eyelids, he had an unblinking stare that suggested a kind of vacant innocence. He never forgot Adrian's admonition to play the role of a simple-minded flyer who didn't know enough to hide anything. His interrogations were straightforward, and he responded with information that stuck to the broad lines of his experiences, taking care never to be vague or to tell an unnecessary lie. This was part of the training he had had back in England. He remained consistent in his story, responding slowly to questions while trying to anticipate where the interrogation was going so he could stay a question or two ahead.

He was well aware of what lay in store should he raise any suspicions. The final stop at that jail for prisoners suspected of sedition or espionage was 'The End Room.' This is where the men and women whom the Gestapo felt were being uncooperative were brought for their final interrogation. If the desired information had been extracted, the prisoner would be sent back into the system and transported to another camp where they lived or died. However, if the desired information had *not* been obtained, then the prisoner was either (a) shot, or (b) burned alive with a blowtorch, and then shot. John sat uneasily listening to one poor German man, screaming, *'Ich bin Deutsch! Ich bin Deutsch!'* But to no avail, as the Gestapo had already decided he was a spy or a collaborator who had chosen not to confess. He was burned within hearing of the other prisoners and then shot. Such brutal tactics made John think carefully about what he would say if his interrogation ever reached that stage.

Sitting in his cell, John thought over the events of the last few days. He was concerned for Michael, but there was nothing he could do. He wondered if Wally and the others were at the new camp now; and if so, what would conditions be like. And he felt certain that the bartender at the whorehouse was trying to hide something from the Gestapo, most likely the ways in which he'd helped other Allied flyers who had come looking for help.

John continued playing his part, while Michael's incompetence in German and in learning the prison routines simply angered the Gestapo, who saw him as a dim-witted Englishman. That didn't stop them from beating him almost to death. In the end, John concluded that the Gestapo had decided they were just a couple of PoWs on the run, and should be shipped on to the new camp with the others.

They were held in solitary for a week, but the beatings had stopped, and the food was marginally better than starvation. During one of their daily exercise outings, a tall, blonde Polish girl grinned at John across the barbed wire that separated the men and women. She was one of the girls who had been forced into work at the whorehouse. They exchanged a few friendly words; she was in for a short stretch because she'd given one of the 'meatheads' the clap. What was startling, though, was that she knew all about John – that he'd come from Barth, had been arrested at the whorehouse, and that he and his friend were about to be shipped out. It made John wonder what other information the Gestapo might have on him, too.

Two long and restless days later, John and Michael were loaded on to a train with hundreds of other recently captured airmen, and set off for the PoW camp that would be their home for the rest of the war, possibly for years. The newly constructed Stalag Luft III was located in the eastern reaches of

Hitler's Germany, so far away from friendly faces as to make the prospect of escape all but hopeless. Still, John was considering trying again.

The first leg of the trip took them a hundred and fifty kilometres south to Berlin, where they turned east and headed another two hundred kilometres across Germany into what is now Poland. John struck up a conversation with an older German guard who sat nearby, looking as unhappy about the trip as everyone else.

John had a gift of being able to talk to anyone about anything. He learned that this quiet man, presumably assigned to guard duty because of his age and non-combative personality, had been a professor at the University of Berlin before the war. The professor seemed happy talking and was indifferent to John getting up and stretching his legs, wandering down the length of the aisle, or simply watching the scenery float by through the windows.

John was making a plan, taking stock of the situation: two guards in his car, and no one paying much attention to anything. He judged that escape would be a simple matter of requesting permission to go for a pee, then slipping out the door at the end of the car and making a jump for it. From there, he would head back to Stettin harbour, now that he knew what to look for and what to avoid.

As the train left the station, John calculated there wasn't much time before they reached the city's outskirts. After that, there would be nothing but an occasional town or village, and then dense forest the rest of the way to Berlin. He was not about to try and hide out there, so he decided to jump from the train around the same place he'd jumped a week earlier.

He kept talking to the guard, gently taking his measure, while he glanced out the windows and kept an eye on where they were. He calculated that he had about ten minutes before he made his move, so he continued with the small talk. It was always safe to ask a soldier about his girlfriend or parents, so John asked the guard about Berlin and if his family was still there. The professor talked about what a beautiful city Berlin was, with its neoclassical buildings, the tree-lined *Unter den Linden*, and the river Spree. It was such a civilized place to live, and far enough from England that there was little danger from air raids. There had been a few, but these hadn't had much impact in terms of damaging the historic sites.

It emerged that his wife and children had been among the few German casualties in a raid the previous November. When John heard this, he realized this gentle man was biding his time, waiting for this prisoner to try something rash, which would give him a reason to carve out some personal revenge. John abandoned his plan to escape. He murmured his condolences, adding that war was a terrible thing, and the professor was silent after that.

Hours passed with nothing worth looking at. Towns crept by, drifting in and out of the window frames. John watched the blank stares of men and women standing on platforms, wondering why their train wasn't stopping. As night came on, the black of the forest enveloped them, and the murmur of conversation in the car dwindled into silence. After hours of dark monotony, Berlin was suddenly all around them, lights blazing and showing no signs of damage or even being at war. It was a living monument to the vitality and strength of the German nation, almost taunting the PoWs to acknowledge the futility of their war against such a powerful adversary.

They turned east as daylight began to break and travelled across a landscape of little more than snowy fields, forest, and an occasional stone building. The countryside looked increasingly feudal, almost primitive as if this part of Germany had only a passing acquaintance with the twentieth century.

No one on the train knew anything about the new camp apart from its approximate location, situated so far from anywhere familiar as to make escape all but impossible. But John wasn't discouraged. Throughout the eighteen-hour train ride to the village of Sagan, all he thought about was how and when he would find his way back to England to get back into the fight.

John was among the first wave of Allied air force prisoners being transferred to this remote corner of the expanding German empire. His train arrived at Sagan on the afternoon of April 15th, 1942, and the three hundred prisoners were escorted from the train on a quarter-mile walk through the woods to their new camp. There was desultory chatter among the boys about where they were, how cold it was, and what might be different about this new camp. Even with the low temperature, it felt good to be outside and to stretch their legs.

New arrivals were brought to the German end of the

A model of Stalag Luft III, North Compound, looking south.

compound where they had their pictures taken, followed by a three-minute hot shower, and a thorough body search. The German guards checked their identification, methodically ticked off names on their lists, and then shepherded them through the gates into their new home.

John thought the camp bore a resemblance to the Minnewaska Resort on Lake Muskoka where friends of his had spent some summers. Located two hours north of Toronto, Minnewaska was ironically now a camp for German prisoners, where some of the most malevolent Nazi PoWs were held.

Stalag Luft III was one of the largest German prisoner of war camps. By the war's end, it spread over sixty acres, had a five-mile perimeter, and housed ten thousand airmen from every Allied country in four sprawling compounds.

The camp had been designed with a number of features intended to make escape difficult, if not impossible. To begin with was the location on Germany's eastern front. Escape would necessitate travelling hundreds of kilometres south through Czechoslovakia and Hungary, north through Poland and into Russia, or back west through Germany.

Twelve-foot high barbed-wire fences defined the camp's perimeter, set two hundred and fifty feet back from the forest of fir trees that surrounded it. Guard towers were positioned at regularly spaced intervals, giving the soldiers who manned them a clear view of virtually all spaces inside the compound, and the open ground outside the fence. Each tower was equipped with searchlights and machine guns. There were twenty-one rough,

Stalag Luft III, looking into the compound from outside the fence.

single-storey wooden huts for the prisoners, with four additional huts at the camp's north end (separated by more fencing) for the Germans.

There were three ways of escaping: over the fence, under it, or through it. Of these, tunnelling was one of the most common and popular, because it could be done secretly and silently. But the Germans had anticipated this and had planned for it. The huts were constructed on brick footings that raised them off the ground so that any digging would be obvious. (A solid concrete block foundation in the centre of the huts encased rudimentary plumbing.) Seismograph microphones had been buried in the ground surrounding the huts to detect any sounds of digging. The elevated huts also provided easy access for special duty guards, known as *'ferrets.'* As well as watching for tunnelling activity, at night they roamed the camp, and English-speaking ferrets crawled under the huts and eavesdropped on the prisoners' conversations. The men quickly learned not to discuss anything important once the compound fell quiet.

The most challenging obstacle was the earth itself, which was an orange-yellow sandy subsoil, a stark contrast to the dusty grey topsoil. It was impossible to conceal. Even traces of the subsoil on the prisoners' clothing would give them away, not to mention its fetid, lingering odour. Worse still, while such loose sandy soil meant easy digging, it was impossible to avoid cave-ins. If anything, the digging conditions were worse than they had been at Barth.

When he first arrived at the camp, John was held in isolation in the Cooler. These cells, used to *'cool down'* new arrivals and to discipline troublemakers, have been portrayed in movies and novels as being bleak concrete chambers used to punish prisoners' transgressions with the torture of solitary confinement. In fact, they were warm, dry, restful rooms, admittedly bare, but refreshingly quiet and vermin-free in contrast to the rooms in the crowded barracks. As spring and summer came on, these cells were much cooler as well, making a week or two's stay with a couple of good books a pleasant break from the throng in camp.

Sergeant-Major Hermann Glemnitz, a veteran pilot of WW I, was known by some of the men as 'King of the Ferrets.' He was the senior non-commissioned officer responsible for escape prevention. He had been at Stalag Luft I, where he and John got to know one another. In the evenings, he would come through the barracks counting heads, and was startled more than once to find John, sound asleep, with his eyelid-less eyes wide open and

Sergeant-Major Hermann Glemnitz.

staring. *'Mr. Weir...? Mr. Weir! Are you dead?'* he would ask, and a sleepy John would reassure him that all was still well.

They developed a friendship out of genuine consideration for one another. Glemnitz was married to a much younger woman, and the boys in camp were always needling him, saying things like, *'When we get out, we're gonna pay her a visit, Glemnitz!'* It drove the poor man half mad.

John reassured him that they were simply boys horsing around, something Glemnitz appreciated and never forgot. He was a decent man, who hadn't joined the Nazis, and was trying to sit out the war without getting killed. He was well-liked and universally respected, but was not one to trifle with. Some even referred to him as 'that bastard Glemnitz,' because of his dedication to uncovering escape attempts.

Unlike most of the guards, he had an appealingly dry sense of humour. The PoWs organized an impromptu game of rugby in the first months of the camp. The ground was as hard as rock, but that didn't seem to dampen the exuberance of the game and the men playing it. A burly Canadian, Ken Toft, captained one team. Glemnitz watched Toft and his side play with interest, as he had never seen the game before. Noticing this, Toft came over to Glemnitz, and said, *'Look, Hermann, this rugby is a great way to burn off your frustrations and it's a hell of a lot of fun. What about getting up a team with the guards?'* Glemnitz watched the men pummel one another, breaking noses and blackening eyes, then nodded said, *'Yes, surely. But only if you let us keep our guns.'*

The food served to prisoners in the cooler was largely limited to bread and water. But the day John arrived at the camp,

Glemnitz came to John's cell in the Cooler and, forestalling pleasantries, put a finger to his lips and pointed at the ceiling. The butt-end of a microphone could be seen poking out of the cement. John nodded, then smiled and shook his old friend's hand. Glemnitz handed John a small box. It contained some bread, cheese, and a bowl of soup. He smiled and left, returning each day with a similar gift. This earned John's enduring appreciation, and he made a point of never betraying Glemnitz's trust over the years they were in camp together.

Once the men had completed the official German processing and entered the confines of the camp, the prisoners came under the command of the *Senior British Officer* (SBO). This officer supervised all prisoners' activities behind the wire. His subordinate officers were charged with vetting out each new

Canadians in Stalag Luft III. Scruffy is in the first row, second from the left, and Wally Floody is in the third row, fourth from the left.

arrival to confirm their identity.

The Allied officers challenged each new arrival with a battery of questions: the name of the squadron he had been attached to, names of men in his squadron and on his crew, details of his squadron's operations, where he had enlisted and trained, and specific questions about his hometown. This was a preliminary screening to collect general intelligence, not unlike the German operation at Dulag Luft in Frankfurt. It was also to prevent the infiltration of German 'stooges' – spies who spoke excellent English and had first-hand knowledge of life in England or North America. They would try to blend into the camp to collect information about RAF operations, or of escapes being planned. Several Germans attempted to slip through this net, but none is known to have succeeded.

Once these questions had been satisfactorily answered, the SBO had established a final safeguard: no man was allowed into the general population until someone already established in the camp had vouched for him. Simply knowing someone was not enough: you had to be vouched for by someone who had known you in the city or town where you grew up, and your information had to match facts already on record. Waiting to be acknowledged in the reception area – a common room in one of the Allied huts stringently policed by the British – could take hours or even days, depending on whom you knew and vice versa.

When John's initial vetting was complete, he drew a blank trying to come up with anyone who might know him from back in Canada. Being among the first wave of prisoners at

A room in one of the huts.

Stalag Luft III meant there weren't many familiar faces, apart from those on the train. And after his arrest in Stettin and delayed arrival at Luft III, he didn't know who was there.

After many frustrating hours, it dawned on him that his Sunday School friend and squadron mate Wally Floody would have been on that train that arrived a week ahead of him. After Wally had confirmed him, he was cleared to join the rest.

When he entered the compound, the British *Intelligence Officer* (IO) was waiting for him and asked John to come for a chat. The safest place to talk was walking '*The Circuit.*' This was a path inside perimeter of the compound, marked by a wire or rail set at knee height, and staked out thirty feet back from the barbed wire fences that enclosed the compound. This defined the boundary of No Man's Land: cross it and you could be shot on sight. But what this circuit also unintentionally created was a corridor of privacy. It was far enough from the tower guards and the other men in the compound to allow for a quiet conversation, as well as a perfect place to be alone with your thoughts. Walking circuits kept many men fit and sane during their years behind the wire, as they walked for hours on end, sifting through worries, frustrations, and hopes.

The IO knew John, if only in passing, from Stalag Luft I. As they walked, he told John his room assignment would be in a hut with Wally, Hank Birkland, Jens Müller, and Zbischek Gotowski. It was like old home week, and John was pleasantly surprised at his good fortune. The IO said that the camp's SBO, Group Captain Harry 'Wings' Day, had recommended rooming them together. Day was a decorated naval officer of the Fleet Air Arm, the air force division of the Royal Navy, and had been SBO at Stalag Luft I as well. 'Wings' was a veteran of several escape attempts, and his irresistibly plucky nickname spoke well-deserved volumes of experience and courage that made him a natural leader and an astute judge of character. Wings had asked the IO to talk to John, and obtain a clearer picture of what he could bring to the 'X-Committee,' as the new camp's escape committee was known.

The IO's questions made John uncomfortable. They were the kind he'd been trained to sidestep: too personal and too familiar. The IO was senior in rank to John, and John politely answered him. He was asked about his friends and his family, where he'd travelled, and what people he knew. John chose his words carefully but was caught off guard when the IO said, *'Weir, who are you?'* John bristled a bit, then made it clear that he was just exactly what he appeared to be: nothing more and nothing less. The IO assured him that he was just follow orders, that he wasn't a Gestapo plant, and that such questioning was routine. John invited him to talk to Wally or any of the others who knew him, but said they wouldn't have anything more to offer than he did. The IO thanked him and went on his way.

John continued walking, thinking about this conversation. It disturbed him. Back at Barth, he had been surprised when he had been invited to the Escape Committee meeting. Newcomers were never included in those discussions. Someone must have been speculating that he had some special talents or connections to share. But he had never spoken to anyone about his special ops training or his work with Adrian. Now he felt he was being scrutinized. But by whom, and for what purpose? It unnerved him.

The warning rail can be seen between the fence and the huts.

He continued walking the circuit by himself, remembering the admonitions of Adrian. He had repeatedly drilled into John that there was never any need or excuse to say anything to anyone that they couldn't figure out for themselves. If you did, you were asking to be made a target. Adrian's words were simple: *'Never forget: you're the most dim-witted boy on the block. And since you know nothing, you've got bugger all to say. Keep your head down, your mouth shut, and be a nobody.'*

Of all the special intelligence training that he'd had, and the experience he'd acquired on operations, this piece of advice was the most helpful in keeping him alive.

Chapter 14

The War Behind the Wire

Stalag Luft III, despite the Luftwaffe's intention of building something worthy of the dignity of air force officers, was nevertheless a bleak place. Lt. Colonel Albert 'Bub' Clark arrived in camp in the summer of 1942 with the first large wave of American prisoners. He was the *Senior American Officer* (SAO), and was welcomed by Herbert Massey, who had become SBO. (Wings Day had been transferred to another camp.)

Clark was not prepared for the disheveled appearance of the place and the men. Some were unshaven and wearing ragged

Prisoners walking circuits in Stalag Luft III.

remnants of the clothing they had been wearing when captured. The huts were unpainted, and a dusty, smoky haze seemed to hang over the whole camp. With the guard towers looming over everything, it was a depressing sight to encounter.

A typical hut in Stalag Luft III held one hundred and forty men. It was equipped with a toilet, a washroom, a kitchen, and had fourteen rooms, four of them small, and intended for senior officers. Each room had three or four triple-decker bunks, with a single double-decker bunk in the senior officers' rooms. Cooking duties were shared among the men in the hut, but the food rations were meagre and the quality was dreadful. In 1943, in Stalag Luft III, a typical daily ration for each man was 2 to 3 slices of black bread, a pound and half of potatoes, a cup of watery turnip or potato soup, and an ounce each of sugar and margarine. Jam, meat paste, and dried fish sporadically appeared as supplements. It totalled about 1,500 calories a day, about half of what an active young man required.

In a May 1941 directive, the Food Ministry in Berlin had dictated the ingredients of one of the staples of the prisoners' diet, black bread. The recipe called for 50% rye grain, the quality typically used for cattle, and the other 50% was made up of sliced sugar beets, tree 'flour' (sawdust), minced leaves, and straw.

It was no wonder that food quickly became a primary concern in camp. The saving grace were parcels sent by the International Red Cross to prisoners of war. They were shipped in light wooden boxes (which the men then used for constructing various things in camp), and the British and Canadian parcels contained such items as processed meat and cheese, tinned fish, chocolate, dried fruit, sugar, margarine, tea, and coffee. They were a godsend, and morale went up when they arrived. In the early years of the war, they were sent at the rate of one parcel per man per week, although this schedule was inconsistent at best. In the last year of the war, the parcels became more and more scarce, often having their contents pilfered by the Germans, who by then were as hard up for food as the prisoners.

Parcels from home were also sent to supplement the meagre rations, and letters from the boys' families and loved ones gave them hope that the life they left behind was still intact.

One challenge was that those back home rarely understood what life was like living in a PoW camp. *'I hope you're getting lots of potatoes because the Germans make such grand gravy,'* John's mother wrote. In another letter, she reminded him to *'...wash your hair with eggs. Remember how I told you to do it: only use the yolks and do what you like with the whites.'* John hadn't seen an egg for months, and wouldn't for another two years.

He had a particular craving for doughnuts, one of those yearnings you develop when you're hungry, and some favourite food is utterly beyond reach. When he was with the squadron in England, he would send telegrams back home, simply saying, *'Dear Klan, everything okie dokie. Send doughnuts. John.'* Once he was settled in Stalag Luft III, his letters home would regularly end with, *'Please send more doughnuts!'*

Chocolate was a particularly valuable commodity in camp and was often used as currency. Again, this was not a concept grasped by one PoW's mother. *'In your last three letters, you have* asked me to send you chocolate. I assume you are kidding and have mailed you underwear. Love, Mother.'

There were head-shaking notes, such as, 'I'm so glad you were shot down before flying became dangerous.' And, 'I'm happy to hear you are with such a nice crowd of boys. I hope the Germans will keep you there.' Which is comparatively less exasperating than, 'Your letter from camp reads like one glorious holiday!' and the philosophical, 'Remember – freedom is only a state of mind.' One mother wrote to say that 'Tom is in another PoW camp in Germany. Maybe you could visit him on the weekend.'

Relationship letters were usually the hardest to laugh off. There were vague implications in one man's love letter from his sweetheart: 'Darling; to think I was only nineteen when you were shot down! I feel so much more experienced now, but you will have to find that out for yourself when you come home…'. Odd remarks such as, 'Darling, I hope you are staying true to me,' were puzzling, but not distressing as some updates from the home front: 'Darling, I've just had a baby. But don't worry – the American officer said he'll send some money.'

The most painful were the dreaded 'Dear John' letters, as with a short postcard that read, 'Dear Jimmy: You were missing for over a month, so I got married,' or the even more painful from one man's (former) fiancée, 'Dear Bob, I've just got married to your father. Love, Mother.'

In the first year and a half of the camp, the Canadians, British, and other Commonwealth countries shared the compound with Americans. John found that the Americans fought among themselves, and the Poles fought among themselves. The British

'... I'm sorry, dear, but I love a soldier.
I know you'll understand...'

and Canadian were the most stable, and the discipline of the British spilled over to the Canadians. He found the Canadians understood the Americans' behaviour better than the English did while much of the time the Americans couldn't understand what the English were trying to say. The English didn't understand the Americans at all. There were many different cultures bumping up against one another, with all the various accents and personalities, but you tended to move within your own cultural circle.

One of the greatest problems facing a prisoner was the tedium of having nothing to do. These young men had enlisted for adventure and had been flying combat missions when they were captured. They wanted to get back into action. But limited rations, the most basic of everyday amenities, and the never ending war undermined their spirits. Keeping fit was

Sports Day in camp, complete with rankings and awards.
The high jumper is RCAF airman Gerry Sullivan.

encouraged for its physical and psychological benefits, such as doing thirty 'circuits'– walking the camp's perimeter – every day. John burned off his energy and frustration with vigorous exercise. He did high-bar gymnastic workouts, ran races, boxed, wrestled, and played rugby, hockey, baseball, volleyball, and basketball.

Twice a day the Kriegies were lined up for *'appel'* – roll call – where ID numbers were called out in sequence to ensure a correct head count. This typically took a half hour, but could stretch on much longer if the head count was off. *Personalkartes* - ID cards with the Kriegie's photograph on it – would then have to be presented and compared against the actual Kriegie. Clothing could be a problem, as civilian outer clothing was strictly forbidden. The Canadians took pains to maintain their

John's Personalkarte, his PoW identification.

uniforms and to properly display their rank, as they found this was another way to boost morale.

The prisoners assembled a substantial library of books that eventually grew to ten thousand titles. Lectures and classes were given in everything from history to electricity to languages. Among the PoWs, there were teachers, lawyers, clergy, and bankers, as well as a complete cross section of skilled tradesmen and professionals. The Red Cross helped make it possible to earn a university degree, with lessons and lectures sent from England.

Card games of all kinds were popular, as were chess and checkers. Concerts and theatrical productions became a feature in camp as well. Men who had been shot down with tickets for the latest West End hit in their wallets were often reassured that the same play was in rehearsal in the camp, and they could see it there. The Germans encouraged this, facilitating costume rental and acquisition of instruments, believing it would keep the PoWs' minds off of escape. The prisoners even requested cameras and film to take photos of the productions to send home. The Germans developed those but were unaware of the

Production of a current West End play.

A concert band in Stalag Luft III.

PoWs reading from the listing of upcoming lectures and classes.

portraits the boys took of one another for forged ID documents, which they developed themselves using chemical and papers obtained from the guards. The men *'tamed the goons'* – bribed them – using chocolate, real coffee, and cigarettes to get news, official ID and travel documents, and pretty much anything they wanted or needed. When necessary, they could (and did) create any number of situations to blackmail the guards to obtain contraband luxuries and necessities.

News was posted by the guards on the camp's bulletin boards, but these were always slanted from the German perspective. Bits of news would trickle in with new arrivals to camp, or in heavily censored letters. The most reliable news source came from BBC radio broadcasts received via the camp *'Canary.'* This was a radio that had been pieced together over many months and was kept constantly on the move around camp to keep the guards from finding it. They could detect its signal, but found it all but impossible to pinpoint. One of the reasons for this was Dick Bartlett, who had been charged with the responsibility of keeping the Canary hidden.

Dick was from rural Saskatchewan and had enlisted in 1938. He'd been inspired by advertisements in his parents' *London Weekly News* and travelled to England to join the Fleet Air Arm because he wanted to fly. Before the war, he earned his commission and had flown the iconic Swordfish biplane torpedo bomber from the British aircraft carrier HMS *Ark Royal* (the same ship John had flown cover for). In 1940, he had been shot down and badly wounded in an attack on the German battleship *Scharnhorst*. By the time he arrived at Stalag Luft III, Dick was

Dick Bartlett in 1939.

a veteran of three PoW camps and several escape attempts. He had an easygoing manner that served him well as he kept the Canary floating around camp. He frequently had to improvise like mad, carrying the radio in a burlap sack back and forth across the compound. When guards would stop him and ask what he had in the bag, he'd guilelessly answer, *'Just some earth for tomatoes,'* or *'Dirty socks and shorts, if you want to have a look.'* His sweet nature never stirred them to bother.

The Canary was both a source of news from home, and a conduit for covert messages. Broadcasts would start with, *'Before we begin, please listen to some personal messages.'* Then would follow a whimsical phrase, occasionally a line from a poem, or a banal tidbit of information, such as *'The underwear is on the line,'* or *'There was a fire at the insurance agency.'* These were coded communications directed to particular resistance cells and individuals who knew to tune in at a given hour. John made a point of listening to those broadcasts.

He realized that the Canary had more potential, and managed to get a message sent back to London. A month later, a package arrived with a handsome set of six heavy metal knives and forks. The Germans had allowed these, as the prisoners had extolled the virtues of the extraordinary cuisine in camp to the Kommandant. John, Wally, and Jens took the new cutlery into the latrine to examine them. They were curiously oversized, and it soon became clear why. When Jens detached the handles, inside were radio crystals for the Canary inside. These strengthened the radio's reception and made it possible for an occasional transmission back to England.

By August 1942, the camp's population had swollen to almost two thousand. Hearing shreds of news from the Allied front – the disaster of Dieppe, defeats in North Africa, ineffective bombing raids – made the boys increasingly restless to get back in to the fight. With that many men penned up together, sooner or later someone would figure out a way to get out. Escape was an ever-present undercurrent in all PoW camps. The challenge and excitement of it, leveraged against the dull monotony of a prisoner's life, fueled their imaginations and bolstered their nerves.

At Stalag Luft III, any escape plan had to be sanctioned by the X-Committee. The Committee provided information and advice, but there was no shortage of inventive attempts. 'Speed Tunnels' were one such example, where one or two men would dig a few feet down into the soft sand of the compound, and then burrow under the wire. The problem was the air: you could only tunnel about twelve feet before it became thin and stale.

John heard about this technique and didn't think it had much promise. But something he was reading sparked an idea for a solution. He talked to Jens Müller about it, and together they devised a scheme where the diggers would shove a metal rod up through the earth as they dug, poking little air holes every couple of feet. It worked beautifully, but as autumn came on, and the temperature dropped, little columns of steam rose from the holes, and the guards would know precisely where a tunneller was digging. They tried digging at night, which masked the steam. But when the honey wagon rolled into camp to haul away waste from the latrines, it sank down to its axles as a tunnel collapsed beneath the weight.

The most interesting variation on speed tunnelling was the 'Wooden Horse.' Three men built a vaulting horse from the wooden Red Cross boxes and used it for gymnastics in the yard. This was carried out to an open area near the warning wire every day, with a 'digger' hidden inside. As the boys practiced their routines, the man inside opened a trap door, below which there was a corresponding soil-covered trap in the yard leading down to the tunnel they were digging. The man inside would climb down into the tunnel and dig like mad while the boys up top did their routines. Earth would be piled back into the base of the horse, and at the end of the day, the routine was reversed and the horse was returned to the barracks, where the dirt was hidden or scattered out in the compound. It took the three of them almost four months, but at the end of October 1943, they escaped and made it safely to Sweden.

There were several men who tried crawling to the fence on their stomachs and cutting the wire, but got a nasty shock in the process. A 'hot' wire had been hidden in the tangle of barbed wire, but it was almost impossible to be sure which one had been electrified. Jens did some experimenting and figured out how to locate it and short it out without making it shower sparks like a fireworks display. But those who made it through the fence still had a long way to go to make it to the woods. As the guards' searchlights swept across the ground beyond the fence, its beam invariably lit up their rear ends crawling the two hundred and fifty feet that lay between the fence and the forest.

Tom Kirby-Green, an RAF squadron leader who arrived in camp with the first wave of PoWs, was very restless to escape. He was too tall to dig a simple tunnel or to crawl unseen under the wire, so he talked to John about his frustration. John suggested he try slipping out with the Bath Parade. (There were special showers in the hospital compound outside the main grounds, which were used to delouse the men.) Tom congratulated John on having a brain after all and made his plans. A multi-talented Polish officer, Minskewich, dyed some RAF tunics to look like German uniforms and dressed four men up in these, Kirby-Green among them.

They waited for the right moment and then slipped in amongst the guards as they marched the prisoners to the

Squadron Leader Tom Kirby-Green.

showers. When they were outside the gate, the four PoWs wearing the phoney uniforms turned left instead of right, and made a beeline for the woods. Luck was with them, as no one noticed. They marched in step, looking every bit the part of a soldiers' working party, and were home free until one of the camp's officers, Hans Pieber, happened to come strolling out of the woods. Kirby-Green, being unavoidably tall, caught his eye immediately. Pieber said, '*Mr. Green! What are you doing out here?*' Tom grinned, and Pieber marched them back through the gate and into the cooler, to a chorus of hoots and hollers from the guys who'd been watching. (Pieber was very popular with the PoWs.)

Some escape plans were intended as a means of obtaining information, or as misdirection for larger operations, or sometimes to help out a friend. There was a guard by the name of Paul, who had served on the brutal Eastern Front. He had been wounded, and ended up as a prison guard at Stalag Luft III. He was an honest fellow, and some of the men were able to bribe him to bring in radio parts and other odds and ends that they wanted. He seemed not to mind as long as he continued to receive gifts of chocolate, cigarettes, and coffee.

Two PoWs, Gwyn Martin and Kingsley Brown, became very friendly with him. They learned that Paul was distressed because a bombing raid had struck very close to his village, and he hadn't had any word of his wife and five children for weeks. They asked him when he last had leave. Almost three years earlier, was the answer. To quality for leave, you had to do something heroic. But he was just a middle-aged man with flat feet.

Kingsley and Gwyn devised an escape in which they would hide in the washhouse until night. At an agreed upon signal, they would 'try' to slip through the front gate, but Paul would catch them, then march them off to the Kommandant for punishment.

It all went according to plan, with Paul shouting and waving his pistol so enthusiastically that Gwyn and Kingsley were afraid he was going to shoot one of them. The Kommandant praised Paul for his fine work, and he was given a week's leave to visit his family. An escape attempt meant two weeks in the cooler, which Brown and Martin were looking forward to as a break from the routine of camp life. But the Kommandant was so pleased with how coöperative the prisoners had been, and how quiet things had been in camp, that he cancelled their stay in the cooler, depriving them of their vacation mini-break.

One brave soul tried slipping out in the honey wagon. He crawled onto the dung and underneath the grass clippings that workmen dumped on top to subdue the stench. Guards routinely jabbed pitchforks into this mess looking for escapers but managed to miss him. However, his very large feet were left poking out and gave him away.

Another ambitious boy had the idea of him and a partner slinging a mattress up against the fence when the guards were distracted, then using it as a spongy ramp to run up and over. Men in the compound started a fight at dusk to draw the guards' attention. He ran to the fence, and made it up and over, and was home free. His sidekick, however, reached the top and then tried to climb down the other side instead of jumping. The clanging and ringing wires made everyone, including the guards, turn around to see what was making all the racket. Even the guards started laughing when they saw what was happening.

John wanted to escape but was very cautious about drawing unwanted attention to himself. The odds were against success, as he'd witnessed over the previous five months in camp and dozens of failed attempts. However, the situation changed in October with the arrival of Squadron Leader Roger Bushell.

Bushell had been shot down in March 1940 and was the veteran of at least four PoW camps, as well as two escape attempts that had been excruciatingly close to being successful. He was a South African who had been an Olympic-class skier, then studied Law at Cambridge and earned a reputation as a formidable defense lawyer. Like so many of his generation, what he wanted to do was to fly. In 1932, he joined the 601 Auxiliary Air Force, also known as the 'Millionaires' Mob,' because of the number of wealthy young men who paid to learn to fly on weekends. When war broke out, Bushell was activated into service with 92 Squadron, and by the end of 1939 he had risen to the rank of Squadron Leader, and been charged with the responsibility for bringing the squadron up to strength. He was a natural leader who had the knack of making tough decisions very quickly.

He had been sent to Stalag Luft III following an exhaustive Gestapo interrogation in Berlin, having been a suspect in the assassination of the brutal SS-Obergruppenführer Reinhard

'Big X,' Roger Bushell (r), with Bob Tuck.

Heydrich in Prague earlier that year. He had been warned that he would be executed if he was caught attempting to escape a third time. While he never spoke of what he went through with the Gestapo, it clearly had a profound impact on him and instilled an absolute hatred of everything the Nazis stood for.

When Roger arrived in camp, his reputation had preceded him. By November 1942, he had been assigned to oversee the X-Committee. He spent the winter months listening to what attempts had taken place, looking for their weaknesses and considering what would be the best options. He had a predilection for tunnels, as these could provide escape for more than one or two men. Over that winter of 1942-43, he decided that all efforts would henceforth be directed towards a unified scheme. His plan involved digging three tunnels simultaneously, which would be named *Tom*, *Dick*, and *Harry*. Should any one of them be discovered, the ferrets would be unlikely to suspect the existence of two other tunnels.

The most audacious component of his plan was to take out 200 men in a single night. All the escapers would wear civilian clothing or uniforms, and all would carry complete sets of forged ID papers that would allow them to pass through train stations and check-points. He presented his plan to the X-Committee with a conviction that fueled the entire operation.

> Everyone here in this room is living on borrowed time. By rights, we should all be dead! The only reason that God allowed us this extra ration of life is so we can make life hell for the Hun. In North Compound [where the British and Canadians were housed], we are concentrating our efforts on completing and escaping through one master tunnel. No private-enterprise tunnels allowed. Three bloody deep, bloody long tunnels will be dug - Tom, Dick, and Harry. One will succeed.

He was not naïve enough to believe that everyone would make it to safety. But he believed that the thousands of German forces that would be pulled away from war duty to track down runaway prisoners would create havoc in German High Command. That alone was worth the effort.

Tunnelling began as the ground began to thaw in early 1943. Bushell decreed that they would dig down ten or twelve feet, instead of three or four. But the sandy subsoil made it all but impossible to dig a tunnel of any length without it collapsing. He sent out word that he was looking for anyone in camp who had experience digging tunnels; he wanted professional input. Wally, Hank, and John had all worked in the mines and were recommended. Bushell asked them to meet with him and the committee.

Roger – Big X as he was known as the head of the X-Committee – wanted to know what they could contribute. Wally said that if they wanted to dig anything that would last, they would have to make some major changes. They had seen the problems at Barth, and conditions weren't any better here. If they were serious about a large-scale tunnelling operation, then they had to start building the tunnels properly. Wally, Hank, and John described some of the techniques they had learned, and how a few of these, applied with some ingenuity, could make all the difference. The X-Committee needed to start thinking differently unless they wanted to see everything come to another dead end. Bushell thanked them, and they were dismissed.

Once they were gone, the committee members began to debate the ideas. Bushell sat quietly, then after about fifteen minutes, he broke into the chatter. Abruptly, he announced that all tunnelling would be stopped immediately and that structural techniques would henceforth be adapted to comply with the Canadians' recommendations. He had decided that Mr. Floody would be in charge of engineering the tunnels, and could make use of anyone he wanted. But he strongly recommended the involvement of Hank and Scruffy from the outset.

That was the start of what came to be known as 'The Great Escape,' the largest such act of resistance of prisoners of war ever attempted.

Chapter 15

The Great Escape

Very quickly, the escape plan became a large and exceptionally well-run operation – an industry, really – within the camp. In addition to the extensive tunnelling taking place underground, six hundred men worked secretly in three main areas: forging; fabrication of equipment such as maps, compasses, and tools; and a tailor shop. Few knew of all the cells of activity that were spread out in various huts and rooms, each operating without the knowledge of the others. Only Bushell and one or two others knew the full picture.

This scale of production was made possible by the extraordinary pool of talent that had been coincidentally brought together by the Germans. Seasoned prisoners brought skills such as map making, logistics, forgery, and the meticulous recreation of complicated travel documents and other essential identification papers. This section became known as the '*Travel Bureau.*'

As designated Master Tunneller, Wally worked closely with John and Hank. He sketched out what the new tunnelling strategy would be. Of the three, *Tom* would be the shortest, running west from Hut 123 into the woods. *Dick* would also run west from Hut 122, slightly south and east of *Tom*. *Harry*, by

Wally Floody (front left), Sam Sangster (back left), Scruffy Weir (back right), and Hank Birkland (front right), all of whom worked in the tunnels.

far the longest, was to run north under the cooler, almost three hundred and fifty feet to the woods. One of the Norwegian PoWs had been a surveyor in civilian life, and he provided an approximate triangulation to calculate the necessary length for each tunnel to reach beyond the fence into the woods. (A fourth tunnel, *George*, was started some months later, and headed east from beneath a theatre that the men built at the sound end of the compound.)

The tunnel entrances were chiselled directly through the concrete and brick foundations that lay beneath the centres of the huts (these supported the small area containing the kitchen and washrooms directly above). Minskewich was an engineer, and had experience working with concrete, as did Zbischek

Gotowski. Cement was plentiful, as it was used by workmen hired by the Germans for camp construction and repair work, and was left in the compound. Using this, Minskewich and Gotowski fashioned a tunnel *'throat'* with an inset ledge. The ledge supported a removable concrete trap that, when inserted, made the tunnel entrance all but undetectable. In Huts 104 and 123, the entrances were located beneath the stoves, while in Hut 122, the entrance was concealed in a shower drain.

First, Wally determined that the entrance to the tunnels would be dug straight down thirty feet before levelling out and moving forward horizontally. It was unlikely that digging at that depth would be detected by the Germans' seismic microphones, and it would also be a more stable stratum of earth to burrow through. Second, the tunnels would be shored up and braced – top and sides – just like the mines in Northern Ontario, especially if the tunnels were of any substantial length.

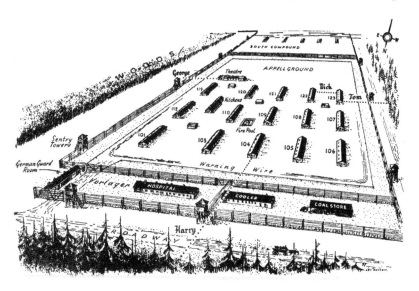

The North Compound, where the tunnelling took place.

While the lumber supply in camp was non-existent (apart from that which could be liberated from the workmen's supplies), each bunk had five to six boards apiece to support the mattress. These were the perfect size for framing, which gave the tunnels a dimension of 2 feet square. At first, the tunnellers used only one or two boards from each bunk, but as the tunnels grew longer and the need for lumber grew, more boards were used, and twine was strung in a zigzagged pattern for a make-shift mattress support. The boards were nailed together, but this proved to be noisy and demanded a constant supply of scavenged nails. 'Pappy' Plant, who was a farmer, suggested that the boards be fastened with tongue and groove joints, which required no nails and was extremely strong.

Looking down the thirty foot entrance to 'Harry.'

'Harry,' the longest tunnel, with shoring on its top and sides, and a trolley cart and railway. Air was distributed via a duct buried below the tracks

Getting rid of the orange-yellow sandy subsoil from the digging was the major challenge. A cubic foot of compressed, hard-packed earth doubles in volume when you haul it out of the ground, and each three and a half feet of tunnel produced approximately one ton of sand. That meant moving tons of earth and finding places to hide it. It couldn't be scattered on the compound's grey topsoil because of its vivid colour. Peter Fanshawe, a Fleet Air Arm pilot who had been put in charge of dispersal, came up with an ingenious solution. Two socks with the toes cut out were slung down the legs of a man's trousers, and a pin held the ends shut. These sock-bags were filled with sand, then as the men walked around the compound, they'd pull a string to release the pin and the sand would pour out down the pant leg and onto the ground in a steady trickle. Those who were responsible for disposal came to be known as 'Penguins,' because of how the full bags of sand hanging down their trouser legs produced a slight waddle in their walk. Whoever was walking behind the Penguins would scuffle the orange-yellow soil into the grey topsoil, and blend the two together. Men were always walking circuits for exercise, so this fit in neatly with the established patterns of life in camp.

The Red Cross also facilitated the disposal of sand. They included flower and vegetable seeds in their parcels, sent in the hope that the prisoners would plant gardens to supplement the meagre food supply and provide a welcome hobby. The X-Committee enthusiastically embraced gardening, which produced fresh vegetables as well as providing another way for the excavated sand to be intermingled with the topsoil.

The subsoil was basically moist sand, so the digging was easy using scoops that had been fashioned from KLIM tins. These were the tins in which the Red Cross sent powdered milk to the camps (KLIM = MILK.) In fact, KLIM tins were used for pretty much everything. John Colwell, an RCAF Navigator, came to be known as 'The Tin Man' and 'The Tin Basher,' because he could make virtually anything out of the tins: clocks, tools, coffee pots, cups, kettles, pots, pans, water heaters, stoves, and even a kitchen sink. (The German officers recognized Colwell's talent, too. When he offered to fashion an artificial tin leg for a fellow PoW, they happily supplied him with tools and materials.)

Creating light to work in the tunnels was a challenge. Lamps were made using leftover bits of fat and margarine poured into KLIM tins, with wicks made from shoelaces. But as the tunnels' depths and lengths increased, the limited light generated by the lamps made it increasingly difficult to see. Also, the smoke and stench of burning fat made the musty air even more difficult to breathe, especially in the deepest recesses of the tunnel at its face. Wally talked about installing electric lamps along the length of the tunnel, but John discouraged this as he feared the wire would make it easy to trace back to the tunnels. So they stuck with lamps and candles. But the stale smokey air became

Duct work made of KLIM tins.

a critical issue.

John approached Jens about devising a solution. Jens had been an engineering student before the war, and with Bob Nelson, a Yorkshireman, together they designed an air duct made of KLIM tins. A wooden trolley had been built in the tunnel to expedite the moving of men and earth back and forth from the face of the tunnel, and the air duct was buried nine inches in the earth beneath the tracks. But the natural flow of air from up top was insufficient, and they needed to figure out how to generate a flow of air through the ducts.

After a couple of weeks of wrestling with the problem, Jens and Bob designed and built an air pump from bed boards, hockey sticks (also supplied by the Red Cross), and a duffel bag adapted into a bellows. When it was compressed, it expelled two cubic yards of fresh air with sufficient force to travel the

The ingenious air pump.

length of the ductwork. More importantly, one man could operate it. As digging progressed, the men kept adding tins to the duct, ensuring the delivery of fresh air right up to the face of the tunnel. And as the tunnel grew in length, the importance of the trolley increased. The trolley's wheels were constructed of wood, and wore down very quickly. Jens suggested wrapping KLIM tin around the wheels, which gave them the resilience they needed, but made them noisy. He then poured water on the rails, which successfully reduced the noise to virtually nothing. Such ingenuity was relentlessly encouraged in all details of Bushell's master plan.

To navigate the length of *Harry*, the longest of the three, the tunnel was dug on a downward slope for about a hundred feet. There it came to a leveling off point known as *'Piccadilly Circus,'* a stope or landing, and was where the tunnellers changed trolleys. The tunnel continued on a level for about another hundred feet to *'Leicester Square,'* the second change station, then sloped uphill again. Determining the length of the tunnel meant allowing for the slopes and rises. This was a calculation that required at least three measurable points of reference, which they simply didn't have. This necessitated some educated guesses to determine what length *Harry* would have to be so that it extended into the fir tree forest to conceal *Harry's* exit. Working with makeshift equipment and insufficient points of reference created a potential margin of error that could be as high as six or seven percent. The boys wouldn't know how accurate their calculations were until they broke through at the tunnel's far end on the night of the escape, which was just one

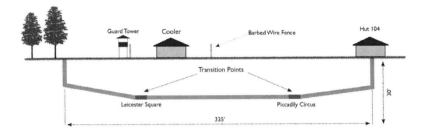

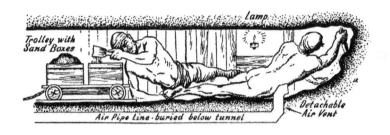

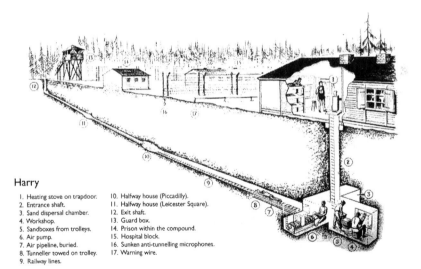

Harry

1. Heating stove on trapdoor.
2. Entrance shaft.
3. Sand dispersal chamber.
4. Workshop.
5. Sandboxes from trolleys.
6. Air pump.
7. Air pipeline, buried.
8. Tunneller towed on trolley.
9. Railway lines.

10. Halfway house (Piccadilly).
11. Halfway house (Leicester Square).
12. Exit shaft.
13. Guard box.
14. Prison within the compound.
15. Hospital block.
16. Sunken anti-tunnelling microphones.
17. Warning wire.

of many aspects of the plan dependent on luck.

Internal security had always been good in camp, but as the plan for the escape evolved, it became a crucial component. George Harsh, who had become a close friend of Wally Floody's, was recommended by Wally to work with the *SAO*, Lt. Colonel 'Bub' Clark, who was *'Big S'*, head of ground security for the camp. In time, when Clark was transferred to a separate compound for the American PoWs, George assumed full responsibility.

He was an extraordinary individual and made a strong impression on John and everyone else who met him. He was somewhat older than most of the PoWs by about fifteen years, and with his white hair, cold blue eyes, and stoic personality, he exuded an inner strength and hardness of character. His extraordinary personal history had formed this, although no one in camp knew anything about him other than Wally.

George was (also) an American who had been born into a prominent family in Atlanta. He attended the University of Georgia in the 1920s, and did all the kinds of foolish things that college boys do when they first taste that freedom of being away from home with a bunch of guys your own age. He and four of his friends, all from wealthy families, would get together in the evenings with a supply of cheap corn liquor, trading challenges and lies, and exploring who they were and who they were going to become.

These college freshmen got to talking about how much fun it would be to undertake a harmless, anonymous crime spree.

George Harsh.

They talked about Leopold and Loeb, notorious university students who, in 1924, had murdered a 14-year-old boy to demonstrate that they could commit the perfect crime. George and his friends thought those two had been cold-blooded and arrogant. Instead, his gang talked about how they could have fun pulling a harmless little hold up at an isolated road house or general store. They would go in, take a few dollars, and then disappear into the night. No one would get hurt, but it could be exciting.

Even after they sobered up, the idea had appeal. They continued talking about it for weeks, debating the pros and cons, making the point that no-one would get hurt. Then came a turning point. One of the boys brought a gun from his parents' house, and within a couple of days they had begun a minor crime wave that lasted for several weeks.

They became known as the *'Polite Gang.'* It was never about the money for them, which was nickel and dime at best. The excitement was that unbeatable rush of adrenaline. They would look for some isolated business, small enough to not have many customers, but large enough to have a bit of cash on hand and not feel the sting of having a bit of it stolen. They drew straws, and whoever drew the short one had to hold the gun when then went in. They would drive to the place that had been chosen shortly before closing time. With the engine running, the boy with the gun and one other would go in and demand cash. Whoever had the gun was usually terrified and shaking with nerves, but the folks they were robbing were even more scared. As they raced away down dark country roads outside, with a few dollars as their trophy, a delirious combination of excitement and relief washed over them.

George's first night handling the gun was at a rural grocery store, typically the safest of places to hit. He walked in with the gun drawn and told the storeowner to put his hands up. For whatever reason, the owner wasn't having any part of this nonsense from a couple of kids, and told them to get lost. George started to panic and shouted at him to hand over the money. A store clerk emerged from the back of the store with a gun and opened fire. George reflexively turned around and shot back, killing the clerk. The clerk's shots had missed George, but hit and killed the storeowner. Badly shaken, George and his friend ran to their car, and the bunch of them drove away. They got rid of the gun, then retreated to the safety of their parents' homes.

It didn't take long for the police to narrow the search. George had tossed his bloodstained clothing into the household laundry, and the family maid reported this. Within days, George and the boy who had gone in with him had been arrested and were put on trial. The District Attorney declared that self-defense was not a legal option as a defense, given that George had gone into the store with the intention of robbing it. The jury took less than a half an hour to find them both guilty. George's friend was underage and hadn't held the gun, so he received a minor sentence of house arrest and probation. But George, who had been the shooter, was sentenced to death. With the help of his family's wealth and influence, the death sentence was commuted to life imprisonment, which in 1927 Georgia meant spending the rest of his life on a chain gang.

The prison camp that twenty-one-year-old George was sent to was one of a few remaining holdovers from a more primitive penal age. Even in the 1920s it was considered to be unconscionably brutal. Known as a 'cage camp,' two hundred and forty inmates were locked into steel cages at night. The cages had been parked on a tract of grassless clay in a haphazard circle around a couple of unpainted shacks that served as mess hall and kitchen, with a latrine and wooden trough for water alongside. A high barbed wire fence surrounded it all. A stock and a sweat box were used for punishment, but the guards preferred using the lash, which was a four-foot long, three-inch wide leather strop used to beat men who committed any one of a hundred minor infractions.

Rehabilitation had no place in the Georgia penal system in those days. One of the first lessons you learned in that prison was that if you wanted to live, you had better mind your own business. George's tenacious will to survive helped him stay alive for twelve soul-deadening years, with the assistance of two 'lifers' with whom he formed friendships. His education and intelligence made it possible for him to work as a trustee with the camp's doctor. He valued any small privilege or escape from routine, and took advantage of any opportunity to keep his mind active and curious, studying all the books in the doctor's collection. His life had been reduced to getting by, day to day, with no hope of any future. In this way, he tried to make the most of each day that he survived serving his life sentence.

One weekend, while Dr. MacDonald, the prison doctor, was away from camp, a guard had a severe attack of appendicitis. With no hospital or treatment nearby, the man was as good as dead without immediate surgery. George persuaded another guard into helping him perform the appendectomy on the now-unconscious man. He had seen the procedure done, knew where the appendix was, and had read a number of physiology and surgery books. Once the cut had been made, the appendix was easy to locate, being so discoloured and distended. George carefully removed it, cauterized the incisions, and stitched the man up. The guard survived, and within six weeks was back on the job.

The other guards talked about what he'd done and wanted

to show George their appreciation. (He had been a model prisoner, and was a favourite of theirs.) One night they came to visit him in the clinic, offered their thanks, and handed him a pouch of pepper. George asked what it was for. One of the guards said that no one would be on watch at four o'clock in the morning, two days from now. So if he happened to go for a walk that night, the chances are that no one would see him. If he did decide to go, he should sprinkle pepper on his tracks for the first couple of hundred yards, which would throw the dogs off his scent. They heard rain was coming, so if he made it to a road, the water would also wash away his scent. All he had to do was to keep moving. They gave him forty dollars that they'd pooled together, shook his hand, and wished him good luck.

In the days following the appendectomy, Dr. MacDonald and the warden had written the Governor of Georgia impassioned letters on behalf of George, pleading for clemency in his sentence. They argued that he had made a foolish mistake when he was barely out of his teens, had served twelve years while none of the other boys had served a day. They felt he had something to contribute to the world, and having him languish in prison served no purpose.

Meanwhile, George had decided to act on the guards' offer of help in making a run for it. At the same time, his sister received notice that he had been granted a pardon based on his age, time served, and his humanitarian efforts in the prison. George was evasive about when and how he left the prison, but he never denied his guilt, which haunted him for the rest of his life. (Ironically, it would take months before he received word from his sister of his pardon.)

It was now 1940. George knew no one in Atlanta would have anything to do with him, so he headed north to Montreal. After a couple of nights drinking beer with a bunch of Canadians who had just signed up, he enlisted in the RCAF as an air gunner (the United States was not yet in the war). He shipped out to in England in 1941, and on his twentieth mission, he was shot down and sent to Stalag Luft III, where he met Wally.

George was older than most, and could appear taciturn and aloof. But despite his cold baleful stare, he was a sweet and gentle man who no longer had friends and family. There was something about Wally's sense of humour and dedication to the escape plan that drew them together in a way that bound them like brothers. Being in Stalag Luft III must have seemed like a summer outing compared to his previous life on a Georgia chain gang, and his self-possessed calm was a great source of strength and confidence for Wally.

With Wally's endorsement, George was assigned to work with 'Bub' Clark on ground security. When the Americans were moved to the South Compound in September 1943, that eliminated Clark and the other Americans from the escape. (George was billeted with the Canadians.) Bushell immediately assigned George the role of Big S. This meant managing the signals when guards entered the compound. Any ferret who came in was logged and tailed until they left. Elaborate signals involving hand gestures, opening and closing shutters, and a variety of sounds were used to give a heads-up to men working on various parts of the production line for the escape, which gave them time to shut down and conceal their work. After entering the camp, it took the ferrets ten minutes to reach Hut 104 (where *Harry* was being dug). From the time the spotters gave a signal that ferrets were on their way, the whole team – two diggers, two guys hauling sand, and the 'pumper' (who worked the air pump) – could get up and out of the tunnel and conceal the entrance, all in under eight minutes.

Bushell knew he was under scrutiny by the Gestapo, and had to distance himself from any suspicion of participating in escape attempts. He went out of his way to be as visible as possible by taking part in rugby matches, enrolling in language classes, attending cultural lectures, and starring in plays. The Kriegies who swapped information with the guards dropped hints that Bushell was out of the escape business. By early 1943, the X-Committee ordered Wally, Scruffy, and Birkland to go nowhere near Bushell. Glemnitz knew them too well, and if they were to be seen coming and going from Roger's hut, or even talking with him in the compound, it would endanger the security of the operation. But this was no great impediment, as virtually all of their waking hours were spent underground.

Down in the tunnel, two-man teams worked in shifts. The front man dug out the earth with his KLIM shovel, pushed that behind him, where the second man loaded the dirt onto a trolley to be hauled back and emptied. Two men could manage five feet of tunnelling during each shift, at which point the tunnel had to be shored up, and new air ducts buried beneath new trolley tracks.

Being strong, modest of stature, and indifferent to claustrophobia, John was well suited to the work. Each morning he was to dig, he would put on long underwear, or sometimes just strip down to the buff, and head down into *Harry* for his digging shift, usually paired with Wally. John was happy to be out of the general circulation of the camp. After his unnerving welcome by the British IO, and the curiosity that arose about his knowledge of coded BBC messages, he wanted to be as inconspicuous as possible. But his real inspiration was Wally. John felt his old Sunday School friend was ordained for the job of engineering and digging the tunnels. He understood mines and shared Bushell's determination not just to escape, but to confound the Germans with an escape on a scale that they wouldn't have dreamed possible. Wally had found his calling, and he put his heart and soul into the successful execution of the plan.

There were some who wanted to tunnel, but couldn't because they were petrified of enclosed spaces. Tom Kirby-Green tried it, but he was a big man and got stuck behind John, who had to crawl back over him, and then drag him out by the legs. When John got Tom out, he was ashen. John asked him why he hadn't told anyone that he was claustrophobic. Tom stammered out that until he got down there, he hadn't known that he was.

On one of Wally and John's shifts, the tunnel collapsed. The guys who had been digging before them had forgotten to put a top board up, and the tunnel caved in burying Wally. John was several feet behind him, loading the trolley with dirt. He heard a *'whump,'* followed by a rush of wind and muffled shouts from beneath a pile of earth. He dug Wally out and dragged him free. They had to rebuild the shoring, then fill the hole in the ceiling where it had collapsed. But such accidents never fazed either one of them for long.

When John was digging, he had a habit of drifting left and downward from the correct trajectory as he inched forward thirty feet underground in the semi-dark. What saved him from going in a circle was following the KLIM tin air duct path beneath the tracks, which he thought was almost as good a guide as having a dotted line. (Engineers came down a couple of times a week with a spirit level to confirm the air duct and the tunnel's trajectory.)

Appel was held twice a day, at eight in the morning and again at five in the afternoon. If he had time, Scruffy would dash in and grab a shower first. After a few hours of underground digging, and drenched with sweat, he smelled pretty foul. Not to mention that you had to pee where you lay. This provided challenges when you had to scramble up top in a hurry. As appel approached, the other boys in Scruffy's hut hustled him into the shower to rinse him off when time permitted. On more than one *appel*, Scruffy didn't have time to shower and came directly from tunnelling. A Hauptmann (a captain), Hans Pieber, on seeing this airman covered in dirt and reeking of sweat and mud, said, *'Mr. Weir, I believe you have been playing in the sand piles, yes?'* Scruffy smiled and said that he was just working on his gardening. Pieber, a likeable, gentle soul who could be a good friend to the prisoners, accepted this. He also did the prisoners small favours, such as lending them his Leica, and even having their photographs developed. He was wise enough to be sensitive to the ever-changing winds of war, an instinct that served him well in the fullness of time.

Corporal Karl Griese, nicknamed *'Rubberneck,'* was despised by all. He was a ferret who had no sense of humour, was aggressive, and looked for any excuse to impose his authority. Outwitting Rubberneck was always a welcome game for the boys. Glemnitz, by contrast, became more reasonable as time went on. He could be impatient with some of the guards, who paid him little respect (they were army and he was air force). On one occasion, he drew his pistol and shouted orders at the sullen guards in a manner befitting his sergeant-major rank. When the guards slunk away, he turned to the PoWs and said, *'How's that for acting, boys?'* He was also heard to say to John and some of his friends, *'Those army Dummköpfes know nothing; so I*

Rubberneck, the ferret that the PoWs hated, poses in the entrance to a tunnel.

tell you: escape!' John loved and respected Hermann, as a friend, an airman, and a gentleman of honour.

The Germans knew that the prisoners were always trying to find ways to escape, and the boys knew that the Germans were always watching, listening, and nosing around, ready to pounce. But neither side knew everything about when, where, or what the other was up to. The ferrets would discover evidence of digging, but then let the prisoners continue to work to give them the illusion of success. At the eleventh hour, they would swoop in and collapse the tunnel and thwart the escape, triumphant in crushing the boys' spirit.

The X-Committee was well aware of this gambit. As tunnelling proceeded, Big X began to encourage all manner of escape attempts, knowing most were doomed. These failed escapes encouraged the ferrets' belief that they were one step ahead of the prisoners' desperate and failing attempts, which in turn minimized any awareness of Bushell's greater plan.

As the camp became increasingly crowded, the Germans began adding new compounds to handle the hundreds of new American prisoners arriving each week. By the summer of 1943, workmen were clearing the woods to the west of North Compound, where all the tunnelling was taking place. This new compound effectively rendered *Tom* and *Dick* useless, as they were headed directly into the area where construction supplies and workmen were preparing the building site. This proximity to the site did have one positive dividend, however. An RCAF pilot, 'Red' Noble, spotted a coil of electrical wire left unattended by the German workmen. He liberated it (John used terms such as *'purloined'* and *'permanently borrowed'* to describe how useful items were acquired), and brought it to Hut 104 where it was used to wire *Harry* for electric lights. Jens had figured out how to tap into the camp's electricity without the Germans being able to trace it. Now they could dig with decent light, and tunnelling began moving faster.

But there were new obstacles. They were quickly running out of places to dump or hide the sand from the tunnels. Since *Tom* and *Dick* couldn't be completed, the X-Committee decided that if they sacrificed one of them, it could be used as a repository for some of the backlog of sand that was choking *Harry's* progress. The Penguins dumped as much as would fit into *Dick*, and then left clues for the ferrets to discover. There was a great commotion when they did, upsetting many of the PoWs who thought it meant a big escape had been blown. The ferrets were exuberant at having discovered such a large tunnel, which they believed was the obvious heart of the PoWs' escape plans. They smugly assumed they had beaten the prisoners at their own game.

To ensure that the tunnel could never be resurrected, explosives were brought in to collapse it. As the ferrets packed dynamite around the end of Hut 122 (where *Dick's* entrance was), Scruffy, Wally, and Hank watched them with interest. Scruffy wondered out loud if they knew *to 'tamp'* the charge, which is the process of correctly packing the dynamite to direct the force of its explosion. Wally said he didn't think they knew anything about what they were doing, and suggested they warn the other PoWs who were watching to move back a couple of dozen yards.

As Scruffy and the others fell back, the ferrets set off their charge. And as Wally had suggested, the Germans didn't have a clue idea about what they were doing. The dynamite blew the back off of Hut 122, showering wood splinters all over the compound, and causing the hut and its chimney to list badly. Some of the boys continued to believe that the Germans had won a victory in discovering and destroying the tunnel. But just thinking about it kept Scruffy, Wally, and Hank chuckling for weeks.

By December 1943, John was down to a hundred and thirty pounds through the combination of hard work in the hot tunnels, and a lack of sufficient food. The PoWs were surviving on watery soup, rotten potatoes, and remnants of Red Cross parcels, of which there were simply not enough to support so many men. Like many of the others, John was slowly starving to death, and had become far more interested in eating than anything else. It was an extremely frustrating and increasingly desperate time.

To make things worse, the digging had hit a wall. There was nowhere else to put the huge volumes of sand excavated from *Harry*. *Dick* had been collapsed, *Tom* was full, and whatever discreet space there had been underneath the huts was packed. With snow now falling, spreading the orange-yellow soil out in the compound was impossible. Although the diggers were near the end of the tunnel, and ready to make the final push, everything had come to a standstill.

Scruffy (front left) sitting with Kirby-Green (rear left), Bischa Gotowski (rear right), and 'Doc' Lybey, who holds G2, their pet cat. As food all but disappeared, and the men were starving to death, kittens were bred from their cats as food. Not an appealing thought, but not really any different than what Fiji had alluded to a decade earlier in Algonquin Park. Scruffy held firm to his belief that you did whatever was necessary to survive.

A party was arranged to boost everyone's spirits. Minskewich had shown Scruffy and the others in their hut how to make his own variety of bathtub gin, although there wasn't much that was like gin-like about it. At the beginning of November, he had mashed up an extra large quantity of potatoes and raisins, added some spittle and other odds and ends to get it started, then let it ferment in cheesecloth-covered barrels buried underneath the huts to keep them cool. After five weeks, the mixture was frothing and ripe.

The barrels were tapped to run off the liquid into a metal pail, which was then heated to condense the alcohol. The final step was distilling the condensate in the shower room using a trombone as a distillation coil. The liquid was brought to a boil and forced through a tube into the trombone. Cold water was then run over the trombone's coils to make the mixture condense further, and the distillate dripped out of the tail end of the horn. To evaluate the quality of the mixture, they lit a teaspoon of it. If it burned yellow, that meant it was poisonous, and so the process would continue until it burned blue. At that point, the liquor was relatively safe to drink and was painstakingly collected a drop at a time.

Remarkably, they were able to produce a couple of gallons of the brew using this convoluted means of extraction and invited guys from the other huts to have a sip. It was *extremely* potent. So much so, that one of the boys offered two squares of chocolate to anyone who was able to drink a small glass of it and still be standing five minutes later. Everyone took the bet; Scruffy too, because how strong could it be? When his turn came, he took his dram and knocked it back, expecting something with a good solid kick to it. He wasn't disappointed. It burned on the way down, which brought about a lot of choking and sputtering. But apart from that, it seemed like a very good tipple, and he considered having a second.

Then something peculiar happened. A curious sensation descended over Scruffy, rather like a fog rolling in, and he decided to set his glass down on the table. But when he tried to, the table disappeared, and his glass seemed to fall to the ground in slow motion. It hit the floor as gently as a feather, and broke apart, with the shards drifting and floating in space as if they were suspended in water. As he tried to make sense of this, a curtain of black descended and he slipped into dreamless and painless unconsciousness.

As far as he could tell, he came 'to' several hours later, although for all he knew he could have been in a coma for a week. Everyone got paralytically drunk. George Harsh wrapped a sheet around himself like a toga and stuck a make-shift crown of thorns on his head. With his mane of white hair and beard, he cut a very biblical image. He walked to the Fire Pool – a concrete water reservoir where the boys sailed model boats – and many swore that George managed to walk three or four steps across the water before sinking like a rock. The only thing left of him was his crown of thorns, floating on the water's surface. When he popped up again, he said, *'Right, boys. Now you can crucify me,'* and then slowly sank back down into the drink.

The next day, everyone was desperately hung over. At *appel*, the Germans were disgusted by the condition of those who managed to stagger out. The huts were a nightmare, with vomit and smashed glasses everywhere, and comatose bodies laid out cold on every surface. The guards had to haul in fire hoses to flush out all the rooms.

It was a party that the boys never forgot.

Chapter 16

Second Sight

As the youngest in his circle of friends, John was fortunate that Wally and the others kept a protective eye on him. Wally, in particular, was worried that John wasn't getting proper sleep because of having no eyelids. He saw how hard John was pushing himself, spending hours underground digging. More concerning was how he dismissed the discomfort his eyes gave him, so Wally put in a request to have a Red Cross doctor come to examine him. The doctor checked John carefully and stated in no uncertain terms that if John left his eyelids as they were, his eyes would become septic, and he would eventually go blind. He recommended that he be sent to a German hospital outside of Frankfurt where a young ophthalmologist was employing some innovative techniques.

John was not pleased. He was determined to stay and see *Harry* finished, and to be a part of the escape, and refused to leave. Wally reminded him that digging was shut down until they could figure out how and where to dispose of the backlog of earth. The Red Cross doctor guessed that the surgical procedure should not take more than a couple of weeks. Wally told John that he might as well go. Nothing was going to happen any time soon, and possibly not until spring.

John was convinced that as soon as he left, someone would figure out how to get rid of the earth, and he would miss everything. But snow was falling, and the ground was starting to freeze. And he didn't want to lose his sight. So in early December, he reluctantly agreed to be sent to the hospital near Frankfurt.

There were two other boys also being sent to Frankfurt for their eye problems. In consideration of receiving special medical treatment, all three swore oaths that they would not try to escape. As curious as this may sound, for the Allied airmen and the Luftwaffe officers, giving one's word was sacrosanct. That code of honour – giving your word – was something most honoured throughout their lives.

Before entraining, the men had to be given inoculations for Typhus. There had been an outbreak of the extremely contagious disease in their region. Hundreds of thousands of prisoners in Nazi concentration camps had succumbed to the disease (Anne Frank being one of them). The orderly doing the injections was distracted by a phone call after giving a shot to a young airman with an ulcerous eye. When he returned, without thinking he gave the airman a second and potentially deadly injection. The airman, not knowing any different, went along.

On the train to Frankfurt, however, he began to feel the effects of too much serum in his system. He began shaking and sweating and developed an extremely high fever. But nothing could be done. By the time they reached the hospital, he was unconscious. The ophthalmologist met them and determined what had happened. As the man's temperature rose, the ulcer in his eye burst, which allowed it to drain. The doctor said the accidental double dose and the resultant fever saved the eye, and possibly his life (because of the danger of septic shock). None of this reassured John regarding his own course of treatment.

The hospital was located in St. Vincent's Marienheim nunnery in Bad-Soden, a village a short distance northwest of Frankfurt on the west bank of the Main River. It sat high on a hill with a spectacular view of the city and was run by an order of German nuns who lived in a convent in one wing of the building. The nurse (a nun) who welcomed John was loving and tender. She brought him a raw egg, which he cracked and swallowed whole in one gulp, the first he had tasted in two years. In the morning, he woke after a long sleep and lay in his hospital bed, enjoying the calm of the hospital and the sunshine streaming through the windows. He was warm and dry, had had something to eat, and was sleeping in fresh sheets and

St. Vincent's Marienheim Hospital and Nunnery in Bad-Soden, outside of Frankfurt.

wearing clean pajamas, with sweet and attentive nurses tending to him. Life was good.

That first morning, the ophthalmologist came to examine him. This doctor wasn't anything like John had expected. He introduced himself as Major Charters, and he wasn't German, but a Scot. David Livingstone Charters had been born in Stirling, Scotland, and came from a long line of Scottish missionaries (he had been named 'David Livingstone' after the most famous of his uncle's missionary colleagues). He had begun his practice in Birkenhead in the north of England, earning the name of 'The Poor Man's Doctor' because he so rarely charged fees to his more needy patients in the very poor neighbourhood in which he practiced..

Charters was in his late thirties when he was captured in Greece in 1941 while serving as a surgeon with the Royal Army Medical Corps (RAMC). He had done many ophthalmological procedures for the Germans in a PoW camp hospital (Stalag IXA Kloster Haina). However, he came into conflict with that camp's Kommandant, who Charters felt was inappropriately meddling in the treatment of both Allied and German patients. He filed several formal complaints, which had an astonishing effect. The International Red Cross intervened, and the hospital was closed down. Many of the patients were repatriated to Britain, but Charters declined and was transferred to the hospital at Bad Soden. He felt he would be of more use there than back at home, and he remained in Bad Soden until the end of the war.

What Charters lacked in his ophthalmologic work was practical experience in plastic surgery, although he had been

Dr. David Charters.

educating himself on effective techniques. Quite by accident, Major Charters found himself at the centre of burn treatment for PoWs in Germany, despite having little pre-war experience with burns or plastic surgery. The *Invalid Comforts Section* of the Red Cross provided an invaluable link with Archibald McIndoe, head of the famous RAF plastic surgery centre in Sussex (at East Grinstead). Sets of highly specialised equipment and dressings were assembled by McIndoe's personal suppliers and sent with detailed instructions directly to Charters in Bad Soden. While the two men had not met, Charters essentially carried on a plastic surgery correspondence course with McIndoe throughout the war. But Charters was clearly a gifted surgeon in his own right and was breaking new ground, especially in the reconstruction of eyelids. When he examined John, he told him in his forthright Scots' manner that he would be his guinea pig. This did not reassure John, who asked for more details.

Charters said he believed he would be able to rebuild at least two new eyelids, and with a bit of ingenuity and luck, he might be able to rebuild all four. It would take time, but they both had plenty of that. The one major drawback was that there was no anesthetic to help offset the pain. (In fact, there *were* small amounts of it at the hospital, but none was for use on PoWs.) Charters went on to explain that apart from the eyes, there was only one place more painful for a man to be cut, which, ironically, was also the best place to get the appropriate skin for the grafting work he would need to do. John described the experience of having the skin on his face and hands peeled off with nothing but petroleum jelly to buffer the pain after he had been shot down and burned. Charters told him, in a rather matter of fact manner, that this eye surgery would be substantially more painful than that. It was his first time doing this particular procedure and estimated that it would take six to eight weeks. He described the stages of the reconstruction.

Throughout the various surgeries, John would have to lie absolutely still, not moving his head or his eyes, otherwise there was a fair chance that Charters could blind him. Above all, Charters reminded John that he had not done this particular surgery before, and they would have to trust each another completely. The odds were probably in favour of him losing his sight; but if they didn't try, John would definitely go blind.

To manage the pain, he told John that he would have to

learn self-hypnosis, which would also take time. Once he was capable of separating his mind from the discomfort, then he would be ready for surgery. John weighed his options but knew this was the only one worth taking. They would start the next morning, and Charters would check on him every day to see how he was progressing.

In the morning, Charters had John lie down on an operating table and stare at the ceiling. He told him to think of the most beautiful place in the world that he had ever seen. He would have to be able to visualize it such a way that he would not only be able to see every detail, but would also be able to hear and smell everything as well. He had to describe the colours and sounds, the fragrance of the flowers and the grass, the bees and butterflies, and everything else that made that place special.

John thought of a Scottish Glen that he remembered as being a most extraordinarily beautiful corner of the world. Charters told him to describe what he saw in his mind's eye, and with as much detail as he could muster. As John began, the doctor encouraged him to keep adding more specifics and forced John to dig deeper and deeper into his memory and imagination. John eventually lost track of time as he talked, and was only brought back to the present when Charters interrupted him and told him he had done fine for their first day.

Every morning for the next six weeks, they went through the same exercise: John visualizing the Glen, exploring its memory and describing the smallest details. Once he had begun, he would gradually lose all sense of time, as the doctor sat quietly beside him. Sometimes hours would pass without

John realizing it, but he wasn't sure if this is what self-hypnosis was supposed to feel like. And how would he know when he had done it successfully? If he was aware of putting himself into a trance, then he must not be hypnotized.

This started to concern him. In the midst of a particularly detailed passage one morning, he started to feel that he had exhausted the subject. He broke his narrative to tell Charters he wasn't getting anywhere with this; all he was doing was repeating the same things over and over again. He didn't know how much longer he could continue this, and how would he ever know if he was ready. Charters told John that he had stuck a needle into his hip thirty minutes earlier, and he hadn't flinched. They would begin surgery in the morning.

The next day in the operating room, John's head was sandbagged on either side so that he could not move it. Charters told John to begin telling his story again, with every bit of detail that he had been exploring over the past many weeks. But this time he would have to tell it to himself. He could not move any part of his mouth or his face. He would have to be certain that he told the story thoroughly, and didn't leave anything out.

There were two main stages to the surgery. The first was the harvesting of skin for transplant. Charters had determined that the best skin to use for reconstructive surgery on the eyes would be a graft from the foreskin; but John had been circumcised, so that limited their options. Charters settled for layers of skin removed from the soft flesh on the back of John's arms. As John lay motionless on the operating table, revisiting his vision of the Scottish Glen in his mind's eye, Charters gently sliced several pieces of skin from the backs of the arms. He laid them in place on John's left upper eye socket, sewed them to the remnant of the eyelid, and stitched the eye shut. It took about a week to begin to heal and determine if the graft would take. When it was clear that it had been successful, Charters repeated the procedure on John's right upper eyelid, again stitching the eye shut.

The problem then became the lack of appropriate skin for the lower eyelid grafts. When he was confident that the two upper lids were healing, Charters had to find some more appropriately fine skin for the reconstruction of John's lower lids. He took slices of skin from the soft tissue on areas of John's legs, which he then grafted them on to his neck for future harvesting. The skin was too thick, but there were no other options. Charters hoped that the graft on the neck would heal and regenerate in a sufficiently pliable form to work on the lower lids, which would take another few weeks. Days passed with John unable to read or even move about because of his lack of sight. What made it worse was that his thoughts kept returning to the camp, which kept him wondering what was happening with the tunnelling.

While John recovered, Dr. Charters turned his attention to a German pilot who had come to the hospital for treatment. The talk on the ward was that he was the nephew of Field Marshall von Rundstedt, one of the most senior German generals. The nephew had been shot down, and the Perspex of his aircraft's canopy had shattered and rained tiny shards into his eyes, blinding him. German High Command wanted to know if Charters could do anything. After an examination, he felt he might be able to restore sight to at least one of the young man's eyes. Berlin was delighted and extended all the resources of the hospital to Charters, including whatever anesthetic he might need.

Charters agreed to undertake the work on the young pilot on the condition he would receive no anesthetic. Since the PoWs had been denied it, Charters said that it would only be fair if the German went without, too. The work would be excruciatingly painful, so it was up to them if they wanted to tell him that in advance. The offer was explained to the young man, and as he was already in agony, he agreed: no anesthetic.

Each day, as with John, the pilot was laid on the operating table with his head sandbagged. Using surgical forceps, Charters would pluck out a fragment or two of Perspex from the man's eyes. Usually, the young man could only bear the removal of a single fragment a day because he was unable to lie still, screaming in pain. The PoW patients got some satisfaction hearing the German's suffer as much as they had suffered. It took several weeks to remove all the splinters, and eventually he had his full sight restored in one eye and about fifty percent in the other.

When the grafted skin was finally ready to be re-harvested from John's neck, Charters stitched it into place on his lower lids. But the whole procedure had taken months, not weeks as John had hoped. It was April 1944 before the grafting and surgeries were complete. Even learning to blink again with his new eyelids took many more weeks.

Soon he was well enough to walk around the perimeter of the hospital. After months of being bed-ridden and having to lie so still, he enjoyed being able to get out and stretch his legs. Apart from a German dentist almost demanding that he pull out all of John's teeth (which were in extremely bad shape, but he declined the offer), his time in the hospital had been a quiet respite from camp life and the war. Most significantly, his eyes had been saved.

Before he returned to Stalag Luft III, John sought out Charters to thank him for all that he had done for him and sang his praises. Charters brushed the compliments and thanks aside. He came from Scottish Presbyterian stock (as did the Weirs), and although brave and dedicated, he always formal to the point of coldness. He was a soft-spoken man with little ego, who was beloved by those he worked with and those he helped. But he deplored any sort of triviality and ostentation, and even declined an invitation to Buckingham Palace at the war's end to collect his MBE. (It was sent to him by registered mail instead.)

The atmosphere around the hospital changed abruptly one morning in the first week of April. One of the doctors took John aside and told him that there had been a mass escape from Stalag Luft III. There were still no confirmed details, but the rumour was that many of the escapers had been shot while resisting arrest. That was all the news they had received. John was stunned, anxious to know if any of his friends had been killed, and what had gone wrong. But no one had any other information.

Having received this terrible news, he stood staring out a hospital window, trying to think how to get more information. Uncle Adrian could help if he could get a message to him, but a letter would take weeks to reach London. He was distracted from his thoughts by a throbbing vibration, which started resonating through the building. He could feel it more than hear it. He looked at the floor, trying to make sense of this. The windows began to rattle, and a *'thromba-thromba-thromba'* became audible from somewhere outside. This was very distinctive and vaguely familiar, but still he couldn't place it. In the distance, he saw what at first looked like a huge flock of birds swaying gently back and forth. He then realized he was watching a thousand RAF Lancaster and Halifax heavy bombers attacking Frankfurt.

The sight of that many enormous aircraft transfixed John, and he didn't give a thought to looking for shelter. As the endless stream of bombers passed over the hospital, he saw them cross the river and release their payloads of five hundred pound bombs. Tens of thousands of tons of explosives were detonated, sending ribbons of fire shooting up through the fog of smoke and ash that blanketed the city. Bomber crews later said they could feel the heat from the fires at ten thousand feet.

The attack knocked out the power and water, which effectively prevented any German counterattack, and left a devastated city in its wake. The hospital's security officer came to warn John that it was no longer safe to venture outside. The citizens of Frankfurt were enraged because thousands of people had been killed, and if he were caught outside, the mob would tear him apart.

About three o'clock that afternoon, another rumbling wave rattled the windows. This time, it was American B-17 bombers coming to complete the mission. Not one German shot was fired as the Americans crossed the Main River and dropped their bombs, completing the devastating attack. Over 30,000 people died in those two raids.

John felt little remorse. For him, at that moment, the raid on Frankfurt was payback for what the Nazis had been doing to millions of people over the past ten years, as well as whoever of his friends might have been shot. The thought of that haunted him, and he was anxious to get back to Stalag Luft III as soon as possible to find out. Perhaps it wasn't as bad as the rumours had made it sound.

Lancasters forming up in Yorkshire for a raid on Frankfurt, 1944.

Chapter 17

The Beginning of the End

John's instinct about the tunnellers' ingenuity had been right. A few weeks after he had arrived in Bad Soden, the problem of disposing the sand from *Harry* had been solved. The Kriegies had built a theatre at the south end of the North Compound, with the Germans enthusiastically supplying materials and tools, seeing its construction and use as energy-consuming distractions for the prisoners that would keep them from their relentless and irksome determination to escape. The

The theatre that the prisoners built.

theatre accommodated approximately three hundred with seats constructed from the wood crates of the Red Cross parcels. The stage and audience were both 'raked,' or sloped, which provided generous space beneath the floors for dumping the dirt. Tons of sand were dispersed under the seats, stage, and in corners of the high ceiling. (In addition, using access from beneath one of the theatre seats, the fourth tunnel, *George*, had been started, headed towards the east fence.)

By January 1944, only six weeks after work had come to a halt, escape plans were back in full swing. The final drive to complete *Harry* was put into motion, and the X-Committee kept a close watch on the best possible weather conditions for the escape. Cycles of the moon, night time temperatures, potentials of inclement weather, and the impending invasion of Europe (D-Day) all played important parts in the choice of the right date. A moonless night was what they wanted, ideally a Friday night and early Saturday, when there would be fewer travellers and more relaxed security at the railway station in Sagan.

Harry was completed in early March, and it was determined that the night of Friday, March 24th would be moonless. They would have to take their chances with the weather. Once the X-Committee had committed to the 24th, there was no turning back. All forged documents had to be dated for that weekend. The date was set.

Principal contributors to the escape effort were offered the first places among the two hundred spots available. The rest were assigned by lottery. John had been given Number 13 in the escape order, but in his absence, his place was assigned to another man. Dick Bartlett, the 'Canary' keeper, had been paired to escape with a Norwegian PoW, but in the days leading up to the escape, it was agreed that it would be safer to have two Norwegians travel together, and Dick agreed to give up his place and move down in the order.

Luck played a great part in the fates of those involved. Wally, George Harsh, and several other key escape personnel were rounded up in early March. The Germans knew that some plan was underway. In an attempt to undermine it, without warning the Germans transferred Wally and George, along and a hundred and fifty other PoWs, to nearby Stalag VIIIC at Belaria, a former slave labour camp four miles away. This twist of fate saved their lives.

Ironically, Roger Bushell had not been one of those removed from camp because of the effective efforts to distance him from the X-Committee's activities. Rumours had been intentionally spread that the *SAO*, Bub Clark, now in South Compound, was the man to be watched, not Bushell. In the months leading up to the escape, Bushell had been heavily engaged in sports and the theatre. He was to have performed as Henry Higgins in Shaw's *Pygmalion* on the evening of March 24th.

When the tunnellers broke through in the early hours of Saturday, March 25th, they discovered that the exit was short of the cover of trees by about ten feet. The estimates for the tunnel's final length, including its rise, fall, and drift, were off by about 3 percent. Heartbreakingly close.

Worse, there was a substantial amount of snow on the ground that showed footprints as the men climbed out of the tunnel, in addition to impeding their trek through the forest to Sagan and the railway station. Seventy-six men managed to escape during an air raid when the camp's lights blacked out. As power was restored, a guard spotted the 77th escaper scrambling out of the tunnel as the lights came back on, and the escape was over.

News of what had happened reached Hitler within twenty-four hours. In a blind rage, he issued a *Grossfahndung* – a national manhunt alert – for the recapture of the men, ordering that all those recaptured to be shot. But the invasion of Europe was imminent, and it had become clear to his generals that the war was already lost. Hitler's most senior advisors, Himmler and Göring, tried to persuade him to be more reasonable. They were already evaluating Germany's relationship with neutral countries, and how they might best negotiate their own shelter from prosecution when the end came. As a result, there was considerable debate and concern amongst these and other senior officers about obeying Hitler's orders to shoot the PoWs. Ultimately, Himmler persuaded Hitler to reduce the number of executions to a list of fifty, who would then be arrested and disposed of by Gestapo agents.

The German High Command removed Stalag Luft III's Kommandant Lindeiner in disgrace for having allowed the escape to happen. A week after his departure, the camp's current SBO, Group Captain Herbert Massey, requested a meeting with the new Kommandant, Colonel Braune. He anticipated bad news regarding the fates of some of the escapees. To ensure that he understood everything that was said, he was accompanied by Squadron Leader Philip Murray to translate and produce an official transcript. Kommandant Braune was clearly uneasy as he glanced at the communiqué that held the news he now had to convey. This is a portion of their conversation from that transcript:

> Braune: I am instructed by the German High Command to state that forty-one of the escapees were shot while resisting arrest.
>
> Massey: How many were shot...?
>
> Braune: Forty-one.
>
> Massey (*to translator*): Ask him how many men were wounded.
>
> Braune: I think none were wounded.
>
> Massey: How could forty-one men be shot in those circumstances and all killed?
>
> Braune: I am only permitted to say by German High Command that forty-one of your men were shot while resisting arrest.
>
> Massey: Have you a list of their names?
>
> Braune. I do not have that information.
>
> Massey: I expect you to provide it as soon as possible.

Hans Pieber, the Kommandant's well-liked adjutant, escorted Massey and Murray out of the office. He asked that they not think that the Luftwaffe was involved in any way in the terrible business. Massey had nothing to say.

In the wake of this, German High Command announced that if there were any further escape attempts, the men would be executed: no court-martials, no second chances, no extenuating circumstances. The Germans posted a notice stating, '*To all*

Hans Pieber.

Prisoners of War: The escape from prison camps is no longer a sport.'

When Scruffy arrived back to Sagan in early June, the new IO was waiting for him. They walked the circuit as they talked. The IO told John they were no longer speaking to the Germans because of the murders. At first, the number of murdered prisoners was thought to be forty-one, but as reports filtered into camp, the final number was confirmed to be fifty, Roger Bushell and Tom Kirby-Greene among them. The man who had taken John's Number 13 position had been recaptured and shot, as were the two Norwegians who Dick Bartlett had given up his place for.

Life in camp had settled down to a bitter routine, with an

To all Prisoners of War!

The escape from prison camps is no longer a sport!

Germany has always kept to the Hague Convention and only punished recaptured prisoners of war with minor disciplinary punishment. Germany will still maintain these principles of international law.

But England has besides fighting at the front in an honest manner instituted an illegal warfare in non combat zones in the form of gangster commandos, terror bandits and sabotage troops even up to the frontiers of Germany.

They say in a captured secret and confidential English military pamphlet,

THE HANDBOOK
OF MODERN IRREGULAR
WARFARE:

". . . the days when we could practise the rules of sportsmanship are over. For the time being, every soldier must be a potential gangster and must be prepared to adopt their methods whenever necessary."

"The sphere of operations should always include the enemy's own country, any occupied territory, and in certain circumstances, such neutral countries as he is using us a source of supply."

England has with these instructions opened up a non military form of gangster war!

Germany is determined to safeguard her homeland, and especially her war industry and provisional centres for the fighting fronts. Therefore it has become necessary to create strictly forbidden zones, called death zones, in which all unauthorised trespassers will be immediately shot on sight.

Escaping prisoners of war, entering such death zones, will certainly lose their lives. They are therefore in constant danger of being mistaken for enemy agents or sabotage groups.

Urgent warning is given against making future escapes!

In plain English. Stay in the camp where you will be safe! Breaking out of it is now a damned dangerous act.

The chances of preserving your life are almost nil!

All police and military guards have been given the most strict orders to shoot on sight all suspected persons.

Escaping from prison camps has ceased to be a sport!

icy tension between the Allies and the guards. Many defiant prisoners would walk up to a guard's face, stand a foot away, and just stare. At *appel*, the PoWs slouched in line and generally demonstrated utter disdain for the whole charade. The guards were incensed but did nothing, and eventually stopped entering the compound unless absolutely necessary.

Auctions were held for the belongings of the murdered fifty, with the proceeds going to their families, and the bidding amongst the men was brisk. Glemnitz was present at the auction, egging the men on with shouts of, *'Bid, gentlemen, bid! Bid!'*

Lectures, sports, and theatre productions continued, albeit with a more subdued, if determined, air. With escape having become so much more dangerous, there was less to keep the boys' spirits up. D-Day and the breakthrough in Normandy gave them hope for a German surrender by the end of the year. News of the D-Day invasion had been communicated from North Compound to the American Compound by a Scottish Padre to a Scottish-American PoW. They both spoke Highland Gaelic, which baffled the Germans, who assumed it was some new code.

But the camp now lacked the unified and exciting sense of purpose that Bushell's escape plan had given everyone. As fragments of good news and bad trickled into camp, spirits went up and down accordingly. The men began to hope that the Allies were on the cusp of a breakthrough, so perhaps the war would be over by Christmas after all. By the autumn of 1944, the invasion of Europe and the increasing desperation of the German army began to choke off the much-needed supply of Red Cross parcels. These essential supplies appeared less and less frequently until there were none at all. The food situation was becoming desperate.

Propaganda continued to be posted on bulletin boards, and German radio broadcasts were piped in over the camp's loudspeakers. Films were shown demonstrating Nazi doctors' medical experiments, presumably to illustrate their contributions to the betterment of humanity. One focussed on an attempt to graft the muscle and nerves from one man's legs onto another's. Another showed an experiment trying to generate twin fetuses.

Slave labourers, who had been working in the camp for years disappeared. An atmosphere of doom hung over everyone and everything.

John's teeth were in terrible shape. Facilitated by the Red Cross, he was sent to a dental clinic an hour's train ride away. When he and his guard escort arrived at an unmarked station, John noticed what he assumed were cattle cars on a siding at the railway station. More particularly, he noticed some young women standing alongside the cars with the yellow stars sewn on their clothing that Nazis required Jews to wear. Women were a rare sight at that time and place in the world, and John couldn't help staring. Some were quite beautiful while others looked wan and forlorn. He assumed they were refugees being transferred from one camp to another.

When the dentist had finished two hours later, John asked him where the girls were from and where they were going. The man shook his head and told John to say nothing about what he had seen. Then he was escorted back to the train. He learned from his guard that the cars were mobile gas chambers.

There had been talk at Stalag Luft III about what was happening at the concentration camps. But even so, he found it difficult to believe the degree to which the Nazis pursued their final solution. There appeared to be little that they were not prepared to do to eradicate traces of their ethnic cleansing. Soon it would be every man for himself.

Chapter 18

The Long Walk

Within the camp, the men pieced together fragments of information about the war's progress. The increasing velocity of the advancing Russians and the crumbling of the Third Reich prompted talk about the chances of the PoWs' imminent liberation, perhaps through an exchange of prisoners. There were also dark rumours of German High Command having issued orders to execute all prisoners should negotiation attempts fail. SBO Massey had been repatriated because of ill health in late 1944. The new SBO, Group Captain D.E.L. Wilson, organized the men to create resistance units if the Gestapo come rolling in without warning. At the very least they would have the chance to go down fighting. And there was always *George*, the tunnel running from beneath the theatre, which was kept active as a storage space for emergency supplies and as a potential refuge.

The approach of the Russian Army from the east was so swift that it displaced all other speculation. By Christmas 1944, the men were hoarding food and preparing for the likelihood of a forced march in the dead of winter west into the heart of Germany. The Germans were going to use the PoWs as barter for their safe passage, and if events turned against them, there was little doubt that they would use them as human shields.

Scruffy made plans with seven others from his hut to travel together. Their group would include Scruffy and two other RCAF pilots, two RAF and one RNAZF (New Zealand) airmen, and two USAAF (American) pilots. The eight planned to share sleeping quarters and combine their resources. They pooled what food they had, and made high-calorie bars of chocolate, barley, and raisins, which could be tucked in a pocket and would keep a man going for twenty-four hours. They packed their kits in similar ways, wrapping bedrolls in white sheets to make it easy for them to spot one another in a crowd of men.

There was constant speculation as to how close the Russians would get before the Germans decided to move. On the afternoon of January 27th, as they were midway through the dress rehearsal of a play at the theatre, orders came in that they were to be packed and ready to move in an hour's time. Even though they'd been preparing for a possible move for weeks, there was still lots of last minute things to do, and there was a hectic rush back to the barracks. John and the others had bags packed with whatever food could be rounded up, including emergency chocolate 'D' ration bars (courtesy of the Americans). A great deal had to be left behind: books, photos, logs, souvenirs, and all the other 'indispensable' odds and ends the Kriegies had amassed over the past three years. (Remarkably, John brought his journal with him and continued making entries during the long walk.)

At midnight, ten hours after they'd been given an hour's

warning, they were still standing by. Many men built last minute sledges to pull their things along in the snow. John and his group of eight had not. He had recommended that they each pack individual and self-contained loads in case any of them had to drop out, although they would travel as a unit and share carrying of the communal food bags. Scruffy concentrated on his clothing. In addition to wearing as many layers as possible, he wrapped a scarf around his midsection, into which he tucked spare mitts and socks. His final touch was a turban fashioned out of a second scarf that one of the boys back at Stalag Luft I had shown him how to put together. It was very effective at shielding the head against the cold.

They finally set off at 2.30 in the morning of January 28th. It was a relatively temperate 35^0 F (about 1^0 C), but there was a cold wind and blowing snow. There were possibly fortunate in not yet knowing that February would become one of the coldest months on record of the 20th Century in Europe, with temperatures falling as low as –25° C (–13° F). That cold would last until the middle of March, with blizzards and drifting snow adding to the misery of being outside without proper winter clothing or footwear. But that was yet to come.

Most of the men were issued a Red Cross parcel, but that was one more thing to carry. These boxes could weigh as much as ten pounds, so many discarded most of the contents and only held on to the chocolate. Such a waste.

They walked through the night, and by early afternoon the next day they had reached the first village on their route. John's back was aching from carrying his pack, and so he and

A sketch of one of the sledges by Ley Kenyon.

the others finally decided to build a sledge. The scene of their impromptu camp was bedlam, with over a thousand prisoners milling about a market square, trading with the locals for bread, cheese, and wood (for fuel), making and wolfing down sandwiches as they went. The civilians were starving, too, so trading was enthusiastic on both sides. You could 'buy' anything you wanted in exchange for one of the few American 'D' ration bars they still had. But they still had another 5 kilometres to walk before they could rest, so they kept moving.

By late afternoon, it had turned cold and dark, and the snow continued to blow. They trudged along single lane roads, with refugee carts and an occasional vehicle passing them in the darkness. One of the Americans had his foot run over by a truck, but thankfully it was only bruised. There was no medical help should it have been broken or worse. That close call demonstrated just how vulnerable and tired they already were, and they'd barely begun their long walk.

As evening came on, it became obvious that there was no place for them to spend the night under cover. The guards' discipline had disappeared completely, and everyone's spirits were sinking fast. Building the sledge during the stop had been the salvation of John's group, but many were on the verge of frostbite. They had to find shelter soon. By 7.30 that evening, the temperature had dropped to -20° C. They had reached the village of Selingersruh, and crowded into a farmer's barns to get out of the cold, eat something, and sleep. They had walked 28 kilometres through a winter storm that first day.

They were on the move the next morning by 8.30, after a wonderful sleep buried beneath five feet of hay, although they were so weary they likely could have fallen asleep on a bed of nails. Their destination was Muskau, thirty kilometres away. On the walk, there were hundreds of odds and ends that littered the side of the road, things the men had jettisoned once they decided there was only so much one could carry in a

snowstorm. Scruffy and his group also discarded anything they absolutely didn't need and picked up whatever they thought they might. Refugees were constantly passing them and begging for chocolate and cigarettes, but no one had anything to spare.

The German civilians they encountered in villages along the way were surprisingly friendly, and with some bartering, the boys put together a meal of biscuits, cheese, and bread, with some hot water to drink. Then they were on the move again. By midday, one of the PoWs had developed a serious case of pneumonia, and was unable to keep up. His fever was soaring, and he had started babbling deliriously when John saw him. He had to be left behind in the hope that he might find medical attention. But from whom, John wondered.

They reached Muskau by 8.00 pm on January 29th, having walked 30 kilometres in twelve hours. It had been another day of blowing snow and sub-zero temperatures. Thankfully, their sledge had worked well on this leg of the walk. The PoWs were quartered all over town: in a theatre, a glass factory, and a pottery. John's group were fortunate to be billeted in a heated horse arena on the estate of Castle von Arnim, owned by the brother of General von Arnim, late of the African Campaign (with Rommel). Their digs were palatial compared to the barn they'd slept in the previous night. Once again, civilians from the town were very friendly, and there was a brisk trading of goods between them. John managed to trade some chocolate for a loaf of bread and some beer.

Three hundred and seventy-five men slept in rows on the earthen floor of the arena that had straw scattered over it. Despite the relative comfort, some were starting to show signs of illness and exhaustion. Two of Scruffy's group – an American and a Brit – had fallen ill with stomach distress, and it looked as though they might not be able to travel the next morning.

After a long night's sleep, John began to feel human again. The arena they spent the night in was warm, and so everyone took advantage of that to attempt to dry out their sodden shoes and socks. That never happened, but at least they were able to make them less wet.

By noon on January 30th, they were told that they wouldn't be on the move again until the following day. They took advantage of the extra time to rest and continue airing out their belongings. Scruffy found a workshop on the grounds, and three of his group built a second sledge. The others went into the nearby town to look for food. Chocolate, sugar, and coffee would get the PoWs anything; cigarettes were like gold. Once again, they found the German civilians to be remarkably friendly, and always eager to trade. The townswomen were especially warm and welcoming and brought them hot water for making tea and coffee.

Ironically, one of the problems that arose was overeating. Having been starved for so many months, when the boys were able to trade for generous quantities of bread and cheese, they would stuff themselves from hunger, then suffer the consequences of stomach ailments. This was a misery when you were trudging through snow and freezing temperatures.

In two days, they had walked almost sixty kilometres on roads that first ran south-west, and then north. But that meant that, as the crow flies, they were only 40 kilometres from Stalag Luft III, which was not encouraging. The snow was beginning to let up, with good and bad consequences. It was easier keeping warm, but it was becoming increasingly difficult to pull the sledges that carried their food and belongings.

The next morning, January 31st, they received word that the two Americans in John's group were splitting off to join up with a contingent of American PoWs, who were being separated and marched to a different destination. Many of the men were now sick, either from gorging on food, the strain of the march, the ever-changing water supply, or a combination of all three. John's hut-mates Sam Sangster and Hank Sprague were beginning to suffer stomach problems as well.

They were fortunate in being able to stay and regroup in Muskau for another day. John and another friend from camp, Ed Bell, went foraging for food in town. It was easier to get in and out than he had anticipated, and he was repeatedly astonished at how friendly the people were. (Especially to Ed, who was tall, blond, and looked Aryan.) There was a perpetual stream of evacuees on the roads, all of whom had less of everything than the PoWs, who always shared whatever they could manage. Every house had at least one evacuee family billeted with them, in addition to the homeowners, but Scruffy and Ed were never turned away from offers to trade. The homeowners were particularly sympathetic upon hearing that John and Ed had been imprisoned for three years.

Word of mouth brought news that the Russians were only about 60 kilometres from Berlin (not far from Muskau), which increased the refugees' fears. The Russians were volatile and seeking revenge for years of German atrocities, and homeless migrants were at the greatest risk. There was also news that the Americans were fast advancing east and had passed the

Siegfried Line, a hypothetical German defensive line that ran approximately along the German borders with the Netherlands, Belgium, Luxembourg, and France. This was encouraging, but it was unlikely that the Americans would arrive soon enough to protect them from the Russians as they swept west across Germany.

That night, the PoWs were on the move again. But sadly another of Scruffy's group, one of the RAF airmen, found himself unable to walk any further because of exhaustion and illness. Scruffy discovered that there was a horse cart that was transporting some of the sickest men to a village where there was medical help, so that was some consolation. Now their group of eight had been reduced to five, and the supplies they were carrying began to be a burden.

At around 11.00 pm, they set off into a windy, cloudy pitch-black darkness. The column of men trampled a swath on either side of the roads they travelled. Three days previously, the Hermann Göring 1st Paratroop Panzer Division had passed the same way. Their tanks had made the roads rutted and uneven, and stripped them bare of what little snow had been left. Walking became extremely difficult. Scruffy's group abandoned the sledge that carried the dregs of their food, as pulling it had become impossible. They ate what they could, and left the rest. All they could hope was that the Germans would supply them with rations when they reached their destination.

Water was also becoming a problem. John had been very careful, making sure that anything he drank had been thoroughly boiled. But back at camp, he had taken a few sips of

water that was 'uncooked,' and by two o'clock in the morning, he was struck with diarrhoea – or *'squitters,'* as the boys called it.

They struggled on through the night towards Spremberg, stopping for a 3-hour rest at around 7.30 am. Now their exhaustion was all-consuming because of illness and having dragged sledges full of gear and supplies along bare roads. By 10.30, they were on the move again, but just barely. Most of the guys were completely worn out. Their reserve strength was spent and they continued to move purely on nervous energy. They reached Spremberg by 2.30 in the afternoon, and by nightfall they were loaded onto railway cars for the next leg of their journey. With forty men crowded into each car, there was just enough room to breathe.

There certainly wasn't enough room for all of them to lie down. Pop Collett took charge. He told the men what to do if they wanted to survive the trip in some reasonable health. They would divide the men in the boxcar into three groups. The first shift would sit, the second would lie down, and the third would stand. Everyone would stay that way for four hours and then rotate. For hygiene, he organized the cutting of a hole in the wooden floor of the car. If anyone was going to be sick or had to relieve themselves, then it went down that hole. That would control the spread of any contagion. There was some food among them, but no water.

There were inevitable displays of temper, but those were minor, and everyone settled down after the first hour or two. But the going was rough: the cars rattled and shook over the irregular rails, and at times it seemed amazing that they managed to stay on the tracks. As dawn came, with no water onboard, and no sign of stopping (apart from a short delay due to an air raid), they were beginning to get desperate.

By dawn on Sunday, February 4th, they were still shut in the boxcars and had had no water for almost twenty-four hours. Scruffy's group, like many others, wolfed down the remains of their food, the general opinion being that what they had inside, they didn't have to carry. The guards had promised water once they reached Hanover, but that city came and went without the train stopping.

At 10.00 am, they reached the city of Verden, where the train finally came to a rest to take on more coal. Scruffy said he knew how to get some water. They cracked open the big door, and he ran up to the engine. As a boy in Algonquin Park, and on his trip out west with Ignatieff, John had done a lot of exploring of the big engines. He had fooled around with the switches, levers, and gauges for the huge boilers; but most vital to their current situation, he had discovered where you could draw water from the engine's reserve tank. There were always pails up front, so he filled two buckets and hauled them back to his boxcar. The boys were in bad shape because of dehydration, but John warned them that as thirsty as they were, the water had to be 'cooked' to get rid of bacteria. Someone got a fire going, while Scruffy banged on the doors of the boxcar next in line and told them he'd bring them some pails, too.

Corporal Griese, aka 'Rubberneck,' the much-hated ferret, was stretching his legs on the far side of the train, when he spotted someone's legs running back and forth beneath one of the cars. He started taking pot shots at them, even though he couldn't see who he was shooting at. It was Scruffy, who wasn't taking any chances, so he headed back to the boxcar. He knew that Rubberneck had been responsible for more than one PoW's death, and that he felt within his rights to shoot at any prisoner who dared leave the train.

Through the long trip, Hermann Glemnitz was an exception in the ways he interacted with the prisoners, although he was not in the group of guards near Scruffy's boxcar. Whenever they made overnight encampments, Glemnitz made a point of ensuring that whatever deprivations the men suffered from, they would always have cover to sleep under at night. He also welcomed the locals who came looking to trade with the men from the dregs of their Red Cross parcels. Again, these were the kinds of exceptional actions that made Glemnitz so unique, and which no-one never forgot.

By 10.00 pm, they had reached the end of the line and detrained. Pop Collett had developed intestinal bleeding, and

Hermann Glemnitz, a great friend to Scruffy and many others.

was sent to a hospital near the camp for treatment. Scruffy was sad to lose him, as he'd been such a wonderful balancing force in the worst moments of the Long Walk and on the train. By that point, more than seventy per cent of the men suffered from gastritis, dysentery, frostbite, colds, influenza, or malnutrition – or more often than not, some combination of them.

They were marched three kilometres to their new camp, *Marlag-Milag Nord*, a German PoW camp that the Red Cross had already condemned as unfit and unsanitary. John's first impression was that it was a ghastly place, little more than a field enclosed by barbed wire with no habitable huts. It had originally been a PoW camp for seamen, but now had no lights, beds, or anything in the way of utensils or tools. There were

bales of wet wood shavings to serve as mattresses, but nothing else. They only had what they had brought with them.

The first night it rained, so Scruffy and his group built a very primitive sod shelter, which, while unglamorous, kept them moderately warm and dry until better quarters could be sorted out. A week later, huts had been cleared and made livable, but that hadn't improved things a great deal.

In Scruffy's room, there were thirty-five men living (and sleeping) in a room seventy feet long by sixteen feet wide. There were three double beds and nothing else. John scrounged pieces of a stove, and from those his group built a workable whole. They scavenged for wood and managed to collect enough to keep a fire burning for three hours each evening. The Germans continued to promise bedding, showers, salt, and cooking equipment, but few of these ever materialized.

As February came to an end, war updates continued to flow in, and the PoWs heard indefinite reports of various cities that had fallen to the Russians. Sagan (and what was left of Stalag Luft III) had been taken, and the port of Stettin, where John first escaped, was about to fall. No-one knew what the

Russians' objectives were, or how far they intended on moving west. But as the winter weather continued to make day to day life challenging, there were more pressing things to think about. The most optimistic among them suggested that there were, at the most, four weeks left in the war.

A few more beds appeared in camp, and the men held raffles for who got them. Some Canadian Red Cross parcels began to appear, which was a god-send. But the liberating Allied forces, moving rapidly east towards victory, effectively created a blockade for supplies as the Army pushed forward. This choked off the flow of parcels and Germans rations as well, making the guards as hard up as the PoWs. The Black Market outside the camp was a thriving source of goods, but the boys had to impose a communal system to control the prices. At first, some bid against others and forced prices up to new heights. During the first week of March, an egg 'sold' for ten cigarettes, and a loaf of bread went for 20.

One PoW named Bryson was shot while trading cigarettes for vegetables. There was an air raid on at the time, and although the camp wasn't the target, its boundary lights had been switched off. In the semi-darkness, Bryson negotiated the deal through the fence with a German NCO. He asked a guard if it was alright for him to cross the warning wire to the fence to complete the transaction. The guard called to another guard in the tower, who didn't answer. He took this as a 'yes,' and he waved Bryson over to the fence, whereupon the tower guard opened fire with a machine gun and hit Bryson twice in the lungs. The guard in the tower kept his searchlight on for the stretcher part to go and retrieve him. Scruffy never heard if Bryson survived his wounds.

Struggling through bitter winter conditions on the journey to *Marlag-Milag,* and now with little food to be found, the men were becoming desperately hungry. Disease became rampant. What meagre food supplies the Germans had been providing ceased to appear. So desperate was the will to live, and so bad the hunger, some resorted to eating the flesh of the bodies of men who had frozen to death or simply dropped dead.

Scruffy, Hank, and Sam had been taming the guards with cigarettes and chocolate, trying to find out what the plans for them were. They were close enough to the North Sea and England that an occasional BBC report was received, and it was clear that the Royal Navy was in complete command of the Baltic. They were treated to a dogfight between a *Focke-Wulf 190* and an RAF *Mosquito.* The Focke-Wulf exploded just out of sight, and the Mosquito flew off with a cheer from the men. Virtually no Germans planes were seen from that point on. With the Canadian and British armies moving quickly towards them, the end of the war was at hand. But BBC broadcasts warned the men not to try to escape. Conditions were extremely dangerous, with many die-hards Nazis shooting anything that moved, and hundreds of thousands of civilians and refugees trying to find some safe harbour. With the Russians possibly days away, the PoWs were safer staying together until the liberating Allied forces reached them. Everyone was on edge. Still, being so close to freedom, some could not resist the urge to escape. There were those who decided to shorten their war by leaving the camp and trying to join the Allied forces driving east towards them. Most of those men simply disappeared.

By early April, food supplies, and wood for cooking and heat, and were in scant supply. Water was only made available for one hour a day, in three twenty-minute blocks, for more than two thousand men. Just outside the camp, large German tanks pulling cannons were seen charging down roads to unknown objectives. As pressures mounted from the encroaching Allied and Russian offensives, the cornered Germans decided to move their hostages to camp near the Baltic port city of Lübeck. In that location, they would have the Baltic Sea at their back, which meant there would be one less flank to defend in the event of an attack. The senior British officers among the PoWs tried to delay this march, believing it was possible that Field Marshall Montgomery's 21st Army Group, which had crossed the Rhine into Germany, could arrive within weeks if not days, and they would be free. The German Kommandant was nervous and indecisive about how best to hold on to their power to negotiate, as the prisoners were their only bargaining chips for whatever the future held.

By April 9th, the decision was made. The Kommandant ordered the PoWs to collect their belongings and prepare to move within four hours. He made clear that failure to comply would result in the use of force. Scruffy could see that the German plan to march two thousand sick and starving men across one hundred and eighty kilometres of war-torn German, without food, water, or medical supplies, would be disastrous.

The men were already struggling day to day, and some of the guards had become paranoid and were inclined to shoot at the slightest provocation. The only beneficiaries of the move, once again, would be the Germans.

Among the PoWs, there were some who had begun to take increasingly desperate measures to survive. Scruffy was convinced that many wouldn't survive this final march, as the Germans were unable to provide food, water, or security. He knew that many of the guards wouldn't hesitate to use their weapons, as they had nothing to lose. The greatest threat, however, would be walking unprotected across Germany, which was still a country at war. The prisoners were bound to encounter fanatical Nazis and Nazi Youth, who had sworn to fight to the end. These were soldiers who not only expected to die in battle but would consider it an honour to do so.

Scruffy had come to suspect that the Germans intended this final leg of their cross-country march as a means of driving the prisoners until they died from exhaustion and malnourishment. Or worse, they were being led to camps where they would be killed in retaliation for the Allies' bombing of German cities (particularly in the region through which they would travel). The bombing raids had caused the deaths of tens of thousands of civilians in the previous two months, and the airmen had been branded '*terrorflieger*' (gangsters of the air). They would never survive if left unarmed and unprotected.

John decided that it was time to put together his own survival plan.

Chapter 19

At Large

Two thousand PoWs and a few hundred German guards set off from Marlag-Milag shortly after 6.30 pm on the evening of April 9th, but had to turn back due to heavy fog and the threat of an air raid. They spent one last night at the camp, then set off again the next morning. The long column moved slowly to maintain control and as a defensive tactic. Attacks by rocket-firing RAF *Typhoons* and *Tempests* had control of the air, and although the PoWs weren't the target, the attacks were often on objectives only a few hundred yards away from their column. It was frequently difficult to distinguish the prisoners from the Germans, which made everyone vulnerable and uneasy.

The first night was spent camped out in the open in a farmer's field. An agitated guard opened fire on a couple of boys attempting to find warmer shelter in the barnyard, and tensions among the PoWs rose to a breaking point in camp.

John went looking for a guard who he thought would be receptive to a proposal. He found a burly, middle-aged man who looked as unhappy about what was happening as the prisoners were. John offered him some cigarettes and led him to a quiet spot in the field. He had a proposal that might save the guard's life. He and three friends were going to leave camp that night and make their own way to Lübeck because he was felt certain that there were going to be serious problems on this final march. Not everyone would make it. If the guard was willing to come and act as a cover, they would work out an amnesty agreement that should keep him out of prison after the war. (The amnesty agreement was not a particularly radical idea; many German soldiers across the continent had already proposed striking such insurance arrangements.)

The guard was wary and said nothing. John said he would write up a contract, and he and the others would sign it, then tear it in half. He would keep one half, and the guard would keep the other. When the Allies liberated them in Lübeck, the guard could show his half of the paper and John would explain how the guard had helped them.

The guard asked what would be expected of him. John said he would be responsible for getting a cart, and finding a fresh horse and driver every few days along the way. He would stay in uniform and carry his rifle to make it appear as though he was escorting four PoWs. But he would have to do whatever they asked of him, and they in turn would do what they had to. The guard thought about it, weighing the dangers of his future freedom against walking cross country and being shot if German troops discovered that they were up to. He said he would have to think about it, as there was a great deal of danger. John told him they were leaving that night, so he had two hours to decide. If it were no, then it would be a simple matter to find someone else. The guard said he would let him know. John went back to the other three and reported what had happened.

He was sure the guard would come through, but had his eye on a couple of other prospects just in case.

Around midnight, the guard found John. They had their escort. He had already located a cart and a driver, who were waiting on the outskirts of the field. John roused his group – Sam Sangster, Hank Sprague, and Ed Bell – and they hit the road.

John had chosen the threesome carefully. They were all Canadians, and he knew them well. He felt confident that they would be more likely to work with him than against him. Sam was a good cook and could speak fluent German, and he had been John's roommate in the last months at Sagan. Hank was a little older and more mature than the others, which would be a good balancing factor. He had been on John's squadron back in

Hank Sprague, who was shot down the day before Scruffy, and roomed with him at Stalag Luft III.

England, and they'd become good friends in those first months. Ed was a good-looking guy, with typically Aryan features: pink cheeks, blue eyes, six feet tall, and a million-watt smile. He would be useful as a *'goat'* when they went foraging for food. He would knock on the front door of a farmhouse and engage the hausfrau's dreamy-eyed attentions, while Sam and John ducked around the back of the house and grabbed whatever they could from the kitchen. Hank would keep watch with the guard in case unwanted German company appeared.

John had decided they would keep on the move that first night and all the following day. Travelling on foot, he estimated they could make three miles an hour. The PoWs from Marlag-Milag with the guards escorting them would be lucky to move at a quarter that speed. With a head start, their foursome would stay out of sight and mind of the others. What's more, as they would be on the road ahead of them, they wouldn't be contending with two thousand other starving men hunting for food and water.

The war was now all but over, but that brought out the best and the worst in people. Many exhausted soldiers had simply tossed away their helmets and weapons, but there were thousands of fanatic Nazis who had dug in and vowed to fight to the death, and would not think twice about charging blindly into murderous machine gun fire in service of the Fatherland.

There were many other dangers. Dead German soldiers' bodies were often left booby-trapped with explosives, and would explode if Allied soldiers attempted to move or bury them. Bombing raids had destroyed most of the major German cities, causing infuriated civilians to lash out at PoWs in some areas; there were many stories of unguarded prisoners having been beaten to death. With the impending threat of the Russian and Allied offensives sweeping towards one another across the continent, and hundreds of thousands of refugees on the move, the retreating German army was trapped and panicking. If you were on the loose and weren't obviously German, you were definitely at threat. No one was safe.

And yet John felt confident they would more likely survive being on their own. He laid down his terms for how things would work. Anyone could split off on their own at any time, but when they travelled as a group, he would call the shots. He knew how to find his way across country and how to live rough. Most importantly, he understood Germans, and was very aware of the dangers they were bound to encounter. The first hard fact was that if and when they encountered armed German soldiers, it would be impossible to know what to expect from them. However, if it became clear that their guard and driving were aiding and abetting prisoners, everyone would be shot, including the German guard and driver. The first wave of Russians sweeping across Germany were known to be brutal; one Canadian soldier described them as being wild men on horseback, brandishing swords and machine guns and showing no mercy. Even the Allies, moving in quickly from the west, were likely to be edgy and fueled by the adrenaline of victory. Without proper identification or uniforms, John's group could easily be mistaken for the enemy.

To protect themselves, John said they would sleep forty feet apart from each other, and fully dressed. One of them would always remain awake. The guard and cart driver would sleep well away from the Canadians. If one of them was in trouble or was caught, he was to yell for all he was worth, which would give the others a chance to make a run for it. During the day, the PoWs would take turns sleeping in the straw-filled cart for a few hours while the others walked. The guard would be uniformed and carry his gun at all times, playing the part of the PoWs' escort. He and the driver would always ride. No more than two days would pass before the guard would find a new driver and a fresh horse in the villages they passed by. No one but the Canadians and the guard was to be told anything about what they were doing or where they were heading. Any

This is the type of horse cart that Scruffy and the others drove across Germany. (These are German soldiers going home at the end of the war.)

food they scrounged would be split six ways, and the guard and driver would get exactly the same portions as the PoWs. They would all live under the same conditions. If the guard or one of the drivers threw his weight around, then John would deal with the problem quickly and decisively.

He made it clear that being in charge had nothing to do with wanting to be the leader. But the simple fact was that he had the skills and experience that would give them a fighting edge. When they ran into problems – and he made it clear that they would – the others must never forget that with the war not officially over, their situation would always be one of kill or be killed.

He decided that they could not chance travelling on the Autobahn, as convenient as it might be, for fear of being stopped. Instead, they would travel on back country roads, using the Autobahn as a guide but remaining at a distance from it to minimize the chance of unexpected encounters. If they ran into trouble, they would head south for a few days and continue travelling parallel to the Autobahn before heading north again. By avoiding main routes, they would also avoid most villages and towns. More crucially, they would circumvent locals who would be bound to spread talk about the dubious and tattered group heading east on back roads. Still, despite all the precautions, John knew it was only a matter of time until trouble appeared.

Their first close call came two days after they had left camp. It was a hot April morning when they approached an overpass that spanned the road on which they were walking. Sam suggested they rest for a bit in the shade it provided. John agreed, but never taking anything for granted, he wanted to make sure the coast was clear. He crawled up the embankment beside the overpass and peered over. On the far side, a couple of dozen German soldiers were stretched out on the grass enjoying the sun. John crawled back down to warn the others about what was waiting for them when they heard a sound that made them scramble for cover. It was a loud and percussive, '*throb-throb-throb-throb.*' Ed shouted, '*Tiffies!*'

The Germans opened fire on the planes, as the Canadians dove into a ditch for cover. The British Typhoons swept down and raked the German troops with machine guns and rockets. When they flew off, there wasn't anything left moving on the Germans' side. Once the smoke cleared, John told them they had to get out of there immediately. If anyone spotted them, they would be suspected of calling in the attack, and would be as good as dead.

From that day on, John was extremely skittish, constantly checking over his shoulder, knowing people would always be suspicious and watching. He was especially wary about someone travelling in the same direction. If anyone gave them a double take, that meant trouble. And if they saw that person a second time, he said that would be an '*us or them*' situation.

They stayed on back roads and passed few people. Towns and villages were regularly skirted, but they occasionally passed through one because it would look more suspicious to be seen avoiding them all. John never felt comfortable or dropped his guard. A saying from his SOE training was, *'Paranoids live longer. That's the curse of having been trained in intelligence.'* As Adrian had stressed the importance of recognition and memory, and the implicit warning of a 'Double Sighting,' John searched his memory to try and remember if he had seen anyone they crossed paths with before. If so, where and when had that been?

Despite the pressure of being constantly on the watch, the journey proved to be a definite improvement over the conditions they had been struggling through for the past ten weeks. They were free to scrounge for food at isolated houses and farms. At one of the first they came across, they traded cigarettes for two dozen eggs. Every man – the guard and driver, too – popped several into their mouths and crunched them straight down, not even pausing to remove the shells. The exercise and fresh air were welcome restoratives after so many years living behind the wire. The guard played his part without question or obvious concern and proved to be very good at tracking down new cart drivers and horses, which meant that there was always a new face and a fresh ride. They settled into a comfortable routine with one man dozing in the back of the cart for a few hours, the guard and driver sitting up front, and the other three walking behind or riding on the cart's tailgate. The weather had turned warm, and the bitter winter march from Sagan to Muskau was a distant memory. They were all encouraged by how things were working out.

One particularly warm day, as they ambled down a quiet country road, John was stretched out in the back of the cart. Ed, Hank, and Sam sat sleepily on the tailgate, with the only sound being the horse and cart on gravel.

The guard muttered something under his breath, and John sat up, alert and anxious. He rubbed his eyes and looked down the road to where a grey German officer's staff car, flags flying, was driving toward them, tossing up a plume of dust behind it. John snapped at the other three to get off the cart, and he rolled off the back to join them. He whispered not to look at anyone, but to shamble along, stare at the ground, and look beaten and defeated. There was no time to say anything else.

The colour had drained from the guard's face as the car slowed down and pulled to a stop a few feet in front of the horse. The guard climbed down and saluted, perspiration pouring off him. In the car sat a colonel, two captains, and three sergeants. The colonel returned the guard's salute and asked him where the next village was. The guard pointed back in the direction they had come from and said he thought it was about four miles. The colonel stood up in the car and looked over the four men skulking behind the cart. He asked the guard what they were doing on that road. The guard explained he was escorting his prisoners to a Luftwaffe camp in Lübeck. Where had they come from? Marlag-Milag. The colonel looked at the cart with loose straw spread out in it, and said, 'A long way to travel like this, no?' The guard nodded and said that there was no other transportation for the likes of them. (In the last six months of the war, almost the entire German army was reduced to the most basic of transportation, usually on foot. Gasoline was extremely difficult to obtain.) The colonel smiled at the guard's response, then saluted and told his driver to drive on. If the day hadn't been so warm, the colonel might have wondered at the sweat pouring down the guard's face.

That encounter was sobering and reminded them of how vulnerable they were out in the open. When they reached the next village, a new horse and driver were found. They moved away from the road they had been travelling on, watchful to see if a squad of Germans was churning up dust in pursuit. When, after a couple of days, no one appeared, John believed they might have got lucky. But they were low on food, which meant they had no choice but to approach a farm or go into a village to restock. When they came to a crossroad, John suggested that he and Hank break off on a road that headed south into a forest where they would forage for something to eat. Sam and Ed would go with the cart and the Germans on the other road that headed north towards the Autobahn to look for some safe place to lie low for a day or two. They would meet back at the crossroad later in the afternoon.

Hank and John headed towards the woods. After walking for an hour, they came across a large, secluded pond deep enough to have a reasonable stock of fish. They sat down, had a wash, and cooled their feet in the water. But their hunger kept them restless. Hank dug through his pockets and came up with a couple of safety pins and lengths of twine he had tucked away for just such an opportunity. John turned over a rotten log and found a worm for each of them, and they tossed their lines in. It didn't take long before they had fish on their hooks, the only fresh fish they had seen in years. They hauled them in and lay back on the bank, full of smiles and self-satisfaction. Hank said something about how the other guys would be impressed at what they caught.

John wasn't listening. He had spotted a platoon of *Waffen-SS* troopers emerging from the forest on the opposite bank of the pond, who were now making themselves comfortable at the water's edge. (Waffen-SS were the armed military wing of the Nazis and extremely tough soldiers.) First one, and then all of them, looked across the pond at Hank and Scruffy. Under his breath, he said to Hank that they had made it that far, and one of them had to survive. When he gave the word, he would run left, and Hank should break right. But before Hank could answer, one of the soldiers pulled out a potato masher – the familiar hand grenade of the German Army – and lobbed it into the pond. It dropped near the middle, and the explosion boiled up the water, bringing dozens of dead fish bobbing to

Young Waffen-SS troopers in 1945. The longer the war lasted, the younger the German soldiers became.

the surface. One Waffen-SS trooper pointed and smiled at John and Hank and their small catch, while the others waded in and started scooping out as many fish as they could carry, all grinning and waving. Following the soldiers' example, they smiled and waved in return, then waded in and stuffed as many fish as they could fit into their satchels. They wasted no time in disappearing back into the forest and headed north to rejoin the others.

They met up with Ed and Sam, who had found a good place to camp that night, and headed there. They had more fish than they knew what to do with and laid them out in the back of the cart to dry. Two Belgians civilians came along, headed in the opposite direction and carrying a small side of pork. They had had their fill of it and were happy to trade for fish. John had also collected a small sack of snails at the pond, which none of the Canadians would touch. To the delight of the Belgians, they were added to the exchange. The day ended as a success, but there was little about it that made John comfortable.

It was now the end of the third week of April. After coming out of one of the coldest winters on record, the weather had turned unseasonably warm. For the four young men who had been underfed and stuck in damp, cold, vermin-infested quarters for years, it was glorious to have fresh air, eat well, and be slowly rebuilding their strength. They crossed the Elbe River and skirted south around Hamburg, which was under heavy attack by RAF bombers. Towns and villages became more frequent as they moved north and east, and the mundane non-military traffic they passed conveyed a sense that the war was finally grinding to an end. It was almost unimaginable that they had managed to make it through in one piece. But John had become increasingly uneasy and talked almost non-stop about being shadowed.

They followed a stream to the outskirts of a quiet town and dismissed their driver and horse. From there, it would be a straight run to Lübeck if all went well. They found a small stone bridge with an inviting pool of water underneath it, with no one around. All of them were filthy, so they stripped off and went for a swim, which made the guard very anxious. He was told to stay on the bridge and keep watch. If anyone came along, he was to keep his rifle trained on them while they were in the water and say that he was making his prisoners take a much-needed bath. Despite the guard's concerns, the four men dove in. The water was fresh and cool, and the air was full of spring. John swam underwater for as long as his lungs would hold out, feeling some welcome release from the tension.

When he came up for air, he was startled to see four giggling teenage girls standing on the bank, holding various pieces of their clothing. As the others resurfaced, the four Canadians fell quiet as they saw they had unwelcome company. They all knew immediately this was dangerous.

In any other situation, it might have been the beginning of a memorable 'Boy Meets Girl' story. There was no doubt that the girls were keen to get to know the boys better (young men were in short supply in Germany at that time), but this was a disaster waiting to happen. If they were caught anywhere near young German women in a situation like this, naked as they were, they would be shot. If they so much as flirted then went on their way, the girls would undoubtedly make it the talk of the village, and the four of them would be hunted down.

John shouted at the guard to get rid of them, but he had frozen with fear and didn't respond. He then told Sam to try and get them to leave, but the girls only giggled some more and playfully moved further away holding the clothes. Sam told the guard to warn the girls they were damned serious. The guard nodded stiffly and shouted at the girls to leave, and gestured with his rifle to emphasize the point. They continued laughing, but dropped the clothes and left with a few flirtatious backward glances.

The four of them quickly got dressed, found a new horse and driver, and moved away from the village while trying to draw as little attention to themselves as possible. John estimated they were still at least four or five days walk from Lübeck. The firing of big artillery guns were a constant presence in the distance, which meant there was an army close at hand; but it was anyone's guess whose army it was. This compounded the dangers they were already facing. John decided they had better reconnect with the main group, as they were in the home stretch of the journey. They headed back towards the Autobahn to search for the column of PoWs to rejoin them.

Walking alongside an orchard on a deserted road, someone began shooting. They couldn't tell where this was coming from, or even if they were the target. Hank spotted the sniper hiding behind a tree, obviously taking aim at them. John told the guard to say something and explain they were prisoners. The guard tried, but with no success. The sniper edged out from his hiding place, and it was clear that he was a Hitler Youth, and had no intention of letting anyone live. He looked about sixteen, and seemed possessed. John recognized him from the village where they'd gone for a swim. He'd been standing at a distance, but had stared so intently that he was impossible to miss.

His reckless firing kept them from being able to move, but he wasn't a good shot. He reloaded and edged towards them with his gun levelled, shouting that they were all going to die. John told the guard to give him his rifle. He loaded a round into the chamber, aimed, and took the boy down. He handed the rifle back to the guard and said they had to get moving. They

Hitler Youth taking target practice. In the last months of the war, they were very young but fanatically devoted to the Fuhrer, and would never surrender. They willingly died for the Reich.

were going to have trouble because of this, and others were probably already on their way. The cart driver was terrified, convinced that he would be next. John told him that, with the guard's help, he would be safe as long as he stayed with them until they reached the Allied camp in Westerau, just south of Lübeck. He nodded his head but said nothing.

They now headed as quickly as they could move for the Autobahn. It would be the only way they could find the other PoWs, assuming they had made it this far. They had no choice but to leave themselves exposed on the main road; there was no turning back or any purpose in keeping to back roads. The close call with the girls, and now with the Hitler Youth, meant that someone had taken notice and were talking about them. He guessed they were still two days away from Lübeck, and hoped they could make it. In the distance, they could see the highway about 3 kilometres distant, which was encouraging.

They heard the trouble before they saw it. A *Kübelwagen* (the German Army's version of a jeep) was approaching quickly. John told the others to ignore it and just keep moving. But it pulled up close behind them and ground to a halt. A Hauptmann barked at them to stop moving. He climbed out with his pistol drawn and approached them. He ordered them to put up their hands, and the guard to lay down his rifle. There was a flurry of questions directed at the guard and the driver, who were now shaking badly. John understood fragments of what was being said, but that was enough.

The Hauptmann was taller than John by about five inches. He took this into consideration when the Hauptmann turned

A Kübelwagen, the German Army's version of a jeep.

his back for a moment. John struck him with all of his strength with a hammer-like blow of his hand, hitting him at a vulnerable spot between his neck and shoulder blade. When dealt correctly, it could be a killing blow, something he'd learned in his SOE training. Being shorter than the man made it difficult, but the German dropped without a sound. John checked him swiftly and said he thought he was dead. But whether he was or not, they had to move now. Everyone had been stunned into silence, so John barked at them that they had to go.

They reached the Autobahn within the hour. The highway looked deserted, and they started walking along its shoulder. They agreed that from this point forward, everything was a threat, and should any vehicles approach, the PoWs would slip down the embankment and hide, leaving the guard and the driver with the cart.

May 1ˢᵗ, 1945 was their second to last day on the road, although they didn't know that yet. There had been no activity on the road when, in the distance, a small convoy of vehicles headed their way. The Canadians jumped off and lay flat on the embankment. A convoy of four German staff cars drove past headed west, the largest with its convertible top open and flags flying, signifying an occupant of senior rank. The cars passed close enough that John was able to recognize Admiral Karl Dönitz, whom Hitler had appointed his successor for control of the Reich. (Hitler had shot himself two days earlier, although no one was yet aware of that.) John thought that the convoy could be a German delegation on its way to meet with Allied commanders to negotiate a surrender. If so, the end of the war was at hand.

However, that also meant that anyone could be a target. John believed that events would quickly boil out of control within hours of an announcement of surrender. They had to find the main group as soon as possible. They got moving, and two hours later came upon an Allied military sign that read, 'Westerau Up.' This was army language indicating that the Allied camp at Westerau was directly ahead.

Their last day on the road, things began to change; they could almost feel something in the air. As they approached Westerau, two kilometres southwest of Lübeck, the guard and driver disappeared without a word. They walked into what appeared to be a deserted village with a couple of dozen buildings on its main thoroughfare, but no sign of where the camp was. An old stone schoolhouse looked promising as a place to take shelter and figure out what to do next.

A German civilian suddenly appeared from between two of the houses, and he started walking down the street, oblivious to them, with a newspaper tucked under his arm. Then a shot cracked out from the schoolhouse, and he fell dead. The four PoWs dropped to the ground to wait for following fire. But whoever had fired the shot apparently hadn't seen them yet, so they stayed lying flat. The schoolhouse door opened, and John saw a group of young, heavily armed Waffen-SS soldiers inside, most of them looking like they were still in their teens.

The Canadians doubled back to find another route to the Allied compound. They came face to face with a British tank that was an advance reconnaissance patrol of the British 11th Armoured Division, which was spearheading the unit's advance

Young Waffen-SS troopers taken prisoner at the end of the war.

on Lübeck. The tank commander challenged them, but they were able to convince him of who they were. They described the pocket of Waffen-SS troopers holed up in the schoolhouse. The commander thanked them, pointed them in the direction of the camp, and his tank rolled forward. Five minutes later, they heard and felt the concussion of the tank's high explosive shells destroying the schoolhouse and the Waffen-SS soldiers inside.

Within an hour, they were reunited with the others from Marlag-Milag, and could rest easy for the first time in weeks. They had survived the brutal Winter March, and a hundred and eighty-kilometre walk across enemy territory.

Word spread quickly that Scruffy, Hank, Sam, and Ed had showed up. Bill Jennings, the Second in Command (2IC) of the camp, who stood six and a half feet tall, tracked them down to debrief them. He had assumed they were dead. After three weeks on the road, the four of them looked tanned, well-fed, and healthy. John had weighed a hundred and twenty-four pounds when he had set out from Sagan, and was a hundred and sixty-one by the time he reached Lübeck. The PoWs they had left behind at Marlag-Milag had been able to scrounge food on their march, but only enough to keep from starving. Still, many had died or gone missing. Jennings said had he known what they were up to, he would have come with them. Bill then debriefed John about what he'd seen and encountered on his walk from Tarmstedt. Scruffy told him their story, giving the carefully considered version that he, Hank, Sam, and Ed had

German soldiers in Lübeck, days before their surrender.

agreed upon, which seemed to satisfy Bill.

When that was done, John went off by himself and was unexpectedly wracked by emotion. He became tearful and inconsolable, leading him to write a long, impassioned letter to Fran describing all he had been through, and all the feelings that were now consuming him. The following day, he pulled himself together and gave the letter to Bill Jennings, asking him to see that it got mailed.

The prison camp they were in was a farm that the Allies had commandeered from a German general. There were few buildings, and so most of the men slept rough in storage sheds and barns. At least they were free of the lice and bedbugs that had plagued them for the past four years. The Germans who had been guarding them were too exhausted to do anything to control the prisoners, and many simply walked away to try and find their way home. As a result, for the first time in three and a half years, John and the others were free men. That being said, *'Do Not Escape'* orders had been posted around camp because security around Lübeck was non-existent. Until the Allied forces met up with them, the farm was their only safe haven.

Outside the camp, it was extremely volatile and incredibly dangerous. The Russians were sweeping in from the east, raping and pillaging everything in their paths. Their officers often gave their men a free pass to do anything they wanted in a city for seven days before imposing order again. German civilians were on the run, carrying everything they owned on their backs and sharing horrific stories about the wrath of the Red Army. Compounding the confusion were the hundreds of thousands of displaced and homeless refugees, ragged and starving, trying to find their way to whatever their new life might be. Tens of thousands of concentration camp survivors, unimaginably emaciated and ill, with nowhere to go, were beginning to be freed. And then there were hundreds of thousands of German soldiers returning on foot from the front, trying to find what might remain of their families and their homes. The more robust among the concentration camp survivors often lashed out with a furious vengeance against these debilitated German soldiers, sometimes physically tearing their former oppressors apart with their bare hands. For several uneasy weeks at the end of April, parts of Germany were considerably more dangerous than anything the soldiers had previously known.

In Lübeck, a unit of vengeful Nazis sank two prison ships in the Harbour. One ship was full of Poles, Gypsies, and other non-Aryans, and the other was full of Scandinavians. This was a tipping point for some prisoners. Hearing what had happened, a group of Scandinavian PoWs in the camp got hold of some guns and headed into to town to even the score. Bursts of gunfire could be heard through the night, and if a German in uniform were spotted looking as though he was trying to hide or escape, he was shot dead on sight.

As Allied tanks and troops arrived and took command of the camp, German soldiers were rounded up and moved into a holding area of their own not far from the Allies. They were allowed out of their compound at 7:00 am to hunt for food, but had to report back at 7:00 in the evening. Many despised having the tables turned and refused to submit to the orders of their former prisoners. To establish authority, a few PoWs were asked to identify guards or German soldiers who had behaved with egregious and inhuman brutality, and would, therefore, be candidates for punishment. Everyone agreed that the universally hated ferret, Rubberneck, was an obvious choice. No one knew what happened to him once he had been identified and hustled off, but he was never seen again. Others were beaten, shot, or crushed beneath the treads of tanks. It was a brutal close to the war. The Germans' rebelliousness was quickly subdued.

Bill Jennings came to Scruffy with questions about a guard who had been arrested and was babbling an unlikely story about some agreement he had signed. He took John over to a security cage where the guard who had accompanied them from Marlag-Milag stood, looking very anxious. John confirmed that it was true, and described how they had signed the contract, then torn it in half. John produced his half, which perfectly matched the guard's. Satisfied that the terrified man was who he said he was, Jennings asked John what should happen to him.

The guard looked grey and beaten and was clearly expecting the worst. John said to let him go; he had got them there in one piece. He had kept his eyes closed when he had to, and wide open when they needed him. He had played his part without complaint and had done them a great service. The agreement should be honoured. The guard was released and he happily disappeared after throwing away his helmet and gun. John and the others never knew his name. It was safer that way for them all.

By May 4th, even though Germany had not officially surrendered, the few remaining German soldiers around Lübeck who weren't being held for war crimes had fled. A new sense of security afforded the PoWs an opportunity to stretch their legs and roam a bit beyond the fences encircling the farm, although Bill Jennings still encouraged everyone to stay close to the camp, as there was safety in numbers. The PoWs had little choice but to stay put and wait for due process to be repatriated.

Civilians in Lübeck were warned that if all weapons weren't surrendered, retribution would be swift and harsh. Within days, there was a mountain of arms in the city square, a storey and a half high: rifles, shotguns, swords, even antiques dating back two hundred years. Four entrepreneurial PoWs talked the guards monitoring this cache into letting them take a couple of dozen of them to pay for a road trip to Paris. They liberated a car sitting next to an abandoned house, its keys in the ignition, and scrounged a dozen Jerry cans of gas from the tank corps. The foursome headed out on the Autobahn for Paris. About a mile into their trip, as the car reached fifty mph, it exploded, having been booby-trapped. The doors blew off comically, like something from the Keystone Kops, and the four were thrown from the car, miraculously unscathed apart from scrapes and bruises. They limped back to camp with their holiday plans in tatters, but with a good story to tell. Another PoW had more success. He broke into a jewelry shop in Lübeck and managed to buy his way south to France with his takings.

John found a beautiful Mercedes convertible but had to return it at Jennings's insistence because it belonged to the local doctor. There was such elation at being free. Just being able to move about without having to watch for the Gestapo, or worry about being shot for looking at someone the wrong way, or accidentally stepping over the wire into No Man's Land, was positively heady.

John relished exploring the rural flotsam outside the city. In a copse of trees, he found an abandoned *Messerschmitt 262*, the world's first operational jet fighter. It saw limited action in 1945 as a multi-role warplane for the Luftwaffe and was dubbed *der Schwalbe* (the 'Swallow'), because the swallow, when in a dive, is one of the fastest birds known. The ME-262 was faster than any Allied aircraft, but its development came too late in the war to transform it into an effective weapon.

He had just put his hand on the latch that would fold down the retractable step used to climb into the cockpit, when a thick Cornish accent stopped him, suggesting that he'd best not pull or open anything. John protested that he didn't see what harm there was in just having a look. A short and sturdy sergeant said he was in charge of the Bomb Disarmament unit, and that the *Schwalbe* had been booby-trapped. If John were to pull down the step that he was about to unlatch, the charge would blow his hand off. If he attempted to open the canopy, there was another charge that would blow his hand off, too. The engine hood had the largest explosive secured to it, which would remove all traces of John if he fiddled with that. John gently withdrew and moved away from the plane. The sergeant said he had disarmed several of them, and invited John to come back in a day or two when he had finished tidying this one up.

An abandoned Messerschmitt 262. Retreating German soldiers frequently booby-trapped anything they left behind.

O n May 7ᵗʰ, two civilians appeared at the camp asking to see if they could speak to 'Scruffy' Weir. Bill Jennings found John sleeping in a barn and told him that there were a couple of *'civvies'* looking for him. John sat up and tried to make sense of this. He was reminded of what had happened at Castletown when the officer had dropped by to say hello. Who would know his name *and* his squadron nickname, let alone how to find him when Europe was being turned upside down? Something wasn't right.

Jennings said that they had been sent to escort him to an airstrip near Lübeck, where he would be flown to Bruges. John said no, that would not be happening. Jennings said they looked straight and had the requisite paperwork and ID, but John shook his head. No one was 'straight' in this part of the world at that moment in time. For all he knew, the men had tracked him down for any number of dubious reasons, from a personal vendetta to a Gestapo execution order. He refused to see them.

Bill left to report this, then returned a few minutes later, asking on what terms he *would* be willing to talk to them. John had thought about this. He said that if they were searched and had their weapons taken from them, he would consider it. He added that they should be checked for ankle pods, one of the tricks he had learned from the intelligence community. When the men were searched, both were wearing them, with knives and pistols tucked inside. John told the men to strip down to their underwear, at which point they were completely unarmed.

He talked to them alone as they got dressed. John said he would keep their weapons. One of the men protested, saying that he was MI5 and was required to carry his pistol at all times. John cut him short, saying that whoever they were, they were most definitely *not* MI5. He told them to try again, and that he would know whether they were telling the truth or not. The two men conferred with one another, and then one of them asked if the letters 'S-O-E' meant anything to him. (During the war years, and for some time afterwards, the SOE was unknown outside of government security circles. But John was very familiar with them through Adrian.) Yes, he said, those letters *did* mean something to him, and he believed they were now telling the truth. Still, he wanted to know why they had come looking for him. There was little they were able to tell him, other than that they had received their orders from Adastral House.

With this, John agreed to go, but only if they rode in the front, and he and a friend sat in back with the guns. They agreed. John collected his things and asked Sam to come along for the ride. The two of them sat in the back and were driven to a nearby airstrip where a plane was waiting. John was still cautious but climbed onboard. The men drove Sam back to the camp.

Inside the aircraft, the pilot introduced himself, but had no more information to offer other than that they were headed for London. He asked John if he would like to have his spirits lifted flying home via Cologne. John said sure, but was curious what he wanted to show him, and who had arranged this flight.

Cologne had been completely devastated by bombing in the past five months. The city had no water, no electricity, and was little more than a shell, much like Frankfurt and Hamburg. Flying over the ruins of the old city eased some of John's bitterness of the past three and a half years. It had nothing to do with the innocent people who had died in the bombing. What this shattered city represented to John was, he hoped, the obliteration of the Nazis and the Third Reich.

A devastated Cologne at the end of the war. Miraculously, the historical cathedral survived fourteen hits from aerial bombing, and remained standing tall in an otherwise flattened city.

Chapter 20

Family Reunion

The plane refueled in Bruges, then landed in England a few hours later. John was escorted to a hotel near Marble Arch for a security debriefing. All PoWs and Evaders (those who were shot down behind enemy lines and evaded escape) were debriefed on their return to England as a matter of course.

In John's case, the questioning quickly became more complicated. Much of what he was asked to talk about was confidential, at least in his consideration, and there were many questions he avoided answering. As a result, he was detained a great deal longer than was normal. His interrogators treated him with suspicion and hostility, believing he was being willfully deceptive. John answered questions about his experiences on the squadron, being shot down and questioned by the Gestapo, and what he had seen in the various camps. But he did not speak of everything that he had seen and done.

His interrogators were arrogant with the exhilaration of the Allied victory and the war's end, declaring that the 'Krauts' had been shown who was in charge once and for all. The immediate post-war was a curious period when there was an almost unbridled optimism for the future. They asked John if what he had seen hadn't convinced him of a permanent and lasting peace. John said no, that he believed there was a new and significant threat: the Russians. His interrogators belittled his comments.

But John held firm about what he had seen and what he believed was coming. He said that the Russians were vengeful after what the Germans had done, and they wanted retribution, and quite possibly a lion's share of post-war Europe. After listening to what he had to say, his interrogators told him he was going to be detained indefinitely for more questioning. He challenged them, saying they had no grounds and wouldn't be able to follow through. One of the men said, *'Because you think you have some hot shot connections. Is that it?'* John repeated that he thought they were bluffing and said nothing more. He had been grilled by far more skilled and cold-blooded interrogators.

The young officers had hit a dead end trying to question him. Like others, they felt he wasn't telling them the whole story, but they had no idea what that might be, nor how to pry any more information out of him. After a second day of non-responsive questions, he was moved under guard to another hotel off Trafalgar Square on the afternoon of May 8th, and locked in his room.

It was VE Day – Victory in Europe – and John could hear the cheering crowds outside celebrating, exasperating him even more. He became extremely frustrated and harangued one of his guards to be allowed to make a phone call. Permission was eventually granted for this, but the guard would have to be present. John agreed.

He had the operator connect him to Air Commodore

May 8th, 1945, VE (Victory in Europe) Day in Trafalgar Square, London.

Chamier at Adastral House, and when Adrian came on the line, his first words were the same as Bill Jennings had been in Westerau: *'Johnny, where the hell have you been? And where the hell are you?'*

All he knew was that he was being held in a hotel whose name and location were unknown to him, other than that it was somewhere near Trafalgar Square. He had been under interrogation since he'd been flown in two days earlier. Adrian said he was glad John had been able to make the connection. John expressed his admiration at having been able to locate him, but he was now being held indefinitely. They were refusing to release him as he was a security risk.

Adrian told John to put the guard on the line. The young

intelligence officer picked up the receiver and listened wordlessly for a few minutes before he said, 'Yes sir,' and hung up. An hour later, a car arrived at the hotel and drove John to the Chamier's.

Adrian wanted to hear precisely what had happened, from the day he had been shot down, to the day that the SOE agents came looking for him in Lübeck. He already knew an astonishing amount: about John's escape from the train, that the bartender at the fateful whorehouse in Stettin was part of a resistance cell, and that Jens Müller, John's friend in Stalag Luft III, was part of Norwegian intelligence. (Jens was one of the three PoWs from the Great Escape who had made it safely to a neutral country.)

Adrian had John recount in minute detail his experiences through the war. Again and again, he asked if John's cover had been compromised; had he done anything that might incite retribution; who had he killed, and more importantly how, why, when, and where. John told Adrian everything he had been through, which was both a relief and an emotional ordeal. He said he felt as though he was being tracked during the last few weeks on the road in Germany. Adrian thought this was very likely. Communications had been intercepted from the Abwehr indicating that a Canadian of interest was at large, and he was to be located and arrested. It appeared the Germans did not know who he was, but that would only be a matter of time. He thought John had been extremely fortunate.

After two days of talking, Adrian said that he had what he needed. But he reminded John that there was much that he must never speak of again to anyone, particularly should he feel a sudden and overwhelming need to unburden himself. What he had gone through and endured had changed him, regardless of how he felt at that moment. He must prepare himself for a psychological, emotional, and possibly even physical backlash that could hit him at any time - perhaps in a few months, or possibly years from now. But that, too, he must keep to himself. That was the price of the work they had undertaken.

Adrian suggested that until he received his orders to return to Canada, he stay with his sister, Nancy, who had a flat a few blocks away. She had just returned from North Africa, where she had been embedded as an SOE agent (which John knew nothing about). Adrian told him to enjoy himself and come to

Nancy was a FANY: a First Aid Nursing Yeomanry volunteer. This fiercely independent organization of women drove ambulances and set up troop canteens under appalling and usually extremely dangerous conditions. But Nancy, like so many FANYs, used their organization as a cover for their real work in sabotage and espionage for the SOE behind enemy lines. Auntie Ted served with the SOE, and she was more than likely the one who recruited Nancy.

terms with being clear of the firing line.

During the weeks he stayed with Nancy, John slept long hours (in a bathtub, as there weren't enough beds in the flat), took day trips, and simply enjoyed himself. Being on the loose in post-war London helped immeasurably with his transition back to civilian life. Everything was rationed, but there was more of most things than he had seen for years.

He got used to people looking at him differently. His surgical scars were mending, and his eyes were beginning to feel normal again; but he had been burned, and those scars would remain. Patty Boyer, a friend of Nancy's, said, *'You're an awfully nice guy, John, but you're no great hell to look at.'*

This didn't bother him. He had been through so much by that point in time that such comments rolled off his back. What *was* challenging were the memories of all that had happened since he arrived in England four and a half years earlier. He had been in touch with Fran by telegram, but she had never received the letter he'd written at Westerau and given to Bill Jennings to mail shortly before he was flown to London.

When John ran into Bill in London, he asked what had happened to it. Bill said that as his commanding officer in camp, he had read the letter and then destroyed it. The despair and darkness it contained were overpowering, and Bill could see no possible good coming from sending it to his fiancée.

John could remember nothing of what he'd written, but Jennings' prudence reinforced what Adrian had told him and what John had already known. He had to keep the wrenching events and the emotions that had defined the final months of his war to himself.

He was going home to Fran, and to a fresh start in life.

Chapter 21

Home

John returned to Canada a month later, in June 1945. His ship landed at Montreal, where his parents and Fran were waiting to welcome him. The returning veterans had been mustered into orderly ranks, while a politician began a rambling speech welcoming them, and thanking them for their service to their country. John weathered about thirty seconds of this before hoping over the barrier and dashing across to hug everyone.

John and Fran were married in October 1945. They had kept in contact the whole time he was overseas, with constant letters back and forth. Both she and their families knew about his injuries, but as Fran said, *'I didn't care one bit about how bad he thought he looked. He was alive, and that was all that mattered to me.'*

They were married for almost 64 years. John said, *'I did all right because I had the right wife. She and I could dance like a son of a gun. Maybe it was subconscious, but I thought if we could dance that well together, maybe we could work well together, too. And that's exactly how it worked out.'*

Coming home could be a difficult transition for most servicemen and women. Frequently, they had undergone substantial changes while in service, but the world they left behind had not. Sometimes 'home' was no longer capable of comfortably accommodating them, and work could be tough to find.

When John returned to '*Civvy Street*' (demobilized back to civilian life), he found it challenging trying to figure out how to earn his living. Work was anything but plentiful. The investment world was familiar ground to him, but a job with *McLeod Young Weir* was not an option. After considering various professions, he applied to *Wood Gundy*, another investment firm in Toronto. They were interested in taking him on, but there were no positions in the city. However, there were opportunities on the road, and so John began driving through rural Ontario, selling securities and bonds from the trunk of his car. One of the things that kept John so vital was his enthusiasm for whatever was coming up next. And so he took on this unconventional 'travelling stock broker' role with affability and a sense of humour about himself.

He had a deep and sincere interest in meeting new people, which always served him well; he had the common touch. After several years on the road, working through small Ontario towns, he had become more successful than the other sales reps at *Woody Gundy's* head office in Toronto. He was offered a position there, where he stayed until he retired (somewhat reluctantly) at the age of 80. Even then, he thought he was too young.

He had been raised to believe that if you didn't make time for others, you would never be any use to yourself. He was one of the founders of the *Canadian Warplane Heritage Museum* in Mount Hope, and *African Lion Safari* in Flamborough, Ontario. He joined the board of *Women's College Hospital* in Toronto, just to lend a hand. But *Women's College* became a significant focus of his energies and extensive community work for the rest of his life.

He got truly involved with whatever he became a part of, and tried to make a difference. He volunteered at the *Warplane Museum* during special events, taking tickets and handing out information. But he frequently enjoyed wearing a pair of battered trousers and a threadbare jacket when he did so. Scruffy liked being able to interact with people and watch them, with no-one taking the slightest notice of him. Few ever knew that the amiable character who tore their tickets and showed them where to park was one of the *Museum's* founders and principal benefactors.

He was always moving forward, never wanting to get too caught up in the past. His philosophy was, *'Look back, but don't stay there.'* But he maintained close contact with the guys from the war years. Brian Floody, Wally's son, remembers laughter-filled evenings at the Floody's when John dropped by to see his old friend, as well as George Harsh. (George lived the last years of his life with the Floodys.) Wally became the advisor to the 1963 film, *The Great Escape.* Dick Bartlett, the 'Canary' keeper, had been approached to do this, too, but had to decline as he was still in active service as a *Lieutenant Commander, Flying,* with the Royal Canadian Navy.

Paul Phelan, John's pal from Camp Borden and Trenton, worked for his family's business, *Cara Operations*, of which John became a board member; Deane Nesbitt joined his father's investment firm, *Nesbitt Burns*; Ormie worked in the chemical industry; and Jeep Neal went into business in Montreal.

They all got together once a year for a barbeque, often at Ormie's beautiful property near Waterloo. At those get-togethers, the ex-fighter pilots could unwind and talk about things that no-one else would understand. There were Stalag Luft III reunions, too, with Wings Day and other old friends in attendance. (Hermann Glemnitz was invited as a special guest of the PoWs to a 1970 reunion in Toronto, all expenses paid.)

Hughie and John remained close for the rest of their lives. Hughie retired from the service as a highly decorated Wing Commander and one of the RCAF's acknowledged 'Aces.' After the war, he became a doctor and worked across Canada. He and John never lived in the same city again, but they got together whenever possible. Driving back to Toronto from one of Ormie's barbeques in Waterloo, they got wrapped up telling stories and making each other laugh. Fran, who had been asleep in the back seat, poked her head up and asked where they thought they were headed. Lost in conversation and chuckles, they had driven a hundred miles past Toronto and were well on their way to Montreal.

There was a saying in the air force: *'There are old pilots and bold pilots, but there are no old bold pilots.'* George 'Buzz' Beurling was generally recognized as Canada's most famous pilot of WWII. Beurling flew with Hughie during the war, and Hughie thought Buzz was technically the finest fighter pilot he had ever known. But he also found him *too* bold and *too* reckless.

John never was. He had learned to analyze a situation carefully before taking action, then to act quickly and decisively. While most men were still pondering what to do, John was already in motion. His ability to analyze, weigh options, and make critical decisions in an instant set him apart. Perhaps this was because he had been raised to think independently, to be self-reliant, and to take full responsibility for his choices, good or bad.

There were so many who had shaped and influenced him. Gordon had been a model of discipline and pragmatic thought and action. He led by example and instilled in John the inestimable value of a life lived for others, as he'd done with the families he had helped escape from Europe before the war. Adrian was endlessly inventive, always looking for creative solutions, and refusing to let standard procedures constrain him. He and John both celebrated the importance of thinking differently. Fiji instilled a life-long love of the natural world. Deane taught him to do his job without getting emotionally wrapped up in it. Roger Bushell astonished John with his focus and single-minded determination. And Wally's fearlessness in the tunnels was always inspiring. There were few people that John encountered in life from whom he could not, or did not, learn something. It was in others that he found the joy of being alive.

He embodied this empathy for others when he was a PoW. In the last year of the war, food had become scarce, and many men had sunk into black holes of depression and suicidal thoughts. Scruffy made a point of talking to them, and helped them find ways to hold on. There were many from Luft III who never forgot what he'd done for them. And like his father, he had endless stores of patience for fellow vets who continued to be challenged by life years afterwards.

But like most, what he had undergone during the war had a profound effect on him. As Adrian had predicted, it came back to haunt him. So many people in his life had died. Pat Chamier, Auntie Ted and Uncle Adrian's youngest son; Paul Henderson, Joe Reynolds, Freddy Watson, and Bruce Hanbury, friends on 401 Squadron; Gardner, his wing man; reckless young pilots he had known who had died in training. Adrian's air cadets, caught in the crossfire of war. And from Stalag Luft III, he knew all of the executed PoWs - *The Fifty*. But Hank Birkland and Tom Kirby-Green stood out, both having been close friends. John kept all those names and faces and emotions deeply buried. But he never forgot.

In June 1944, British Foreign Secretary Anthony Eden addressed Parliament, promising that 'Exemplary Justice' would be served on those responsible for the murders in Stalag Luft III. Finding those who were guilty could take many years; but for John, that did not matter.

Walking through London in the weeks before he had returned to Canada in 1945, a stranger materialized beside him, and said they were seeking justice for '*The Fifty*.' Would he help? John immediately pledged his support. A dead drop (to exchange information) was arranged, and the stranger vanished again into the crowd. He was working on behalf of a covert mission, well underway, that sought to methodically track down all of the Gestapo directly involved in, and responsible for, the executions. Although there was no obvious connection to Adrian, John knew that *Acquisitor* was playing a part.

Adrian died in 1974, but John's relationship with the network never ended. Post-war, its focus continued to be finding and identifying war criminals. When his services were required, he would receive a phone call at his office – never at home – and the voice on the other end would recite a string of numbers. John would make note of these, eliminate the irrelevant ones, and then call from an outside phone booth. A voice would give John the specifics for his assignment, frequently as a part of his business trips. *Acquisitor* always knew when he was travelling abroad, although John never had any idea how. It was common for him to receive a phone call a few days before leaving, with an assignment specific to the country to which he was headed.

Such as Austria, where he travelled to visit clients and went skiing every year. Or in Switzerland, where he'd gone for a friend's daughter's wedding (his assignment was tracking down a Nazi who had stolen millions in jewels from a Russian family during the war). In both countries, he never lost the feeling of being watched and followed. An assignment in the late 1970s had particular personal resonance for him. A business trip to Buenos Aires brought him a mission to locate and identify two

Nazis who had had direct involvement in the execution of *The Fifty*. He found them, and in time, *Acquisitor* ensured that exemplary justice was served.

His most difficult assignment was monitoring an elderly war criminal who had created a new identity, and assimilated himself into an upscale neighbourhood in Canada. Despite his maintaining a scrupulously low profile, *Acquisitor* had found the man, and John was given the assignment of keeping him under surveillance. He was aware that any connection made between him and this fugitive could put his family at risk. But he continued to honour the code by which he'd been raised: if you were *able* to do something that was of importance, then you *must* do something.

To the end of his life, John believed that Hitler's Nazi culture continued to thrive, and was being passed down to third and fourth generation descendants of the war years. He never ceased to question the critical importance of gathering intelligence to defend against potential attacks. With Scruffy, such vigilance had been bred in the bone.

Adrian's warning about the past revisiting John came late in his life. There was so much that he had seen and done – all the people and events that he had managed to keep buried within himself. That was part of the pact with *Acquisitor*. It was also one he'd made with himself at the end of the war.

But those years of holding so much locked away eventually took their toll.

Thirty years after he had rebuilt his life in Canada, John's subconscious began reliving experiences and emotions that had long been forgotten. This began dramatically with nightmares from which he could not be roused. When he awoke, his body was drenched in sweat, although he had no memory of his dreams. Then fragments of the past slowly began to revisit him during his waking hours, and the past became a part of him again.

Like all combat pilots, John and Hughie had been in a state of extreme anxiety when they scrambled and flew off into battle, but without having any conscious fear. Being in combat was a blur. Engine noise and adrenaline blotted out everything but the endless and immediate 'Now.'

It was not until years later that John began to recall that when he landed after a dogfight, his tunic and flight gear were soaked through with sweat. (Fighter pilots often lost pounds during combat.) In those days, Scruffy would unbuckle his parachute, head to the Mess, and gulp down a quart of milk and a couple of Mars bars before he began to feel anything like himself again.

Combat veterans' bodies absorbed inconceivable levels of stress. They managed to do what had to be done by forcing the violence they encountered back into the darkest recesses of their minds. That, compounded with the loss of friends, forged memories that their subconscious minds and aging bodies could not forget. John's body relived those intense and nerve-wracking moments, when (in Patrick Bishop's words, author of the wonderful *Fighter Boys*), the young pilots "*...crossed the threshold of fear and became warriors.*"

Shortly after he turned eighty, John gave a Remembrance Day talk at the *Albany Club* in Toronto about his wartime experiences. He shared the crazy things that he and the other boys had got up to, and had his audience entranced and laughing.

Then he was suddenly overcome by a wave of crippling emotion and tears, and had to abruptly excuse himself, unable to continue. The past had come roaring back into the present without any warning. After that, he declined such invitations.

Some months later at a party, a friend's son showed John a plastic model of a Messerschmitt. It looked exactly like the *ME-109* that had killed Gardner and nearly killed him. Anxiety and panic completely overtook him, and he began to shake. He had to ask that the toy be taken away. His subconscious mind and body remembered vividly what he had laboured consciously for so long to leave behind.

Towards the end of his life, there were many things he found himself unable to talk about. For so many years, he'd been trained to keep his thoughts to himself, and to melt into the background with a friendly smile. His father and Adrian had instilled in him the same sensibility: keep your thoughts to yourself. Looking unremarkable was a good place to start.

But that came at a price.

When we reflect on what the men and women who served their country in wartime have endured, it would be wise for us to consider everything their subconscious minds and bodies continue to struggle with, and try to put to rest.

John spent the remainder of his life keeping far too much

buried deep within himself. He chose to live his outward existence with the fullest possible grace, purpose, and appreciation of all that life had given him.

In June 2009, John's phone rang. He had been unwell, and was resting on a couch in his living room, but happened to be near the phone. He answered in a quiet voice, and a stranger's voice read off a string of numbers. However, he was already gravely ill with an undiagnosed illness, and died three months later without ever managing to return the call.

Chapter 22

Postscript

On a cloudless afternoon in late September 2009, several hundred men, women, and children found their way out to the south field of Upper Canada College in Toronto. It would be reasonable to assume that the people, who ranged in age from toddlers to those well into their nineties, had just left a commencement ceremony, or perhaps had been the audience at some school entertainment.

What was unusual was that the well-dressed crowd remained on the grassy field, making conversation with one another and behaving as though they had no particular or better place to be. They *were* where they wanted to be.

Around two o'clock, a throaty rumble came from the southwest. Slowly everyone's eyes turned skyward to watch the silhouette of an unfamiliar aircraft come into view, flying directly towards them before making a wide and lazy circle over the field. It was a four-engine Lancaster bomber, quaint in comparison to the size of modern aircraft, but in its active years during World War II, one of the largest planes in the air. One of its four engines had been *'feathered,'* or effectively shut down, as a salute to the man that the crowd gathered below had come to celebrate. Feathering a bomber's engine is not a typical tribute to acknowledge the death of a fighter pilot. A more traditional salute would be a flypast of a squadron, flying in formation, with the fallen man's position in the formation left vacant. But the rare sight of this vintage aircraft acknowledging the passing of an extraordinary man was extremely moving; unexpected and rather graceful, and then gone as quickly as it had appeared.

It had been flown from the *Warplane Heritage Museum* to honour John 'Scruffy' Weir, whose memorial service had just taken place at UCC. The mood was a friendly get-together, an informal service enlivened by fond remembrances, a shared sense of the loss of a friend, and enlivened by the song, *'I'm Getting Married in the Morning'*, from *My Fair Lady*, one of John's favourites. There was nothing typical about any part of the event, rather like the man himself. Each person who knew him celebrated their own memory of an extraordinary man: inquisitive, mischievous, steadfast, and brave.

And above all, a true survivor.

John 'Scruffy' Weir in Stalag Luft III, July 1942.

John in front of Women's College Hospital in Toronto in 2003.

367

Hermann Glemnitz (left) and Wings Day (right) at a reunion in 1966.

John (centre) with Wings Day (right) at a Stalag Luft III reunion in Toronto, 1966.

Fran in uniform, 1942. She was working for Research Enterprises Limited (REL), located in Leaside, Toronto. REL created technologies for Canadian, British, and American military forces throughout the war, as well as for the BSC, SOE, OSS, ISI, Camp "X", and possibly MI5. Radar and Aztec were developed at this facility.

Wally Floody, Charles Bronson, and director John Sturges during the
making of the film, "The Great Escape" in 1962.

Steve McQueen, Angus Lennie, and Wally Floody during the
making of the film, "The Great Escape" in 1962.

401 Squadron flying in formation in 1941.

John Weir at the Royal Canadian Military Institute, 2001.

UNREMARKABLE

ACKNOWLEDGEMENTS

The idea for this book began when I first met John in 2001, but took on substantially more weight in 2006 when John and I began our long collaboration. We worked together on the telling of his story until shortly before his death in 2009. Since then there have been many to whom I am indebted for their support and encouragement.

First and foremost is John *aka* Scruffy Weir. Without the unquestioning trust and generosity of spirit that he showed me throughout our partnership, this book would have been without its heart and soul. He is missed.

The Weir family were all supportive and helpful: John's children, Suze, JS (John Scott Sr.), and Ian; Mary (McCormack) Bunnett, Fran Weir's sister; and of course Fran (McCormack) Weir.

Dr. Hugh Godefroy, Squadron Leader, DSO, DFC & Bar, who was every bit as delightful in later life as he must have been when he and John were stirring things up in their youth.

Garfield Mitchell, Douglas Bassett, Dr. Gail Regan and the Langar Foundation, Dr. Frederic Jackman, The Jackman Foundation, and the F.K. Morrow Foundation for their support of the ongoing Testaments Archive work.

The Canada Council for the Arts, and the Toronto Arts Council provided much needed financial assistance in the final drafts of the rewrite of the book.

Janet Joy Wilson of Penguin Random House Canada has been ever supportive and a generous friend. You're extremely good at what you do!

Donal Foley was my stalwart co-worker on some much of the original research. Without his support, I could not have accomplished nearly enough. Mark Laurie was also there in the early days, and has always provided thoughtful and pragmatic feedback.

Barb Duncan and Pierre Lalonde, both of who have always been tireless supporters of the Testaments of Honour archive, must be mentioned. Brian Floody (Wally's son), Jamie Jordan (Jimmy Jordan's son), and Anne Dumonceaux (Dick Bartlett's daughter) were all generous with their time and memories. Jamie was also a great help in final copyediting.

The many RCAF and RAF veterans who spoke with me and generously shared their experiences of these war years, including John Acheson, Tom Lane, Grant McRae, Dick Bartlett, Clem Pearce, Al Wallace, Dick Corbett, Tony Cowling, Jim Finnie, Harold (Red) Hayes, Jim Kenny, Tony Little, Lorne Shelter, John Colwell, Geoff Marlow, Jack Fleming, Don Cheney, Jack Gouinlock, John Dix, Bonnie Joan Graham, Jim Kelly, Art Kinnis, Ian Ormston, Art Sager, Cy Yarnell, Stocky Edwards, Don Lush, Don Morrison, Bill Paton, Gilles Lamontagne, and Bert Coles. Rob Davis and his detailed website on the Great Escape.

Special thanks to Stephen Boake, Laura Marquez, and Designwerke Inc. for their wonderful work on the book jacket design. Work with them if you can.

Barbara Heathcote was a dedicated and thorough copy-editor and promoter. Thank you, Mom! And Dr. Isobel Heathcote. Although she is my big sister, she is also a first-class editor for both copy and content, and was a tremendous help with an earlier telling of this story. Any remaining errors are the author's alone.

And my two lovely daughters, Elizabeth and Maggie, who are always an inspiration, as well as collaborators. Elizabeth, for her help with scanning and spreading the word, and Maggie, for her creative help with titles and other content. Thank you, my sweethearts.

Blake Heathcote
2015

BIBLIOGRAPHY

Ash, William and Brendan Foley. *Under the Wire: The World War II Adventures of a Legendary Escape Artist and "Cooler King".* London: Bantam, 2005.

Bailey, Roderick. *Forgotten Voices of the Secret War: An Inside History of Special Operations in the Second World War.* London: Ebury, 2008.

Binney, Marcus. *Secret War Heroes: The Men of Special Operations Executive.* London: Hodder & Stoughton, 2005.

Bishop, Patrick. *Fighter Boys: Saving Britain 1940.* London: HarperCollins, 2003.

Borrie, John. *Despite Captivity: A Doctor's Life as Prisoner of War.* London: William Kimber, 1975.

Brickhill, Paul. *The Great Escape.* New York: W.W. Norton, 1950.

Brickhill, Paul. *Escape – or Die.* London: Pan Books, 1957.

Buckham, Robert. *Forced March to Freedom.* London: Sentinel, 1995.

Burgess, Alan. *The Longest Tunnel: The True Story of World War II's Great Escape.* New York: Grove, 1990.

Carroll, Tim. *The Great Escape From Stalag Luft III: The Full Story of How 76 Allied Officers Carried Out World War II's Most Remarkable Mass Escape.* New York: Pocket Books, 2004.

Chamier, J. A. *The Birth of the Royal Air Force.* London: Pitman, 1943.

Clark, Albert P. *33 Months as a POW in Stalag Luft III.* Golden, CO: Fulcrum Publishing, 2004.

Clutton-Brock, Oliver. *Footprints on the Sands of Time: RAF Bomber Command Prisoners of War in Germany 1939-45.* London: Grub Street, 2003

Copp, J. Terry and Richard Nielsen. *No Price Too High: Canadians and the Second World War.* Whitby, ON: McGraw-Hill Ryerson, 1996.

Edy, Don. *Goon in the Block.* n.p.: Don Edy, 1961.

Foot, Michael Richard Daniel. *SOE: An Outline History of the Special Operations Executive 1940-1946.* London: British Broadcasting Corporation, 1984.

Forrester, Larry. *Fly for Your Life: The Story of R.R. Stanford Tuck, DSO, DFC.* London: Mayflower, 1979.

Gill, Anton. *The Great Escape: The Full Dramatic Story With Contributions from Survivors and Their Families.* Philadelphia: Review, 2002.

Godefroy, Hugh. *Lucky 13.* Stittsville, ON: Canada's Wings, 1983.

Harsh, George. *Lonesome Road.* New York: Norton & Company, 1971.

Hinsley, Francis Harry. *British Intelligence in the Second World War.* Cambridge: Cambridge University Press, 1979.

James, Jimmy. *Moonless Night: The Second World War Epic.* South Yorkshire: Pen & Sword, 2006.

Macintyre, Ben. *Agent Zigzag: A True Story of Nazi Espionage, Love, and Betrayal.* New York: Broadway Books, 2008

Marks, Leo. *Between Silk and Cyanide: A Codemaker's War, 1941-1945.* London: HarperCollins, 1998.

McIntosh, Dave. *High Blue Battle.* Toronto: Stoddart, 1990.

Mignet, Henry. *The Flying Flea: How to Build and Fly it.* Translated by the Air League of the British Empire. London: Samson, Low, Marston, & Co., 1936.

Miller, Russell. *Behind the Lines: The Oral History of Special Operations in World War II.* New York: St. Martin's Press, 2002.

Nicheol, John and Tony Rennell. The Last Escape: The Untold Story of Allied Prisoners of War in Germany. London: Viking, 2002

Pattinson, Juliette. *Behind Enemy Lines: Gender, Passing and the Special Operations Executive in the Second World War.* Manchester: Manchester University Press, 2007.

Perrin, Nigel. *Spirit of Resistance: The Life of SOE Agent Harry Peulevé DSO MC.* Barnsley: Pen and Sword, 2008.

Philpot, Oliver. *Stolen Journey.* London: Hodder and Stoughton, 1950.

Shores, Christopher and Clive Williams. *Aces High: A Tribute to the Most Notable Fighter Pilots of the British and Commonwealth Forces in WWII.* London: Grub Street, 1994.

Simmons, Kenneth W. *Kriegie.* New York: Thomas Nelson, 1960.

Smith, Sydney. *Wings Day.* London: Collins, 1968.

Soward, S. E. *One Man's War: Sub Lieutenant R.E. Bartlett, RN Fleet Air Arm Pilot.* Victoria, B.C.: Neptune Developments. Albuquerque: Neptune Development, 2005.

Vance, Jonathan F. *Objects of Concern: Canadian Prisoners of War Through the Twentieth Century.* Vancouver: UBC Press, 1994.

Wells, Mark K. *Courage and Air Warfare: The Allied Aircrew Experience in the Second World War.* London: Frank Cass, 1995.

Willatt, Geoffrey. *Bombs and Barbed Wire: My War in the RAF and Stalag Luft III.* Kent. Parapress, 1995.

Made in the USA
Middletown, DE
25 January 2017